AMERICAN STORIES

BOOKS BY CALVIN TRILLIN

An Education in Georgia
Barnett Frummer Is an Unbloomed Flower
U.S. Journal
American Fried
Runestruck
Alice, Let's Eat
Floater
Uncivil Liberties
Third Helpings
Killings
With All Disrespect
If You Can't Say Something Nice
Travels with Alice
Enough's Enough (And Other Rules of Life)
American Stories

CALVIN TRILLIN

AMERICAN STORIES

TICKNOR

& FIELDS

NEW YORK

1991

For information about permission to reproduce selections
from this book, write to Permissions, Ticknor & Fields,
Houghton Mifflin Company, 2 Park Street, Boston, Massachusetts 02108.

Library of Congress Cataloging-in-Publication Data

Trillin, Calvin.
American stories / Calvin Trillin.
p.   cm.
ISBN 0-395-59367-0
I. Title.
PS3570.R5A8   1991
814'.54—dc20   91-15939
CIP

The pieces in this book first appeared in *The New Yorker*.

Printed in the United States of America

AGM   10   9   8   7   6   5   4   3   2   1

To Robert (Slowly) Lescher

CONTENTS

Outdoor Life / 1

Telling a Kentucky Story / 22

The Life and Times of Joe Bob Briggs, So Far / 41

Rumors Around Town / 73

A Couple of Eccentric Guys / 98

Competitors / 137

Right-of-Way / 155

Goldberg Can Go Home Again / 177

You Don't Ask, You Don't Get / 199

I've Got Problems / 223

Covering the Cops / 243

Zei-da-man / 263

Afterword / 289

AMERICAN
STORIES

OUTDOOR
LIFE

CENTRAL OREGON is an outdoor sort of place. Edwin Dyer, who moved to a Central Oregon town called Sisters in 1969, was an outdoor sort of guy. He had grown up in cities — mainly Portland, and then Eugene, where his father worked as a printer for the University of Oregon — but he always felt attached to the country. When Dyer was in his mid-forties and his children were getting nearly old enough to think about families of their own, he wrote down some of what he remembered from his childhood, and all he had to say about Portland, where he lived all but a few of the first fifteen years of his life, was that he had hated it. His reminiscences about his childhood concentrated on the summers he had spent on his grandparents' farm, near Yamhill, Oregon — an old-fashioned farm where the plowing was done behind a team of draft horses, and butter was turned in the parlor in the evenings, and baths were taken in a washtub in the kitchen, and the beef was butchered right out in the farmyard, and Grandpa's way of announcing a trip to the outhouse was to say, "I'm going to see Mrs. Murphy." What Ed Dyer tended to recall about his boyhood was hunting and fishing and horseback riding and Boy Scout hikes. What he remembered about high school was shop class and the rifle club. After high school and a hitch in the Navy, he got married — he and his wife, Tona, met at a Mormon church function — and got a job with an organization that could offer a career in the outdoors, the United States Forest Service. When he moved to Central Oregon, six years after joining the service, it was to work at the Sisters ranger station, which is responsible for the trees and wilderness trails and campgrounds and mountain lakes in the northwest quarter of a vast and magnificent patch of the outdoors called the Deschutes National Forest.

Sisters is the first town travelers come to when they drive through the central pass of the Cascade Mountains from what people in Oregon call the Valley — the Willamette River Valley, where most of the state's population is concentrated in a string of cities that includes Portland and Salem and Eugene. When the Dyers moved to Sisters, it was a quiet old logging town of six hundred people, known to a lot of travelers in Oregon as the place they stopped for gasoline and a short chat about the rigors of mountain driving, but it was beginning to change. In the seventies, outdoor sorts of places like Central Oregon were beginning to appeal to a lot of people from places like the Valley and the coastal cities of California — people who talked about getting out of the rat race or finding a slower pace of life or trading some income for convenience to a wilderness trail and a mountain lake. A number of people who had passed through Sisters on their way to ski on a nearby mountain or to camp in one of the national forests started thinking about moving there. It's practically inside the Deschutes National Forest. From just about anywhere in town you can look across pastureland or ponderosa pines and see the snowy peaks of spectacular mountains known as the Three Sisters. In the mid-seventies, the commercial district of Sisters, which had always consisted of the nondescript hodgepodge of stores customarily found in old Western towns, began to take on a look that a lot of visitors found attractive. When Black Butte Ranch, a huge tract of private land that cuts into the national forest about eight miles west of town, was developed into an expensive vacation-home complex, the developer, as an alternative to putting in a shopping center, financed the wooden façades and rough-cedar posts and board-and-batten siding and ersatz balconies that can transform a place from what old Western towns usually look like into what people think old

Western towns ought to look like — a process now known in the West as Westernization.

Sooner or later, the shops behind the Western façades had names like The Cook's Nook and The Hen's Tooth and Nancy's Fancy's and The Elegant Dromedary. Partly because a large ranch just outside town has found some customers right in the area for the exotic and costly beasts it breeds, the animals seen grazing in the pastureland around Sisters include not just the customary Herefords and Black Angus but also llamas. The developer of the Black Butte Ranch complex eventually completed a more modest development on the edge of Sisters called Tollgate — it was named not for a thruway exit but for the nineteenth-century toll operation that provided the money to keep the mountain pass clear — and gave its streets names like Oxbow and Lariat and Saddle Horn and Stagecoach. Some of the old-timers in Sisters have grumbled a bit about the fancying up and the summer tourists and the parking problem. Some people in Sisters like to ask exactly what you'd do with a llama worth twenty thousand dollars. ("You sell it to someone who's willing to pay twenty thousand dollars for a llama.") Still, considering the changes Sisters has seen, it is not a place where people seem to dwell on contention. What they tend to talk about is whether to go cross-country skiing after work or how their dogs did at field-obedience class or when the wilderness trails might be dry enough for horse-packing trips. They talk about the outdoors. When they're asked why they live in Sisters — why they took a pay cut to move from Los Angeles, why they came over from the Valley before they were certain a suitable job was available — they are likely to answer by making a sweeping gesture toward the Cascades and saying something about "the quality of life."

Maintaining the wilderness trails became one of Ed Dyer's responsibilities not long after he began working at the Sisters station, and they were his pride. He estimated that, on foot or on horseback, he covered six or seven hundred miles on the trails every year himself. He presided over trail-maintenance crews funded by the Forest Service and whatever government program happened to be in operation — the Comprehensive Employment and Training Act or the Youth Conservation Corps or the Young Adult Conservation Corps. He acted as liaison with equestrian groups that made use of the trails. As a Scoutmaster, he was known for organizing and leading "fifty-milers" — week-long backpacking trips that covered a full fifty miles on the wilderness trails.

After several years in Sisters, the Dyers had moved to the outskirts of Redmond — a much larger, more conventional Central Oregon town twenty miles to the east — so that the children wouldn't have to take a twenty-mile bus ride every morning to get to the nearest high school. Even before the move, though, the entire family was active in the Redmond Mormon church. Both Ed and Tona Dyer taught Sunday school. Ed Dyer had become Scoutmaster of the church's Boy Scout Troop 26 within a year of his assignment to Sisters. Dyer had never really left Scouting. Years before his own boys were old enough to be Boy Scouts and years after they had gone on to other things, he went through a constant round of troop meetings and courts of honor and campouts and fifty-milers. It was said around Redmond that Troop 26 did consistently well in amassing merit badges and producing Eagle Scouts. Ed Dyer was given any number of awards. Scouting, in the view of another member of the congregation, was Dyer's "prestige thing, his ego trip."

Being a successful Scoutmaster may bring a certain kind of prestige, or at least some community appreciation, in an outdoor sort of place like Central Oregon. There are a lot of places — indoor sorts of places — where it would bring no prestige at all. There are a lot of places — places that value social skills and appearance and sophistication — where Ed Dyer might have had some difficulty fitting in. Even his friends acknowledged that once he had you cornered he could tell you a lot more about a fifty-mile hike than you wanted to know. The Western clothes he wore when he was out of his Forest Service uniform did nothing to disguise the fact that he had put on a lot of weight over the years. He was not thought of as someone who always knew precisely what to say at precisely the right moment. But Ed Dyer was someone who seemed to have found a niche in Central Oregon. Through Scouting and other good works, he had become a valued member of the community.

He had his wilderness trails and his hunting and his horseback riding. Behind the Dyers' house, two or three miles toward Sisters on Highway 126, there was a patch of pastureland where he kept a couple of horses. Dyer rode on the trails, and he rode in the Deschutes County sheriff's posse. He and his wife — a rather retiring, soft-spoken woman with a strong commitment to the Mormon Church — not only raised four children of their own but occasionally took in children of friends and relatives when help was needed. In Central Oregon the Dyers had carved out a pretty good life for themselves — except for what was, much later, always referred to as Ed's problem. His problem was pedophilia — homosexual pedophilia. He could not control his sexual desire for young boys.

The Mormon Church does not have a professional ministry. The leader of a Mormon congregation — in Mormon terminology, the leader of a ward — is a layman who is known as the bishop. In 1982, the bishop of the Mormon ward in Redmond got some disturbing news about Ed Dyer. One of the Scouts in Troop 26 had told his parents that Dyer made a sexual advance to him during an overnight camping trip. Dyer's version was that he had inadvertently touched the boy while they were sleeping in a tent together, and the boy had panicked. But it turned out that there were other stories of sexual misconduct concerning Dyer and Scouts in Troop 26. Ed Dyer was asked by the church to resign as Scoutmaster.

Aside from that, the church leadership had trouble figuring out exactly what to do about him. The first step was easy. The president of what the Mormons call a stake — a stake is roughly the equivalent of a diocese — has a high council that at times sits as a sort of ecclesiastical court. The court has the power to excommunicate a Mormon. It can also simply reprimand him. In Dyer's case, it took a middle course — what the Mormons call disfellowship, a sort of probation that is based on a period of repentance and rehabilitation. The church authorities did not inform the civil authorities of the allegations against Dyer.

It could be said, of course, that the church was simply trying to avoid embarrassment, or even lawsuits: if the accusations against

Dyer were true, after all, the Redmond ward had for twelve years had a pedophile in a position of trust and intimacy with young boys. The Mormons would offer some other explanations for not having gone to the police. It was always possible, for instance, that the accusation by the Boy Scout was untrue or exaggerated; Dyer apparently told some members of the congregation that it was all a mistake and he was being treated unfairly. It could be argued that the fact that the inquiry had started within the church gave it the equivalent of the confidentiality traditional between priest and penitent — although there is no indication that Ed Dyer confessed to anything. It was presumably also true that the Mormons had difficulty facing an issue that a lot of them considered appalling and repugnant. Apparently, those in the ward who came to know about Ed Dyer's problem rarely discussed it. "It's the sort of subject you avoid because it's distasteful," one of them said later. "It's something you just don't want to believe has happened."

For whatever reason, it was about a year before the high-council court prepared to convene again to consider refellowshipping Dyer. By that time, though, one high-council member had heard what seemed to be a corroborating allegation from the time Dyer still lived in the Valley, and had learned that Dyer had put up notices in places like gunshops announcing that he was certified to give the hunting-education course required in Oregon for any hunter under eighteen — notices that could, of course, be seen as a device to meet boys. That member was asked by the stake president to undertake an investigation, a role provided for in Church rules. The boys in Troop 26 were reluctant to say anything, but the investigator began calling around to young men who had been Boy Scouts in Redmond in the past. He spent just about full time on the investigation for three weeks, and at the end he gave the stake president a thirty-page dossier, accompanied by tape recordings that, with the permission of his informants, he had made of several telephone conversations. The report indicated that the incident with the Boy Scout in the tent was not an isolated incident but part of a pattern that went back at least twenty-five years.

The stake president did not reconvene the court to consider refellowshipping Dyer, but some time passed before he decided what to do instead. Part of the delay may have been caused by preoccupation with other matters. In August of 1983, one of the Dyers' sons, a young man of nineteen named Lance, was found to have leukemia. The members of the ward rallied around to help the Dyer family through the months of treatment — treatment that turned out to be of no avail. Lance Dyer died of pneumonia in May of 1984. It didn't seem to be the best time to pursue a case against Ed Dyer. Also, according to a member of the church who was familiar with the case, Dyer "kept saying he was going to turn himself in." It had been the high council's understanding that during the disfellowship period Dyer was going to seek counseling and was going to avoid situations that would put him in the company of young boys. Apparently, the council concluded that Dyer had not complied with that understanding, because when it finally convened as a court, in late 1984, the decision was to excommunicate him. "I stayed away from kids for a long time," Dyer said some time later, when his problem was finally being dealt with in a court of law. "And then Louis came along."

Like Ed Dyer, Susan Birdsell Conner grew up loving the outdoors. She lived on the outskirts of Santa Barbara, California, where her parents owned a beauty parlor and her father dabbled in real estate. From the time Susan and her twin sister, Sharon, were eight or nine, they both knew that they were going to be veterinarians, and they both knew that they were someday going to live in a place where the horses were back of the house rather than miles away in a boarding stable. Their mother can summon up life with two aspiring veterinarians in one sentence: "We had cages all over." Like many identical twins, the Birdsell sisters were a lot more comfortable with each other than with other people. By the time they entered school, they had used a private language with each other so long that they had to be treated for slight speech impediments. They enrolled together at the University of California at Davis, and in 1967 they graduated as veterinarians. Both married Davis veterinary students who planned to practice as equine veterinarians. It was a double wedding.

Sharon got to Sisters first. She and her husband, Eric Sharpnack, moved there from Point Reyes, California, in 1978 and took over the Sisters Veterinary Clinic. She concentrated on small animals; he treated horses, and on a number of occasions llamas. Susan had been living in the East with her husband, a racetrack veterinarian named Edward Conner, and their two sons. She and her husband were divorced in 1976, and after a couple of years she and the boys moved to Oregon, where she eventually joined the Sharpnacks' practice. Not long after that, Sharon and Eric Sharpnack were divorced. Seventeen years after the double wedding, the Birdsell twins — both divorced and both with two children — were in practice together as the sole partners of the Sisters Veterinary Clinic.

They seemed to be among those people who were well suited to Central Oregon and might have been uncomfortable in a place less focused on the outdoors. "I don't think they'd even know how to dress up," a friend says of them. Susan Conner bought a house in Tollgate — a simple rough-cedar house that had nearly an acre of ponderosa pines and a paddock in the back. Tollgate, like Black Butte Ranch, is virtually inside the national forest, and she took great joy in being able to ride from her own paddock onto the forest's trails and logging roads. She became particularly active in what is known locally as wagon driving — leisurely caravans of horse-drawn conveyances that might range from sulkies to restored buggies to covered wagons.

Susan had one problem not shared by her sister. Sharon Sharpnack's children were both girls, and their father was still in Sisters. Susan Conner's boys had virtually no contact with their father, who remained in the East. Her younger son, Brian, was an outgoing boy who had adjusted with relative ease to the move to Oregon and life in Sisters. But her older son, Louis, was more diffident than his brother and more obviously in need of a father figure. That was why Susan Conner was so pleased when, during Louis's eighth-grade year at Sisters Junior High School, he met an avuncular outdoorsman from the Forest Service named Ed Dyer.

Louis Conner, who was then fifteen, seemed a couple of years younger than he was — a slim, nice-looking boy with sandy hair and a quick, shy smile. He had his mother's love of animals and the outdoors. He belonged to two 4-H groups — one having to do with horses, the other with dog obedience and showmanship. He was gentle and unassertive, the sort of boy who tends not to register on his classmates in a large school. The adults who came in contact with him — teachers, 4-H leaders, Susan Conner's friends — thought of him as a polite young man, eager to be befriended by them. "Every year, there are boys, and sometimes girls, who adopt you," James Green, Louis's science teacher at Sisters Junior High, has said. "You could tell he wanted to talk to an adult — particularly a man."

In the spring of 1984, just before Easter vacation, Jim Green asked the Forest Service if it was possible to have someone come out and instruct his eighth graders in the proper use of the national forest. The Forest Service sent Ed Dyer. Green and Dyer gave a three-day course on how to exist in the wilderness — how to use a compass, how to read a map, how to pack a horse, how to survive in an emergency. During the visit, Dyer said he was looking for someone to hike the trails with him — to take part in "camping and skiing and different things in the outdoors." As Dyer later recalled it, Louis Conner "turned around and said, 'I'd like to be your friend and go with you.'"

By that time, as it happened, a member of the Mormon congregation had informed an acquaintance on the Redmond police force that Ed Dyer had been disfellowshipped because of allegations of sexual misconduct with Boy Scouts. The informant suggested that it was a matter the police should investigate, but eventually it became obvious to him that whatever investigation had taken place was not going to lead to an indictment. It may be that the Redmond police had problems with the statute of limitations. It may be that there were problems with jurisdiction; a lot of the crimes that were alleged, after all, had occurred on hikes and encampments far outside the Redmond city limits, in the Central Oregon outdoors. It may be that the police were reluctant to launch a vigorous investigation of good old Ed Dyer or that, like some members of the church, they were simply unable to face the possibility that what was being said about the man who had been entrusted with so many boys for so many years was true.

Louis worked that summer as a volunteer helping to maintain trails in the national forest. He began to talk about the possibility of making the Forest Service his career. Ed Dyer and Louis did a lot of things that a father and son would do in an outdoor sort of place. They went deer hunting together. Dyer gave Louis a shotgun. When the time came for Louis to buy a horse, Dyer helped him pick one out. Dyer often dropped by the house in Tollgate. He offered to supply the Conners with firewood. He had discussions with Susan Conner about how Louis was doing in school and what sort of friends he should be meeting. The adults who knew Louis — the woman who led his 4-H horse group, for instance — thought it was "really nice that he could have an older friend who was interested in the same things he was." Susan Conner was delighted. She thought that her worries about the absence of a father figure for Louis were over.

Of course, neither Susan Conner nor Louis Conner nor their friends knew why Ed Dyer had resigned as Scoutmaster of Troop 26 two years before he met Louis at Sisters Junior High. They were not Mormons. They knew nothing of the deliberations concerning Ed Dyer in the stake high council. They knew nothing about an investigation by the Redmond police. Sooner or later, though, the Forest Service was told of the information that the police had about Ed Dyer. As a result, the ranger in charge of the Sisters Ranger District walked into Dyer's office in February of 1985, closed the door behind him, and informed Dyer that he would no longer be permitted to work with young people unless other adults were present. The allegations in the hands of the police had not been proved, of course, and the ranger apparently tried to be balanced in responding to them. Recalling the ranger's instructions later, Dyer remarked, "He said, 'Well, just be prudent. Don't put yourself in a situation where you're set up.' And I followed those rules."

Dyer did not interpret the rules as applying to his relationship with Louis Conner. Louis continued to be Dyer's companion in

the outdoors — although there were times when he seemed reluctant to go on outings with Dyer, and periods when they didn't see
each other at all. Susan Conner thought that Louis might be getting
tired of Dyer's stories or that he was beginning to prefer the company of boys his own age. Dyer persisted, though, and eventually
Louis would accept one of his invitations. Dyer took him elk hunting. Two or three times Dyer took him to an event called a Mountain Man Rendezvous, a weekend encampment at which men dress
in buckskin clothes and hold marksmanship contests with black-
powder muskets and drink a lot of modern-day beer. In the summer of 1985, a little more than a year after their meeting at Jim
Green's science class, Dyer arranged for Louis to work as a member of the Youth Conservation Corps crew maintaining trails.

Meanwhile, the informant from the Mormon Church, having
tried both the Redmond police force and the Deschutes County
Sheriff's Department with no success, turned to the state police.
The state police were interested. They didn't foresee any jurisdic-
tional problems. They weren't troubled by the fact that so many of
the allegations were beyond the statute of limitations; the behavior
pattern of a pedophile tends to be so unvarying, they told their informant, that incidents within the statute of limitations would almost certainly be turned up. The case was assigned to Lynn Fredrickson, a state police detective who has a reputation for dealing
sympathetically and effectively with young people. New names of
boys who knew Ed Dyer were not difficult to find. On June 18,
1985, Fredrickson showed up at the Sisters ranger station and
asked to speak to a summer Youth Conservation Corps employee
named Louis Conner.

Louis acknowledged nothing, but when Dyer learned of the interview he agreed to talk with Fredrickson. Eventually, Dyer admitted having initiated sexual encounters with Louis. He said that
on a number of occasions he and Louis had engaged in mutual
masturbation. When Fredrickson reinterviewed Louis, he gathered
that Louis had felt trapped. When his mother had found him reluctant to accompany Dyer on outings, he hadn't known how to explain his reluctance without telling her what he couldn't bear to

say. He had been worried about displeasing the man who had settled into a role so much like a father's. He had been worried about his job and his hope for a career in the Forest Service. Louis's story about what had happened on the outings matched Dyer's story. Another boy — a boy named Keith, who had met Dyer at a church supper — told a similar story. Charges of sexual abuse were filed against Ed Dyer.

For a while, it looked as if prosecuting Dyer might necessitate Louis's testifying in open court. Louis was obviously reluctant. The prospect of being labeled a homosexual filled him with dread. "He wanted to cooperate with the process," a clinical social worker who saw him at the time has said, "but he wanted to keep it a secret." Still, both Louis and his mother were determined that he would testify if that was required to convict Ed Dyer. It turned out not to be necessary. After protracted negotiations, a plea bargain was made: in return for Dyer's guilty plea to two charges of second-degree sexual abuse, the district attorney of Deschutes County agreed to recommend concurrent sentences and to drop any investigation of similar charges. Instead of a trial, there was a sentencing hearing — in Bend, the seat of Deschutes County — to consider questions of punishment and treatment and restitution.

There was testimony from the mothers of both boys involved. "Before I knew all this had happened, I had said that I thought Ed would be blessed for his interest in my son," Keith's mother said. "But I know now that that's not true, because his interest was selfish. It wasn't to help my son or to love him. He simply used him." Susan Conner answered questions about how much had been spent on counseling for Louis, who still seemed to her depressed. Although the one news item carried in local papers about the case, a tiny item in the *Redmond Spokesman*, had not mentioned the names of the boys involved, she said that some kids at school had brought up the subject with Louis. "He doesn't want to go anywhere on weekends," she said. "He doesn't want to be around other high school kids, because he thinks they're going to talk to him about this, and because of his depression." She had decided, she said, that she was in need of counseling as well: "My son blames me for this, because I encouraged him to go with Ed, because I thought Ed was such a wonderful person."

Most of what the judge heard, though, was mitigating evidence presented by Dyer's lawyer. Tona Dyer, speaking in a soft, sad voice, said that her husband was a kind man and a good father. A couple of men who knew Dyer through the Boy Scouts testified that he was sincere and law-abiding and had made a great sacrifice of his time and energy in the years he spent as Scoutmaster of Troop 26. It was brought out that Ed Dyer had already suffered for his crimes. He had, in effect, lost his job — the Forest Service had allowed him to take early retirement — and that job had been the center of his life. ("It meant a lot to me to work in that job," Dyer testified. "I really enjoyed it. It was a way of life. It wasn't just a job.") He had been forced to leave Scouting. He had been excommunicated by his church. Although two of the counselors who met with Dyer had come to the conclusion that he was without remorse — they thought he regretted only that he got caught — Tona Dyer testified that they were mistaken. "He's been very depressed, and he is very remorseful," she said. "He just sits around or lays around . . . He feels really bad because of what he's done and how people feel toward him. He feels really bad. And he feels bad for the people he's hurt. More than, I think, anyone realizes." Mrs. Dyer said she had known about her husband's problem for years. "It does bother me," she said. "But I feel that you don't always look at the thing that someone does wrong. You look at the other qualities a person has, too. And I think if you care about someone you expect that these people are good and maybe they'll be able to crack this problem. And I do care about him."

Dyer himself was on the stand for some time. He denied that he had used his position as Scoutmaster as a way of arranging sexual encounters. "It might be construed that way, but it wasn't intended that way," he said. "That was not my reason for staying in the program." Dyer said that he had always wanted to seek help but had been afraid it would mean arrest and the loss of everything — his job, his family. "Most of the boys that I molested by their terms, by the terms of the law, I really loved," he said. "I didn't want to hurt them." Then he looked at Louis Conner, who was sitting in the courtroom. "I know that Louis back here, sitting there, I know that he probably hates me now, because of the problems I brought on him and his family," Dyer said. "But I truly did love him and enjoyed his company and all the good things we did. And I'm painfully regretful of that problem and that situation. And if there was any way I could erase it, and make his life better, I would sure do it."

Dyer may have been right about Louis's hating him. Louis was angered by a lot of what was said at the sentencing hearing, particularly Dyer's answer to a question about who had initiated the encounters between him and the boys: "It was mutual part of the time and part of the time maybe mostly myself." Partly because of Louis's fear of being labeled a homosexual, the question of who was to blame was terribly important to him — in the words of one counselor, "he needed to be real clear that it was not *his* fault that this happened" — and Dyer, despite his guilty plea, seemed reluctant to accept the blame. Just after the guilty plea, Susan Conner had angrily informed the district attorney's office of a telephone call from Dyer in which he had told her that the encounters had come about by mutual consent, and that Louis would be free to make his own decisions on such matters as soon as he had his eighteenth birthday. Also, Louis, as he sat in the courtroom, knew what he had been afraid and ashamed to tell Detective Fredrickson: on two or three occasions, his sexual contact with Ed Dyer had gone beyond the mutual masturbation that Dyer had admitted. The district attorney's office had eventually learned of those occasions. Presumably, one reason Dyer had finally agreed to plead guilty was the knowledge that if Louis Conner testified he would be testifying about sodomy.

There was nothing in the judge's decision that might have made Louis feel better about what was happening. Although the presentencing report had recommended a considerable time in jail, Dyer was sentenced to serve only twenty days, more or less at his own convenience. The judge also ruled that Dyer would have to enter a counseling program for sex offenders and would have to be on supervised probation for three years and would have to avoid associating with boys under eighteen. He was not specifically forbidden to see Louis Conner, even after the prosecutor pointed out that Louis, who may have looked only fifteen or so, would be eighteen before the year was out. "From what all the witnesses have testified to, why you're a fine fellow, with a good work record, who's done a great deal for the community," the judge told Dyer. "If you feel positive about yourself, why these episodes aren't going to mar your life, and you can make the best of it."

Presumably, Louis had been angry even before he got to the hearing. Two nights earlier, he had taken out the shotgun Dyer gave him — a .16-gauge single-shot. He had removed most of the stock. He had sawed off the barrel about six inches from the trigger. A sawed-off shotgun is, of course, easier to conceal than a full-length shotgun, and is also more maneuverable. For targets more than a few yards away, there is a sacrifice in accuracy and power. A sawed-off shotgun is not an effective weapon for hunting deer. What it is used for is killing someone at close range.

January 22 was a bleak day in Sisters. A cold rain fell intermittently. The stunning view of the Cascades didn't exist. It was a Wednesday, five days after the judge in Bend had pronounced sentence on Ed Dyer. As on any other school morning, Louis Conner climbed onto the bus that took him to high school on the edge of Redmond. He was wearing the blue parka he normally wore to school. Hidden underneath his parka was the sawed-off shotgun. At Redmond High School, Louis got off the bus with the other students, but he didn't go into the school building. He walked back down Highway 126 in the direction of Sisters — toward Ed Dyer's house.

Dyer's pickup was not in the driveway. He had gone to a swap shop in Bend to see what he might get for a set of sleigh bells he was ready to part with. On the way back, he stopped in Redmond to chat with a friend. In a cold, driving rain, Louis Conner stood in a field waiting. Two hours later, Dyer still hadn't returned. Finally, Louis, soaked and shivering, knocked on the door and told Tona

Dyer that he was there to see her husband. She was concerned by his presence. Her husband, after all, had been instructed by the judge not to associate with boys under eighteen. She asked Louis in, though, and told him to stand next to the wood stove to dry out. Twenty minutes later, Ed Dyer showed up. When he was told that Louis wanted to talk to him, he said he'd have to call his probation officer first. The probation officer told Dyer that he should not talk to Louis. Dyer was instructed to drive Louis back to Redmond High School immediately. Tona Dyer, who didn't drive, was to accompany her husband and Louis, so that they wouldn't be alone. The three of them walked out to the pickup. Ed Dyer and Louis Conner had exchanged hardly a word. At the pickup, Dyer opened the door on the driver's side and then went over to lock what he called his sport shed — the place he kept a lot of his outdoor equipment. As Dyer returned to the truck, Louis stepped out from behind the driver's door, holding the shotgun. Tona Dyer thought she heard her husband say something like "No, Louis!" Louis shot him in the chest.

Dyer was still standing when his wife ran into the house to call an ambulance, but she was certain that he had been mortally wounded. In Redmond, a few miles away, Lynn Fredrickson, the state police detective who had filed charges against Ed Dyer, was eating lunch in his car when he heard the report of a shooting on Highway 126. The address sounded familiar, and he asked the dispatcher who lived there. When he was told that it was the home of an Edwin Dyer, he thought he knew what must have happened, and he headed for Dyer's house. Before he got there, an ambulance had arrived, and the crew had seen that there was nothing to be done for Ed Dyer. It was Fredrickson and his partner who found Louis, an hour or so later. He was standing in a field about three quarters of a mile from the Dyers' house. He offered no resistance.

In Oregon, any sentence imposed by a juvenile court, the court that normally has jurisdiction over everyone under the age of eighteen, expires on the defendant's twenty-first birthday — so a juvenile defendant who is, say, seventeen cannot be locked up for more than four years no matter what he has done. In the case of certain serious felonies, though, a district attorney can move in juvenile court to have a defendant who is fifteen or older remanded to the adult court system, where no such limitation on the sentence exists. The criteria for making the decision include the previous criminal record of the juvenile and the protection required by the community and the "aggressive, violent, premeditated, or willful manner in which the offense was alleged to have been committed." The district attorney of Deschutes County announced that he would attempt to have Louis Conner remanded to the adult court system and tried for murder.

It was not a popular decision. There were people in Deschutes County who said that there was no reason for any trial at all. For some people, Louis Conner had become a sort of hero; at the very least, he seemed more the victim than the offender. Although the risk would have been too great, it occurred to Louis's lawyers that if they elected to try him in the adult court system, where his fate would be determined by a jury rather than a judge, it was unlikely that any jury would convict Louis, no matter what the evidence. It's possible that there were people in Deschutes County who agreed with the district attorney that Louis was guilty of murder. It's possible that there were people who, whatever their views on how the case should be dealt with legally, were disturbed by indications that in the public mind Louis Conner, the timid boy who dreaded the thought of being labeled a homosexual, had, in the tradition of the Hollywood Old West, transformed himself into a hero with one blast of a gun. If there were such people, they kept their opinions to themselves. In letters to the editor and gossip at the cafés and late-night talk in the bars, the prevailing opinion was that Ed Dyer had got what was coming to him.

In Sisters, at least, that view was often expressed after a qualifying observation about how nobody has a right to take the law into his own hands. Most of the people in Sisters are not the sort of people who condone violence or preach vengeance. It's the sort of place whose response to what had happened included inviting two specialists on the problem of sexual abuse to come to town and conduct a symposium. Still, people in Sisters were disturbed at what seemed to be a disparity in the way the county had treated Ed Dyer and the way it was treating Louis Conner. "I think people don't blame Ed or Louis but the judicial system," Eric Dolson, the editor of the weekly paper in Sisters, said as the remand hearing got under way in Bend. "People like to think that the guilty are punished and the innocent are protected. It's part of our sense of security. If they think there's reason to believe that's not true, it upsets them." By the time the remand hearing began, about two months after Ed Dyer was shot to death, a defense fund for Louis Conner in Sisters had raised more than eight thousand dollars.

The deputy district attorney who represented the state in the remand hearing — Roy Miller, the same deputy district attorney who had prosecuted Ed Dyer — basically argued that the three and a half years until Louis Conner's twenty-first birthday was not enough time for the state to have him in custody, whether the custody was considered treatment or punishment. Miller argued that the crime had in fact been premeditated. The shotgun had been sawed off two days before the sentencing hearing that so upset Louis; there was no indication that Dyer had said or done anything to provoke Louis just before the shooting. Louis's lawyer, a former Eugene prosecutor named Stephen Tiktin, said that it was Louis who had been the victim — the victim of "sexual abuse perpetrated by a homosexual predatory pedophile." Louis had been willing even to undergo the embarrassment of testifying in open court in order to bring the man who victimized him to justice, Tiktin said, but the sentencing hearing convinced him that "the system had failed." The state presented witnesses to support its contention that there were facilities in the adult correctional system appropriate for Louis; the defense presented witnesses to support its contention that Louis was a natural victim who would be "fair game as soon as he steps into the bowels of the penitentiary."

The witness who seemed to speak with the most authority was Dr. John Cochran, the senior forensic clinical psychologist for the State of Oregon, who was called by the prosecution but testified in favor of the defense contention that Louis should be treated as a juvenile. Cochran turned out to be a pudgy man with a mustache and a thoughtful expression that made him appear personally concerned even when he happened to be speaking of test results that sounded rather technical. In a way, Cochran's testimony amounted to a retelling of the story of Ed Dyer and Louis Conner, this time in psychological terms. Cochran described Louis as a naive and passive and dependent boy, less mature socially and emotionally than the average boy his age. More than most boys, Cochran said, Louis had a need for the approval of others, to the point of being willing to subject himself to "abuse or intimidation to avoid rejection or abandonment." In other words, Cochran said, Louis was an easily manipulated boy who was perfect prey for Ed Dyer — "a pedophile extremely experienced at grooming people like Louis." In Cochran's view, the stress Louis was under once the investigation of Dyer began was magnified by Dyer's response to the charge against him. "As the circle began to tighten, instead of protecting his pseudo-child he abandoned him," Cochran said of Dyer. "Once in court, instead of making a clean breast of it he blamed Louis." The result, Cochran said, was "a massive amount of betrayal." According to Cochran's interpretation of the events, Louis had not gone to Dyer's house with the intention of shooting anybody; the shotgun was an "equalizer," a way of making certain that the larger man paid attention. Louis desperately wanted to find out why Dyer had said in court that some of the sexual encounters had been initiated by both of them, Cochran said, and Dyer's adherence to the probation officer's instructions not to talk to Louis was, ironically, the last straw: "The usual coping methods that Louis has were obliterated." Cochran testified that the combination of events required to drive Louis Conner to violence would be unlikely ever to occur again. He was, in Cochran's term, "a situational offender."

To no one's surprise, the judge held that the juvenile court would retain jurisdiction over Louis Conner. In holding for the defense, though, the judge, John M. Copenhaver, was careful to separate himself from the notion that Ed Dyer had got what he deserved — the notion that sexual offenders should be "destroyed like rabid dogs." In announcing his decision, Judge Copenhaver said, "Sexual abuse does not mean that a person's life has no value to us. The loss of any life diminishes the quality of life in our community."

Shortly after the remand hearing, Louis Conner's lawyer sent the tort notices required if he intended to file suits in civil court against the Redmond Police Department and the United States Forest Service — suits that would presumably allege negligence that led to Ed Dyer's remaining in the company of boys even after his background was known. There were two more hearings remaining in the criminal case against Louis. From what the judge and the defense had said in court, it seemed clear that they both believed what Louis had done fit the legal definition of manslaughter, but there had to be a hearing on that question. And there had to be a hearing — what juvenile courts call a dispositional hearing — to decide on a sentence. While those hearings were being prepared for, the judge let Louis remain at home. Susan Conner found her son in relatively good spirits. "People expect him to be depressed," she said. "But for the first time he doesn't have the cloud of Ed Dyer hanging over him."

A month after the remand hearing, Judge Copenhaver ruled that the shooting of Ed Dyer had been manslaughter. A couple of months after that, those involved in the case gathered again in Judge Copenhaver's courtroom for the final hearing in what was officially called "In the Matter of Louis Robert Conner, a child" — a hearing to decide what should happen to Louis. Deputy District Attorney Roy Miller was there to argue that Louis should be sent to the MacLaren School — the sort of institution that used to be called a reform school, and, under ordinary circumstances, the place where a juvenile found guilty of something as serious as manslaughter would go. The defense, backed by the counselor who had been treating Louis, argued that he should be sent home. The Deschutes County Juvenile Department, which normally comes to such hearings in agreement with the district attorney, suggested a middle course — a small, unguarded residential facility that emphasizes intensive counseling. The Juvenile Department's representative testified that the department would prefer to see Louis go home if the alternative was MacLaren, but that one disadvantage of sending him back to Sisters was that the community "might be too supportive," because "Louis is seen as a hero."

Judge Copenhaver took the middle course. He suspended a sentence to MacLaren and ruled that Louis should instead spend six months at ACCORD, a house in the countryside a few miles from Bend which is a sort of adjunct of a nearby facility called the J Bar J Boys Ranch. The day after the decision, a few people from Sisters were quoted in the Bend paper expressing disappointment that Louis had to serve any time anywhere, but a lot of people thought the judge had made a sensible choice. "I think the decision had as much to do with the community as with Louis," a lawyer who has followed the case said after the dispositional hearing. "Given the nature of the offense, it's sort of hard for a judge to say, 'Well, don't do it again,' and send Louis home. He couldn't give the message to the community, 'Go ahead and shoot these guys.' "

Susan Conner had known that a boy who killed someone was not likely to be sent home, but, partly because she had read of something like that happening in a similar case in California, she had gone to the hearing with her hopes up. "I should be really happy," she said not long after the sentencing. "I guess I am happy." Ordinarily, boys sent to ACCORD or the J Bar J Ranch have done nothing more serious than take a car that didn't happen to belong to them. ACCORD is on a few acres of land; the facilities of J Bar J, just down the road, are available. It's the sort of place that tries to take advantage of its access to the Central Oregon outdoors. There are, of course, horses at J Bar J. To build confidence, the boys do rock climbing and mountaineering. Particularly during school vacations, they're encouraged to work outdoors, for wages. In the summer, they often work for the local parks and recreation department, maintaining trails.

1986

TELLING A
KENTUCKY STORY

I N THE SPRING OF 1984, Tom Chaney, a friend of mine from
Horse Cave, Kentucky, wrote me a letter that, as he might have
put it, surprised me some. Tom and I met through a shared interest
in pan-fried chicken. That was in 1976, when he was working as an
editorial writer for a newspaper in Covington, Kentucky, a town
just across the Ohio River from Cincinnati. I was spending a few
days in the adjoining town of Newport, having been attracted by a
proposal of the mayor's to span the Ohio River with a gigantic
monorail system that would finally forge the historic link between
Riverfront Stadium, in Cincinnati, and a banquet hall he operated
on a bluff in Newport. A reporter on the Covington paper who was
considerate enough to look for ways to lighten the load of a traveling man had arranged for me to have dinner at Tom's house because of Tom's renown as a pan-fryer of chicken. Tom turned out
to be a serious pan-fryer, all right, but from the start I thought of
him more as a Kentucky storyteller — the sort of creatively digres-
sive talker who seems to have so many relatives (or "kinfolks")
back home that almost any subject can bring to mind a story about
at least one of them.

As it happened, there was plenty of material for a storyteller
right where we were, across the river from Cincinnati. Stories
abounded about the mayor with river-spanning ambitions, a televi-
sion-repair-shop proprietor known as Johnny TV Peluso, or simply

Johnny TV. It was said that Johnny TV was the sort of public official who had distributed eggs to the poor one Christmas, had been sued some months later for failure to pay his egg bill, and had offered to settle for half, on the ground that the eggs were small enough to have been produced by pigeons. For years, Newport had been notorious as the scene of gambling and assorted wickedness, and just about everyone in town knew the story of the conspiracy in 1961 to drug a reform candidate for sheriff and arrange for him to be found in bed above the Tropicana nightclub with an exotic dancer named April Flowers. Although Miss Flowers was not among those indicted for the conspiracy, she did have her Kentucky colonel's commission revoked — a penalty enabling her, so the story went, to bill herself from then on as "the only defrocked Kentucky colonel." At the time of my visit, none of the local storytellers had a story about how April Flowers came to be commissioned a Kentucky colonel in the first place. I suspect that this gap in the oral tradition has been filled by now.

Tom knew some stories about Covington and Newport, but it was clear that his heart was in Horse Cave — a town of two thousand people, in the south-central part of Kentucky known for burley tobacco and for limestone caves so spectacular that showing tourists through them has been a local industry for as long as anyone can remember. When I met Tom, he had spent only one full year in Horse Cave since his graduation from high school, in 1955. He had attended Georgetown College, near Lexington ("a small Baptist college for small Baptists"), and had put in two years at a Baptist seminary in Louisville. He had been a graduate student and teacher in Texas and Arkansas and Kentucky and Iowa. He sometimes described himself as "a reformed Baptist preacher and a reformed college teacher." But he seemed to be one of those people whose wanderings cause them to cling all the harder to an identification with their home ground. He looked a bit like someone who might have a patch of corn-and-tobacco land near Horse Cave — an ample man who favored blue jeans and wore a red beard that always seemed to have a pipe jutting out of it. He still talked more like a rural Kentucky storyteller than like a Baptist preacher or a college teacher or an editorial writer. There may be a lot of small-town boys whose exposure to years of graduate school got them into the habit of saying "*Ciao*" as they took leave of friends; Tom always said "See you directly." At that first fried-chicken dinner, he informed me that he was in fact someone who owned a patch of corn-and-tobacco land outside Horse Cave. He had bought it with his Aunt Daisie, who, Tom said, had decided as a widow in her seventies to prove that she was a better farmer than her husband, Hobart Carter, had been. ("She doesn't want all the land in the county — just what joins her.") Then he told me a story or two about Uncle Hobart.

When I met Tom, he was about to add "reformed editorial writer" to his curriculum vitae. He was going home to manage the farm he owned with his Aunt Daisie. Together with two friends, he had a plan that sounded almost as audacious as Johnny TV's monorail: they intended to found a professional repertory theater in Horse Cave. Tom was looking forward to being a farmer and he was looking forward to starting a theater. Most of all, though, he was looking forward to going back to Horse Cave. In a way, Tom was like a lot of people a decade younger who, in contrast to their parents, thought that deciding where they wanted to live was more important than deciding what they wanted to do there — except that Tom, instead of wanting to live on the coast of Oregon or in the high desert of New Mexico, wanted to go home.

Tom's attachment to Horse Cave was intertwined with an attachment to his family. He had always been close to his Aunt Daisie, who had no children of her own. During a year he spent at home teaching English at Caverna High School — that was in 1964, the year after his mother died — he had become particularly close to his father, an insurance man known to just about everyone in town as Boots. In the late seventies, I stopped in Horse Cave a couple of times and got to know Tom's family. I had a country-ham lunch at Porter's, in Sulphur Well, with Tom and his Aunt Daisie — a cheerful, quick-witted woman who, I noted at the time, had spent fifty-one years in the Hart County school system and seemed none the worse for wear. Tom and Boots and I had dinner at the home of Tom's sister, Ann Matera, who lived with Boots and her own family in the house she and Tom had grown up in. Ann's husband — Jerry Matera, an Italian-American from White Plains, New York, who had become the editor of the *Hart County News* — seemed very much at home in Horse Cave, but, just to be on the safe side, Tom and Boots told me, they tried not to let a family meal pass without saying that if the couple ever split up "we'd keep Jerry and send Ann on her way."

I ate pan-fried chicken with Tom and his father at a restaurant near Mammoth Cave, and remarked at the time that pan-fried chicken, which takes a long time to prepare, was the sort of food that should be eaten with people who are good enough storytellers to make a thirty-minute wait easy to take. Both Tom and Boots qualified on that score. Boots, who was more or less retired by then, had once been the man who handled patronage for the Democrats in Hart County — a task, Tom later told me, that he somehow managed to complete year after year without enriching himself in the process. Boots could tell stories about bootleggers and stories about tourist-fleecing and stories about his kinfolks and story after story about politics. He could tell the story about the time in 1932 that a Republican named J. D. Reynolds got so frustrated with Democratic vote-rigging that he sat on the ballot box in Precinct Seven and refused to move all day — forcing the Democrats, who had never been fussy about which precinct someone was registered in, to go off and vote somewhere else. Tom and Boots were sharing an office in the late seventies — they referred to it as Bogus Enterprises, Inc. — and Tom had presented his father with some elegant personal stationery that included the legend "Widows Tended — Lies Told — Whiskey Hauled."

In the years that followed, I heard from Tom occasionally by mail. In 1983, we exchanged letters after I learned of Boots Chaney's death. That was the last I heard of Tom until the letter that surprised me some. It began, "Friends should let each other know when they change addresses. I have moved, much against my will, to the Federal Pen in Lexington."

·   ·   ·

Late one morning a few months later, I knocked for a long time on the front door of the Horse Cave Country Inn without getting a response. Finally, Tom Chaney came to the door. He was wearing blue jeans. He still had a red beard, and there was still a pipe jutting out of it. "Sorry, I'm just getting some bread into the oven," he said, moving back toward the kitchen to get on with the task. "The thing that worried me most about being in the penitentiary was that it might destroy my taste buds. Fortunately, they appear to have survived."

All I knew about Tom's time in the penitentiary was that his sentence, a year and a day, had eventually been reduced, so he actually served only three months. I also knew that he had pleaded guilty to what the government called manufacturing a controlled substance and conspiracy to manufacture a controlled substance, and what Tom had described in his letter as having "leased some land to folks to grow corn, knowing corn was not all they would grow." By the time I learned of Tom's release, he had found himself the manager of the Horse Cave Country Inn, a bed-and-breakfast place that had opened right across the street from the house he grew up in. Tom said he would fill me in on the bare bones of the story before we had to leave to pick up Aunt Daisie and drive out to Sulphur Well for a country-ham lunch.

It all began, he said, when he was approached by Donnie Nunn, a former sheriff of Hart County, and was asked how he felt about growing marijuana.

"The former sheriff?" I said.

Tom said that with some sheriffs the line between what is legal and what is illegal could get blurred. "It's like Dad used to say about income tax," he went on. "Folks like H & R Block see what's legal as ending at a cliff, and if you get too close to the edge the ground might crumble and you fall in. Dad saw it like a river flowing through a swamp: as long as you didn't sink, you could wander pretty far out and claim you're on dry ground."

The Nunns have long been active on the Republican side of Kentucky politics; Donnie Nunn's cousin Louie Nunn served a term as governor of the state. Three or four generations of Chaneys and

Nunns have known each other, Tom said, but the families have not been close. In fact, he told me, Aunt Daisie's older sister had been sent to Texas in 1913 to prevent her from marrying a Nunn, and, more than seventy years later, she was still there. The talk of older generations reminded Tom of a story about Donnie Nunn's grandfather, known to everyone as Uncle Wash, who was a tobacco-chewer notorious for his lack of concern about where he got rid of tobacco juice. According to the story, Uncle Wash was sitting in the lobby of the Helm Hotel, in Bowling Green, one day, casually spitting tobacco juice on the floor while a porter desperately tried to maneuver a spittoon to a strategic spot next to him. "By God, son," Uncle Wash finally said. "If you don't quit moving that damn thing around, I'm going to spit right in it." After a few more Uncle Wash stories, it was nearly time to pick up Aunt Daisie.

Two days away from her eighty-seventh birthday, Aunt Daisie seemed to be in good health except for some arthritis that was giving her trouble with her legs. "How are you?" I said as Tom helped her into the car.

"Well, I'm about out of the running," she said, in a cheerful voice that made it plain that she considered herself well in the running.

"Oh, she's just got a little hitch in her get-along," Tom said.

Aunt Daisie didn't seem to have become less active since the last time I'd seen her. In fact, she told me later that she had recently attended her first cockfight — something she had been meaning to get around to for years. She rather enjoyed it, although she warned that it wasn't for the squeamish. "There's right smart blood involved," she said. On the way to Sulphur Well, we passed the farm where Aunt Daisie and Boots had grown up — the Chaneys' home place. We drove through communities that had made do with rather primitive one-room schoolhouses as late as the mid-forties, at which point Aunt Daisie became school superintendent and managed, in an eight-year reign, to close ninety-eight of the one hundred one-room schoolhouses left in Hart County. We passed by settlements best known for having adopted official names that sounded more respectable than the names by which local people knew them — like Hiseville, which most people still refer to as Goose Horn. Aunt Daisie was reminded of a time when she was studying at Western Kentucky and heard a Metcalfe County boy inform some fellow students, in a tone of newly learned sophistication, that he was from Savoyard, Kentucky. " 'Oh,' I said. 'You mean you're from Chicken Bristle.' "

When we arrived at Porter's, Tom came around to open the car door for Aunt Daisie. "What can I do to help?" he asked.

"You can look off somewhere," Aunt Daisie said, with a short laugh.

Porter's is a neighborly place that keeps a supply of country hams hung on a hatrack just inside the door. The ham we ate was splendid, although the first bite reminded me that I might have still been a bit thirsty from the last time I'd had it. The lunchtime conversation eventually turned to what Tom sometimes calls "the marijuana thing." Aunt Daisie said she had been astonished when she heard, early that morning in July of 1983, that Tom had been arrested and was being held for arraignment at the state police barracks in Bowling Green. She agreed with Tom about what Boots Chaney's reaction to the incident would have been: "Damn it, Tom! I told you never to mess with those Nunns."

"I was studying American literature, and I got involved with William Faulkner and Robert Penn Warren," Tom said. "And through them I began to see something about someone defining himself through what his family was and where he came from." We were sitting in the Horse Cave Country Inn, talking about how Tom's experiences in academe — what appeared to be, as he put it, "getting so far from my raisin' " — had in some ways helped to steer him back to Horse Cave. He said that he hadn't really been ready when he came back in 1964, partly because he was still sufficiently self-conscious about his break with the Southern Baptist Church to feel guilty every Sunday when eleven o'clock came and he was at home. Tom had been ordained while he was at the seminary — he continued over the years to perform marriage ceremonies for friends — but he had left both the ministry and his belief. One reason, he told me, was that the Southern Baptist Church's intransigence on the race issue "made preaching love and brotherhood like hitting your head against a wall"; another was that, as he put it, "I got to thinking that there wasn't any Truth with a capital 'T,' or if there was I didn't have access to it."

By the time he came home for good, though, he felt comfortable in Horse Cave. "He has been a member of the Horse Cave Rotary since 1976," a pre-sentencing report submitted by his lawyer said. "As a member of the club, he has been active in all of its programs and projects, including a major role in organizing the Horse Cave Tobacco Festival . . . He has been a frequent speaker at the Horse Cave Rotary Club luncheons and at other Rotary Clubs in the region . . . Along with his colleague, Joe V. Graber, Mr. Chaney conceived the idea of a professional repertory theatre in Horse Cave . . . He has been vice-president and president of the Green River Dairy Herd Improvement Association." In speaking appearances, Tom normally just told stories — stories about his kinfolks or about politicians or about preachers. Sooner or later, I suppose, he would have acquired stories about the Horse Cave Tobacco Festival and the Green River Dairy Herd Improvement Association. He was, after all, back where his material came from.

The Horse Cave Theatre has actually survived, even though it has resolutely mixed Shakespeare and Shaw and Tennessee Williams with the light comedies that might be expected in a small-town summer theater. The bed-and-breakfast inn Tom was managing had been started — in a place Tom often visited when it was his cousin Caroline's house — partly on the strength of tourist business generated by the theater. For a time, Tom served as chairman of the theater's board of directors; he even acted in a production of Preston Jones's *The Last Meeting of the Knights of the White Magnolia*. Eventually, though, he drifted away — partly because he felt some tension with the director over what amounted to proprietorship. "It has to be someone's theater, and he naturally thought it should be his," Tom told me. "It's like the story they tell in Edmonton about the stranger who came to town and asked directions to the Church of Christ. 'Well, that's Mr. Joe Martin's church over there,' the man he had asked told him. 'And Mr. Barlow's church is yonder. Church of Christ? I don't believe he has one here.' "

Tom's farming ventures with his Aunt Daisie did not go well — not the corn-and-tobacco farm, not the dairy herd, not the feed store and mill. It may be that Tom was simply not cut out to be a farmer or a businessman. It may be that he ventured into agriculture at exactly the wrong time. Farmers in Kentucky, like farmers in most parts of the country, were suffering from a precipitous increase in interest rates without a corresponding increase in crop prices. The pressure on a lot of farmers was intensified by a steady drop in land values. By the spring of 1983, when Donnie Nunn approached Tom about raising marijuana, Tom and Aunt Daisie were in what he describes as "pretty ticklish financial straits." Nunn was not riding high himself. Around the time he served as sheriff and Republican precinct captain, he had been widely considered a shrewd and powerful politician. In the years that followed, though, he had found himself with a lack of steady employment and a drinking problem and some difficulty recuperating from a serious car accident. Even those who don't like Donnie Nunn say that one thing he never lost was his power of persuasion. When I asked Daymond Humphrey, the present sheriff of Hart County, what Donnie Nunn was like, the sheriff described him this way: "Donnie could come in here and sit down and talk you out of your shoes."

"Well, it's like the Kentucky poet Wendell Berry said about the fox," Tom said when I asked him about his conversations with Donnie Nunn. "He makes more tracks than necessary, and some in the wrong direction." Tom was among half a dozen Hart County farmers who agreed to lease their corn land for raising something they knew wasn't corn. Nunn assured Tom double protection. Since Tom would simply lease the land — people from another county would be brought in to tend the crops — he could plead ignorance. Also, Nunn said, the three law-enforcement officers whose responsibilities included policing such activities — Sheriff Humphrey and two members of the Bowling Green state police detachment, Robert Sheldon and Ron West — were in on the scheme.

Tom had no trouble believing this part of the pitch, and not simply because he knew so many stories about sheriffs whose relationship with bootleggers had not been purely adversarial. Nunn was an old friend of Sheldon's and had done some serious favors for him in the past. It was rumored in Hart County that Sheriff Humphrey himself raised marijuana somewhere near Cub Run, in the northern part of the county, and shipped it to Colorado hidden in truckloads of firewood. Nunn did approach Sheldon, who reported the conversation to his superiors and from then on spoke to Nunn while wearing a recording device. Sheriff Humphrey, who says that what he sent to Colorado in truckloads of firewood was firewood, was also approached, and also began wearing a recording device. From then on, Donnie Nunn was the unwitting point man of a sting operation. One interpretation of what happened to the scheme is that Nunn simply outsmarted himself by trying to put the fix in. When the arrests came, West told reporters that if he and Sheldon and Humphrey hadn't been approached they would probably never have known that the marijuana fields existed. It may be that Donnie Nunn was not cut out to be an organizer of marijuana-growing conspiracies. Someone who holds that view told me, "He's got a big mouth on him, but a big mouth is all he's got."

When people in Munfordville, the seat of Hart County, tell courthouse stories, some names come up again and again. Just about any lawyer or judge in the county, for instance, is likely to have a supply of stories about a large clan called the Hortons, some of whom are troublesome and some of whom have been downright dangerous. "They was a mean set of people," Sheriff Humphrey said of the older generation of Hortons one day while he and some lawyers were trading stories. Charlie Williams, Tom's lawyer, likes to tell the story of the old lawyer in Glasgow who became convinced that the Hortons were one of the ten lost tribes of Israel. A story about the Hortons is likely to lead eventually to a story about moonshine — a couple of the Hortons apparently made moonshine of surpassing quality — and maybe even to a story about mixing marijuana plants in with more conventional crops.

"He's got a peculiar way of growing corn," someone said one day when a few people were sitting in the back of Charlie Williams's law office telling stories. The remark was made about a prominent local landowner who was suspected by some of raising marijuana, and it was followed by a long silence.

"Yes, it's odd," someone else said.

"What's so odd about it?" I asked.

"Well, he didn't harvest it, for one."

In organizing his marijuana-growing scheme, Donnie Nunn did not approach the sort of people widely suspected of growing corn in a peculiar way or the sort of people whose names were the staple of courthouse stories. The farmers he recruited had never had any serious run-ins with the law. Although Tom does not claim to belong to that narrow section of the population which spent most of the sixties and seventies on college campuses and did not try even one joint, his own smoking habit would have been better served by a field of pipe tobacco than by a field of pot. Several of the other farmers involved seem like the sort of rural people who are only dimly aware that some folks somewhere smoke marijuana cigarettes. Even now, the sheriff describes them as "respectable people, hardworking people — not the sort of people who end up in court all the time on assault charges." Their respectability was apparently part of their appeal.

Most of the farmers involved had financial problems. "It was people just like myself, who needed to get up on their feet a little better financially," I was told by one of the farmers, an angular, serious-looking man with a weathered face. We were talking in the kitchen of his farmhouse. His son was mowing the lawn outside. Through the kitchen window I could see rows of corn. I found it odd to sit in a farmhouse kitchen and talk about marijuana cultivation with a man who could have posed for one of those photographs which are meant to show the resilience of the American family farmer. It could be argued, of course, that respectable farmers in Hart County have less reason to be shocked than farmers in some other places at being approached about growing a substance that is widely used but clearly illegal: they live, after all, in a county that is both legally dry and full of people with drinking problems. Throughout Kentucky, though, there must be a lot of marijuana grown by the sort of people nobody would suspect of growing it. Kentucky is hardly a stronghold of the counterculture, but the *Louisville Courier-Journal* was reporting as early as 1980 that marijuana was thought to have overtaken tobacco as the state's leading cash crop — at a time when its annual sales of tobacco were five hundred million dollars. The Louisville papers have written a lot about the legal and social issues involved, but, inevitably, some of the headlines about marijuana begin to have the routine sound of a farm report on corn or soybeans ("POT CROP REMAINS NEAR TOP IN NATION DESPITE DROUGHT"). Whatever various states have decided about whether marijuana ought to be a criminal issue, the sort of farmer Donnie Nunn was able to recruit seemed to be an indication that a lot of ordinary farm people no longer considered it a moral issue. The farmer I talked to in his kitchen had worried about breaking the law, and had worried even more about the possibility of getting caught. But he hadn't had the feeling that what Nunn had asked him to do was morally repugnant. Neither had Tom. Both of them seem certain that they never want to become involved in such activities again, but both of them seem to be only half joking when they refer to marijuana as "a supplemental cash crop."

Tom considers Randall Skaggs a pretty good storyteller. Skaggs is a rotund, affable man who lives with his family in a modern brick house in a town twenty miles or so north of Horse Cave. I heard some Donnie Nunn stories from Skaggs. We were in the room that Skaggs had created by finishing his basement — a large area dominated by pictures of racehorses and racks of trophies won by softball teams and Little League teams that Skaggs had coached. Skaggs told me the story about how Nunn, while running for sheriff, managed to get the support of two neighboring farmers in the

Three Springs area who hated each other but had in common a pride in how many votes they controlled and an opposition to Nunn's candidacy ("So then he told the other one, 'I'm going across the road to give that son of a bitch a cussin' now, because I heard he has done made the statement that he controls every vote out on these roads and he's going against us' "). He told me about how Nunn had been advised by his father, who had also been sheriff of Hart County, to store up political favors by staying active even when he was out of office ("If a bumblebee and a grasshopper are in a race, take sides"). Skaggs knows Donnie Nunn well, because he was once Nunn's deputy sheriff. He went from that to the insurance business. He eventually settled on a career as a professional gambler — an occupation for which he has never offered any apologies, pointing out, as a Kentucky bootlegger might, that what he does is legal in some places and illegal in others and done all over. Skaggs was among those indicted for having participated in Donnie Nunn's scheme; he was accused of having made some introductions that linked farmers in Hart County with some people in Marion County who were looking for a place to grow marijuana. It all came about, Skaggs said, through someone he had met in a poker game — a man he described as among those "we in the business call honorable people: they don't bet on ballgames that are already over; if they owe you three hundred dollars, they don't forget about it." Randall Skaggs and Tom met in their first few days at the Federal Correctional Institution at Lexington.

More than any of the other people arrested, Randall Skaggs is still engrossed by the case. He has transcripts of the secret recordings made by Sheldon and Humphrey. He has copies of the tapes. He has a lot of questions. If the local law-enforcement people launched an undercover operation of such effectiveness and probity, he asks, why was one of the state policemen transferred far from his home and the other one encouraged to retire? The local law-enforcement people have questions of their own. Sheriff Humphrey says that he and Sheldon and West — "three country boys" — had a perfect case going until higher-ups took charge. In an affidavit included among the documents that Charlie Williams submitted in arguing for a reduction of Tom Chaney's sentence, Sheriff Humphrey said, "The affiant has had numerous opportunities to bust and has busted local people who have grown marijuana in small amounts, but this operation presented a chance to apprehend the big operators and money men. Because the arrests were made prematurely, before harvest, and at a time when there was no hope of discovering the identity of the principal organizers and money men, the affiant feels that his efforts were for naught and that only the least culpable people were finally apprehended." The inside story of Donnie Nunn's marijuana operation, like a lot of stories in south-central Kentucky, has a lot of versions.

The story that Randall Skaggs tells about Tom in the penitentiary took place in those first few days of their term, when they were in a large dormitory area that is used for new prisoners and for prisoners who have lost their room privileges because of some infraction of the rules. "One day, we were playing a card game called pitch," Skaggs told me. "We were teaching two other guys, so Tom and I each took one of the inexperienced players. It was Tom's bid. He didn't say anything for a long time. It seemed like a couple of minutes. Maybe it was forty seconds. Finally, I said, 'It's your bid, Tom.' He still didn't say anything. He just sat there staring out the window at this concrete wall and the rain. I said, 'Tom — it's your bid.' It seemed like a minute passed. Then he said, 'What in the hell are we doing here?' "

Tom doesn't have many stories about life in the penitentiary. The Federal Correctional Institution at Lexington is a low-security prison, but it's still a prison. It has strip searches and more regulations than anyone feels confident of being able to obey all at the same time, and some guards who, in Tom's words, "like to play some really demeaning games with you to keep you off balance." But it's the sort of prison that has rooms instead of cells and has daily visiting hours. Although Tom said that "not all the unpleasant people were guards," an inmate of Lexington does not live with the constant fear of physical danger that he might have in a lot of American prisons. Tom worked as an orderly in a dormitory, a job that left him most of the day to read and write. He began trying to encompass some of the stories he had learned from Boots in pieces of fiction. A school friend who lives in Lexington came out to see him a couple of times a week; the friend's wife sent him something in the mail — maybe just a political cartoon she thought he might like, but something — every single day. In the view of the farmer I spoke to in his farmhouse kitchen, Tom seemed to have the resources to do time pretty well. "They weren't able to hassle Tom a lot," the farmer told me. "He did O.K. He could've made it sittin' on a rock if that's what it come down to."

"He couldn't see the inside of me," Tom said when I reported that assessment. "Those three months seemed like three years to me." According to Tom, being in prison tends to make someone wary, with a heightened sense of his surroundings. Most prisoners, of course, also have a heightened sense of time. In one of his letters from prison to Charlie Williams, Tom said that it all reminded him of the story about the hog.

"What's the story about the hog?" I asked one day as we were chatting at the Horse Cave Country Inn.

"Well, there are two hog stories," Tom said.

"That goes without saying," I said. "What's the appropriate hog story?"

"Well, there was a farmer who owned a shoat and a persimmon tree," Tom said. "And as the persimmons got ripe and fell off the tree the shoat was eating them. And he liked them so much that he soon ran out of ripe persimmons on the ground. So the farmer went out and picked up the shoat and held him up to the tree. And he was eating the persimmons off the tree with the farmer holding him up when a neighbor came out and saw him doing this and said, 'Well, I reckon you *could* fatten a hog that way, but it'd sure take a lot of time.' And the farmer turned, holding the hog up there, and he said, 'Shoot, don't you know time don't mean nothing to a hog?' "

The day before I left Horse Cave, Tom was busy preparing for a gathering that evening of some people at the Horse Cave Country

Inn to have dinner and tell stories. The group included people from two or three counties who were known as storytellers — and a few people who were considered excellent listeners. It also included three men who were known to do a little guitar-picking and fiddle-playing and singing. Tom had met once before with the same group, shortly before his arrest. A lot had changed in his life since then. He was an ex-con. He was a felon. He had added "reformed farmer" and "reformed mill operator" to his résumé: the holdings that he and his Aunt Daisie owned together had been sold just before he went to prison, in an effort to stave off bankruptcy.

Still, a lot had not changed. It had never occurred to Tom not to return to Horse Cave when he was released from prison. In the months between the time he pleaded guilty and the time he reported to Lexington, he hadn't been snubbed by his neighbors; in fact, some of them had told him quietly that, whatever he had done, they considered him their friend. His arrest hadn't seemed to change anyone's view of Aunt Daisie or of Jerry Matera or of Ann Matera, who is the city clerk of Horse Cave. Tom couldn't think of anyone whose attitude toward him had changed drastically after "the marijuana thing" except, perhaps, one banker. The gathering of storytellers was to include two former state judges — James Gillenwater, an attorney from Barren County who had served as county judge, and Cass Walden, a retired circuit-court judge — but as we discussed the event that morning Tom didn't seem apprehensive about that causing any awkwardness. What he did seem apprehensive about was the news, conveyed by Charlie Williams the day before, that Judge Gillenwater insisted on sending over some groundhogs for Tom to cook for dinner. "He keeps saying that they're the cleanest animals there is," Tom told me, without enthusiasm. A few minutes later, Williams phoned again. Judge Gillenwater, having realized that Tom wasn't quite certain just how to cook a groundhog and was not looking forward to finding out, had suggested that Tom cook anything he wanted to and then try groundhog at the annual varmint supper the Judge holds every winter. Tom, greatly relieved, decided to pan-fry some chicken.

The guests started showing up around seven. Both judges were there, along with a couple of lawyers who had considerable experience in giving judges their respectful attention. The musicians included a surveyor, a man who works for the telephone company, and a young lawyer who could sing anti-coal-company songs with titles like "Black Waters." Jerry Matera came over from across the street to listen. Charlie Williams came with the other lawyer in his firm, Chuck Pritchett, and a friend of Pritchett's from Letcher County who could tell tales of eastern Kentucky. Williams does some writing, and, like Tom, has an inclination to see the goings-on in his home territory as stories: Pritchett says that the first thing Charlie Williams asks a new client is to provide his family tree.

For décor, Tom had put out an old ballot box that Jerry Matera bought at a courthouse auction, and as the guests arrived it naturally provoked the story of J. D. Reynolds's sit-down strike — which inspired a story about some inflation in vote-buying a number of years ago. ("So old Aunt Lucy straightened up and said, 'Mr. Abe, I done cast my last fifty-cent ballot.' ")

As everyone got settled in the living room, Judge Walden asked Tom how long he had been managing the inn.

"Well, just about ever since I got back from the penitentiary, Judge," Tom said.

The pan-fried chicken was as good as I remembered it from Covington. After we had all had our fill, everyone gathered in the living room again for some stories and music. The prospect of music started someone talking about a one-legged fiddler named Keen Bradley, and that, in due time, led to a story about a one-eyed Baptist preacher in Monroe County who can be called Brother One-Eye Haynes ("It was rumored that he had his eye put out in a bawdy house in Nashville"), and that led to a story about a revivalist I'll call Pappy Hawkins, who was a successful traveling faith healer until a confederate he was about to heal of blindness and paralysis stood up in the middle of a long healing prayer and said, "By God, I've got to have a drink." That eventually led to Tom's doing a sermon about a sermon, complete with those odd snorts that some low-church preachers use as a sort of punctuation when they get warmed up: "And this preacher, he had not cluttered his mind with education — huh. He had left it like God intended it to be, empty — huh . . . And he never knew the taste of whiskey . . . And he said one Sunday, 'Brothers and sisters — huh — our text today is Song of Solomon 2:12: The voice of the turtle is heard in the land. Now, brothers and sisters — huh — I don't — huh — know what this Scripture means, but let's read it one more time — huh . . . I still don't know what it means.' "

Judge Walden and Judge Gillenwater both had stories about Buck Williams, an unschooled but remarkably acute black man from Chicken Bristle who was said to be so multitalented that he could have qualified as an expert witness. ("I pull calves. I shoe horses. I shoe mules. I castrates colts. I relieves old men of their water. And I have fried more fish for the Republican Party than any living man in this county.") There were stories about a legendary midwife and stories about a local man who had given his daughter the name Passing the Fair Shores Bryant. ("Oh, yeah, I knew her — they called her Passie.") Then Tom told the story that Boots used to tell about his half-great-uncle Doc and Doc's wife, Skillet. I figured it was only a matter of time until we got to Uncle Wash, and then it occurred to me that Uncle Wash stories could lead to stories about his grandson, Donnie Nunn. There is no reason, after all, that generational digression can't go in either direction. It occurred to me, in fact, that it's probably only a matter of time until "the marijuana thing" gets folded into the Kentucky storytelling. The chain could easily start with a story Tom had once told me about Uncle Wash:

"They tell a story about Uncle Wash. You know, Uncle Wash couldn't read. And one day he was down at the barbershop, looking at the *Courier-Journal* like he was reading, except it was upside down. And there was a picture of a ship on the front page. Someone said, 'What's in the newspaper, Uncle Wash?' And Uncle Wash said, 'Well, I tell you one thing: there's been a bad shipwreck.' "

"That reminds me of Uncle Wash's grandson, Donnie Nunn. Now, that old boy could talk."

"There was that time Donnie went over near Horse Cave where Tom Chaney was running this mill —"

"Boots Chaney's boy. Now, there was a man who could tell a story — old Boots Chaney."

"— and he started talking to Tom about this farmer in Metcalfe County who raised corn. And he said this old boy had a peculiar way of raisin' corn . . ."

1984

THE LIFE
AND TIMES OF
JOE BOB BRIGGS,
SO FAR

THE PROBLEM WAS how to deal with trashy movies. It's a common problem among movie reviewers. What, exactly, does the film critic of a main-line American daily newspaper do about movies like *The Night Evelyn Came Out of the Grave* and *Malibu Hot Summer* and *Bloodsucking Freaks*? Does he pick one out, on a slow week, and subject it to the sort of withering sarcasm that sometimes, in his braver daydreams, he sees himself using on the executive editor? Does he simply ignore such movies, preferring to pretend that a person of his sensibilities could not share an artistic universe with such efforts as *Mother Riley Meets the Vampire* and *Driller Killer* and *Gas Pump Girls*?

The *Dallas Times Herald* had that problem, and in late 1981 it seemed to have more or less stumbled onto a solution. The assistant managing editor for features, Ron Smith, had asked the movie reviewer, a young man named John Bloom, to look into the question of why drive-in movie theaters, which were folding in most places, still thrived in patches of the country that included the area around Dallas. Bloom came back with a proposal: he could review the sort of movies that play in Texas drive-ins — they are sometimes called exploitation movies — through the persona of a fictional drive-in customer who was actually able to distinguish between a successful zombie-surfing movie and a zombie-surfing movie that didn't quite work. "I had been thinking about doing a

column from someone with a personality that is completely opposite of what we think is tasteful," Bloom later said. "I had been
saying to Ron, 'What would happen if a movie critic loved *I Spit on
Your Grave* and hated *Dumbo*? What if this guy suddenly had an
aesthetic revelation and started looking at Charles Bronson as an
auteur?' "

Bloom first suggested a reviewer named Bobo Rodriguez. He envisioned Bobo as a "kind of all-purpose ethnic, like Andy Kauf-
man's foreigner: you don't know what nationality he is but he's
quintessentially foreign." Smith rejected Bobo Rodriguez as a character Dallas minorities were bound to find offensive no matter
how many times they were assured that the real target was pretentious film criticism or respectable Anglo moviegoers. The character Bloom came up with instead was a young redneck he called Joe
Bob Briggs. Smith liked that idea. He decided to give Joe Bob some
space in the back pages of *Weekend*, the paper's Friday entertainment tabloid — a low-priority operation that was generally
avoided by reporters and was probably best known to readers as
the part of the *Times Herald* most likely to come off on your
hands. In January of 1982, the *Times Herald* ran Joe Bob Briggs's
first movie review, under the heading "JOE BOB GOES TO THE
DRIVE-IN." The movie being considered was *The Grim Reaper*,
in which the title character "likes to kill people and then chew on
them for a while." Joe Bob liked it.

In an accompanying piece introducing his new colleague to the
readers of the *Times Herald*, John Bloom said he had met Joe Bob
at the snack bar of the Century Drive-In, in Grand Prairie, Texas,
during an all-night Bela Lugosi marathon. According to Bloom, Joe
Bob was, at nineteen, a drive-in authority of enormous experience:
he had seen sixty-eight hundred drive-in movies, and had still
found time for at least three marriages. Experience had not
brought a strong sense of responsibility. Only a month or so after
the column began — a month during which John Bloom found a
Brazilian film called *Pixote* to be "powerful" and "unsettling," and
Joe Bob praised not only *Mad Monkey Kung Fu* ("We're talking serious chopsocky here") but a snakebite horror movie that his girl-

friend of the moment, May Ellen Masters, refused to watch with her eyes open — the new columnist disappeared. (Bloom had taken some vacation time.) Bloom finally reported that he had found Joe Bob — in jail, in Bossier City, Louisiana. Joe Bob had been arrested for beating up an auto mechanic named Gus Simpson, who not only had sold Joe Bob's baby-blue Dodge Dart for parts to Junior Stebbens, of Mineral Wells, but also had been discovered by Joe Bob with the perfidious May Ellen Masters in a room at the Have-A-Ball Tourist Courts. By that time, it was clear from the volume of inquiries about Joe Bob's whereabouts that "Joe Bob Goes to the Drive-In," which Smith had envisioned as an occasional feature or maybe even a one-time event, had become a Friday staple of the *Times Herald.*

Eventually, Bloom's authorship became a sort of open secret in the Dallas newspaper world, but for the better part of a year it was a real secret even from the people who worked in the *Times Herald* newsroom. A lot of readers believed that the Joe Bob Briggs column was in fact written by a nineteen-year-old redneck who had seen sixty-eight hundred drive-in movies. "They bought that," Ron Smith said later, sounding amazed as he recalled it. "There were people on this staff — serious newspaper people — who bought that." Many of those who finally became suspicious, of course, settled their suspicions on John Bloom. He was, after all, the only person on the paper who claimed to have met Joe Bob. He was the movie reviewer. His initials were similar to Joe Bob's initials. Close readers might even have noticed that when Bloom wrote about Joe Bob in those first weeks of shepherding the column into the paper he fell into rather Joe Bobbian phrasing himself — as when he wrote that Joe Bob's adventures around Bossier City had left his head looking like "the inside of a Big Mac after it's been left on the dashboard three or four days," or when he wrote that Joe Bob's previous car had been ruined at the Ark-La-Tex Twin "when a dough-head in a Barracuda crunched his rear door and scared Dede Wilks half out of her halter top." Bloom's basic defense against the accusations of authorship was that he could hardly have been less like Joe Bob. A soft-spoken, reserved, almost withdrawn young man who had graduated with honors from Vanderbilt, Bloom drove a Toyota instead of a baby-blue 1968 Dodge Dart. He spoke with a trace of a Southwestern accent, but it would have been difficult to imagine him using Joe Bobbisms like "He don't give a diddly" or expressing his admiration for an actress by saying "Bootsie is not just another humongous set of garbanzas." An admirer of foreign films, Bloom wrote essays on the *nouvelle vague* while Joe Bob was rating movies according to the amount of innards displayed ("We're talking Glopola City") and the number of severed body parts that could be seen rolling away and the number of breasts exposed ("the garbanza department").

Bloom wanted Joe Bob to "talk about movies the way most people talk about movies: they give the plot, with emphasis on their favorite scenes, then they sum up what they think of it." Joe Bob tended to tell the plot ("So this flick starts off with a bimbo getting chained up and killed by a bunch of Meskins dressed up like Roman soldiers in their bathrobes"), and his summaries eventually developed into his best-known trademark: "Sixty-four dead bodies. Bimbos in cages. Bimbos in chains. Arms roll. Thirty-nine breasts. Two beasts (giant lizard, octopus). Leprosy. Kung fu. Bimbo fu. Sword fu. Lizard fu. Knife fu. Seven battles. Three quarts blood. A 39 on the vomit meter . . . Joe Bob says check it out."

What some readers wondered about such material was not who was writing it but how it got into the newspaper. The short answer was that it was sneaked in. Ron Smith and Bloom, playing around with ways to handle a section of the paper that even the editors didn't read very closely, hadn't taken the Joe Bob gimmick seriously enough as a long-term proposition to consult any of the sort of editors Joe Bob began referring to in print as high sheriffs. If a gathering of top editors had been presented with a formal plan to run a truly tasteless weekly column by a fictional trash-movie fanatic, Joe Bob Briggs would presumably have gone the way of Bobo Rodriguez. The *Dallas Times Herald* was a lively newspaper, but even lively newspapers are cautious institutions. As it was, the Joe Bob column impressed itself on the consciousness of the paper's principal editors after it had begun gaining a foothold with the readers. Not long after that, it became apparent that "Joe Bob Goes to the Drive-In" was on its way to becoming the most talked-about feature in the paper. "You can't imagine what incredible appeal it had in those early months," someone who was at the *Times Herald* at the time has said. "When the Friday paper came out, everyone in the newsroom stopped whatever he was doing to turn to *Weekend* and find out what outrage Joe Bob was perpetrating now." The same thing was happening all over town. Friday was Joe Bob Day among young professional people who worked in the shiny new office buildings of downtown Dallas. Friday was also Joe Bob Day among folks who, in the words of one *Times Herald* reporter, "were grateful that there was finally someone in the paper who wrote normal."

The top editors of the *Times Herald* were constantly being reassured that the perpetration of outrages was all right. It was satire, they were told; it was not really written by some crazed redneck, after all, but by the thoughtful and enlightened John Bloom. But they were still uneasy about running Joe Bob's column. Daily newspapers have never been comfortable with satire. Daily newspapers have never been comfortable with columnists who perpetrate outrages. Then, in November of 1982, the *Wall Street Journal* ran a long front-page story by G. Christian Hill headlined "AFICIONADO OF TRASH AT THE TIMES HERALD IS A BIG HIT IN DALLAS." The *Journal* piece conferred an almost instant legitimacy on "Joe Bob Goes to the Drive-In." The high sheriffs at the *Times Herald* breathed easier. The Los Angeles Times Syndicate — whose parent company, the Times Mirror Company, owned the *Dallas Times Herald* — offered Joe Bob a syndication contract. A young woman who had met Bloom through handling the advertising for some Dallas exploitation-movie distributors became a literary agent on the spot and sent a Joe Bob Briggs book proposal to fifty editors whose names she got out of a guide to the publishing industry. Joe Bob wrote the proposal's covering letter himself. Since it was important correspondence, he used his special stationery — the stuff decorated with reproductions of movie posters for drive-in classics like *Doctor Butcher, M.D.* and *The Slumber Party Massacre* and *Vampire Playgirls.*

The letter began, "Dear Big Shot Publisher: Cherry Dilday is typing this sucker up for me, so if we got technical problems, I'm telling you right now, I'm not responsible. Cherry claims she got a typing diploma from the Industrial Trades Institute on Harry Hines Boulevard, but I know for a fact that she left school after two weeks to go to the dog track in West Memphis with Dexter Crook. She'd probly amount to something today if she'd stayed for the full three. Correct me if I'm wrong, but I've been told you're interested in getting filthy rich off my book." Several of them were. Joe Bob signed a contract with Dell.

Among large American cities, Dallas has had a reputation for being run, rather smoothly, by an oligarchy. While other cities of the Old Confederacy were battling over the demands of the civil rights movement, for instance, whatever desegregation could not be avoided in Dallas was arranged quietly from above by a group of conservative white businessmen called the Dallas Citizens Council — a fact often mentioned to explain why Dallas's black community has been slow to develop aggressive and independent leaders of its own. The Citizens Council also installed slates of city councilmen. Jim Schutze, who does an urban-affairs column for the *Times Herald,* has written that until 1978, when city councilmen began being elected in single-member districts instead of at large, Dallas was, in effect, a "well-run predemocratic city-state." The oligarchy's newspaper was the *Dallas Morning News* — an appropriately sober, locally owned, journalistically conservative paper whose editorial page is even now described occasionally as Dixiecrat. Until the mid-seventies the *Morning News* dominated the Dallas newspaper market. Its competition, the *Dallas Times Herald,* was an afternoon paper that had a smaller circulation and carried advertising that ran more toward Kmart than toward Neiman-Marcus. Like a lot of afternoon papers, the *Times Herald* concentrated on local coverage — particularly the juicier murders. The joke names for the two papers in Dallas were the *Morning Snooze* and the *Crimes Herald.*

In the middle seventies, all that changed. The Times Mirror Company — a huge, expansionist communications corporation whose empire includes the *Los Angeles Times* and *Newsday* — had bought the *Times Herald* in 1969, in a deal that included five-year contracts for the management that was in place. As the contracts expired, the *Times Herald* launched an ambitious campaign to overtake the *Morning News* and become the preeminent newspaper of Dallas — a prize of considerable value, since the Dallas market was expanding daily in the Texas boom that had been touched off by the Arab oil embargo and fed by Sun Belt migration. The *Times Herald* gradually transformed itself into an all-day paper. New editors were hired from papers like the *Washington Post* and the *Philadelphia Inquirer,* and the new editors brought in eager young reporters from all over the country. The news coverage was aggressive, and the editors made it clear that they were unconcerned about which powerful citizen or potential advertiser might be in the line of fire. A sign on the newsroom wall said, "THE ONLY SACRED COW HERE IS HAMBURGER." The newsroom took on the sort of élan that in the early sixties was associated with the *New York Herald Tribune*. Reporters were encouraged to come up with stories that had what the new managing editor, Will Jarrett, called "pop" or "sizzle." The editorial page found a moderate niche in that vast area of opinion that lay to the left of the *Dallas Morning News,* and it put forward late-twentieth-century views on racial and social issues. The *Times Herald* solidified its position as the newspaper that concerned itself with the problems of Dallas's minorities, but, in a way, the new version of the paper seemed to be directed toward a new Dallas audience — the people who had moved to the Sun Belt from the North and the younger Dallas natives who had turned away a bit from the economic and cultural conservatism of their parents. It worked. In 1980 — at the height of the boom — the *Times Herald,* which had started many laps behind, almost pulled even with the *Morning News* in circulation.

John Bloom was among the brightest of the *Times Herald*'s new crop of bright young reporters. Will Jarrett had remembered him from a summer Bloom spent as a college intern at the *Philadelphia Inquirer*. Jarrett found Bloom in Nashville, where he was editing a country-club magazine, and hired him, despite the fact that two other editors who met him thought he was too shy to be a reporter. Bloom says he was the paper's "fluff specialist" for a while — the reporter papers depend on to write their way out of a story on the first day of spring or a story on the new baby giraffe at the zoo — but he also worked on stories about mistreatment of Mexican-Americans taken into police custody and about a resurgence of the Klan. After only two years on the paper, he was chosen to be what the *Times Herald* called its Texas Ranger — a reporter who roams across the state looking for stories. In 1978, he left to join *Texas Monthly*, a magazine whose young nonfiction writers were bringing it a national reputation, and then, toward the end of 1981, he returned to the *Times Herald* as the movie reviewer. Only a couple of months later, he went to the Century Drive-In in Grand Prairie and discovered Joe Bob Briggs.

There are any number of people on newspapers around the country who could easily be imagined sliding into the character of Joe Bob Briggs — people who wrap themselves in the blue-denim cloak of childhoods in places like west Texas or south Georgia — but John Bloom was not among them. Nothing about him suggested that he might harbor within him a wild nineteen-year-old redneck. Bloom was the son of schoolteachers — Southern Baptists from Texas who, fairly early in his childhood, settled in Little Rock. It was not a childhood spent beating up auto mechanics or watching trashy movies at drive-ins with the likes of May Ellen Masters and Cherry Dilday and the other girls Joe Bob was always describing as "dumb as a box of rocks." As an infant, Bloom had contracted polio, and he spent part of junior high school with a withered right leg in a brace. He grew into a tall, exceedingly thin, almost theatrically handsome young man with pale skin and a thatch of black hair and a barely perceptible limp. In person, John Bloom would have fulfilled the expectations of a reader who had a strong vision of what a sensitive commentator on the *nouvelle vague* should look like, but he would have been a surprise to readers who had followed the ragged adventures of Joe Bob Briggs. When he is asked why he didn't acknowledge authorship of "Joe

Bob Goes to the Drive-In," he sometimes says, "I was almost afraid people would feel disappointed if they met me."

Although Bloom obviously didn't turn out to be too shy to be a reporter, he never really became part of the newsroom crowd. At both the *Times Herald* and *Texas Monthly,* his colleagues thought of him as a sort of outsider, who was likely to have odd hours and odd friends. Editors considered him enormously talented and also quietly intent on having his own way. Partly because Bloom had written long, thoughtful pieces for *Texas Monthly* on an articulate fundamentalist minister and on the Wycliffe Bible Translators, he was sometimes called John the Baptist. People who knew him on *Texas Monthly* tend to use the same phrases when they talk about him, which might suggest a unanimity of opinion except that one of the phrases is "You never really feel you know him." They sometimes spoke of him as Good John and Bad John — the Good John seen as sensitive and intelligent, the Bad John as cold and manipulative — and not many of them felt close enough to him to know which was the actual John Bloom. Neither Good John nor Bad John seemed to presage Joe Bob Briggs. During Bloom's time at *Texas Monthly,* some of his colleagues felt him to be edging toward the right politically but certainly not to the sort of right represented by Joe Bob Briggs, who once wrote that he wasn't terribly happy about being syndicated in San Francisco because "it goes against my principles to write a column for communist-speaking cities." Looking back recently at Bloom's days on *Texas Monthly,* the magazine's editor, Gregory Curtis, said, "I wasn't surprised he could become someone else, but I thought he might have turned into a Baptist preacher."

However unlikely it was, though, John Bloom could, when it came time to write Friday's column, transform himself with great ease into Joe Bob Briggs. Bloom seemed to be among those writers who find the use of an alter ego or a pseudonym liberating: he has said that producing a Joe Bob column took him about three hours, counting the time spent watching the movie. Almost from the beginning, Joe Bob wrote about his own life as well as about such matters as the transvestite wrestling scene in *Chained Heat.* Joe

Bob might start talking about how he'd asked Junior Stebbens to do a complete overhaul on the Toronado he bought after the demise of the Dodge Dart or about how the young woman he always referred to as Ugly on a Stick "went down to Tex Pawn and tried to get a 30-year breast improvement loan," and almost forget to get around to the movie he had just seen. He always printed letters from readers — preference given to hate mail — and he always showed no respect in his replies. ("We're talking jerkola at the minimum. We're probably talking wimp.") Jim Schutze believes that in those early months Bloom, through local references and an ear for local language, created not just a generic redneck but someone representative of the people who had been left out of the new Dallas — "the people on the fringe of Dallas, this Yankee island, who were country, who had to drive in for work in their pickups."

Bloom saw Joe Bob not simply as a redneck but as a particularly smart, diabolical, anarchistic redneck who was "full of latent sexual and violent energies" — someone who wasn't afraid to say anything. What a country storyteller named Gamble Rogers once said of the ornery and fearlessly outspoken cracker was a central feature of Joe Bob's character: "He don't care. He flat do not care." In fact, Joe Bob took pleasure in saying whatever seemed likely to offend someone, and his response to finding out that what he said had indeed given offense was to say it again. (Writing in *Patriotic Gore* about a Tennessee cracker who was an alter ego of a midnineteenth-century journalist named George Washington Harris, Edmund Wilson said, "One of the most striking things about *Sut Lovingood* is that it is all as offensive as possible.") It was a characteristic that made people turn to Joe Bob first thing on Friday morning — wondering what he might have gone and said now, and wondering how long he was going to get away with it.

It was also, of course, the characteristic that made the high sheriffs at the *Times Herald* edgy. Early in Joe Bob's career, they established a special system under which each Joe Bob column was read by two copy editors, both of whom had instructions to summon an assistant managing editor at any sign of trouble. It isn't unusual for Texas writers to use a plainspoken character like Joe Bob. Molly

Ivins, a popular *Times Herald* columnist who's based in Austin, tends to find her best material in the true adventures of Texas politicians — the gubernatorial candidate, for instance, whose fear of AIDS was so strong that on a trip to San Francisco he wore shower caps on his feet while standing in the hotel bathtub — but she also refers often to a sort of all-purpose Texas ol' boy she calls Bubba. Having such a character write the column himself, though, presented some special problems. One of them was what some people called the Archie Bunker factor — the problem of whether the column was making fun of Joe Bob or of the people Joe Bob was making fun of. Also, part of Joe Bob's impact was based on his saying something the readers would not have expected him to say. Although Bloom has always denied any strategy beyond trying to make jokes, there was a feeling at the *Times Herald* that Joe Bob had to "up the dosage" every Friday. "John's the sort of guy who wants to push and push," one of the high sheriffs has said. "Like a college editor trying to get a bad word in the paper." At times, he was precisely like a college editor trying to get a bad word in the paper — the only difference being that the word's excision would provide Joe Bob with a joke about being muzzled by the high sheriffs or by "the jerkola french-fry head communist censors in Washington."

A couple of years after the column began, an editor's note in *Weekend* said that Joe Bob, mentioning such irritations as "too many high sheriffs" and "too many guys named Todd living in Dallas," had left what appeared to be a letter of resignation, written on a page torn from a Big Chief spiral notebook. "Life is a fern bar and I'm out of here," Joe Bob wrote. "I'm history." But Joe Bob was back the next week, praising a movie called *The Being* for an "excellent slime glopola monster with moving mouth." By that time, there were people on the *Times Herald* who thought that the steady increase in dosage would inevitably make Joe Bob history sooner or later, and one editor had offered the opinion that the high sheriffs might consider the advantages of simply picking an opportune moment to have Joe Bob's Toronado spin out on the interstate.

It would obviously be unusual under any circumstances for a newspaper to kill its most popular feature. It would have been particularly difficult in the circumstances the *Times Herald* found itself in. By the time the Joe Bob Briggs column had become established, it was clear that the race with the *Morning News* was being lost. There were any number of theories to explain what had happened. The *Morning News*, partly because of the competition and partly from the infusion of some new blood in management, had greatly improved, making up in thoroughness what it might have lacked in sizzle. Its editorial page still might not have given great offense to those who drafted the Dixiecrat platform in 1948, but its news department had, in Will Jarrett's grudging words, "kind of started practicing modern journalism." ("Newspaper competition is usually like high-low poker," Molly Ivins has said. "But in this case both players went high.") Meanwhile, the *Times Herald* was having some problems. For a variety of reasons, it was without strong editorial leadership for a while. There was a newsroom power struggle that sapped a lot of the paper's energy. Some observers outside the paper thought that the management had never learned the prescribed Dallas method of getting along with the business leaders — people who have assumed the synonymy of their interests and the city's interests for so long that they routinely describe any story not respectful to business as "anti-Dallas" — and some reporters inside the paper grumbled that management was beginning to get along with the business leaders too well. Some people thought that the *Times Herald* had, in covering all of those extra laps necessary to catch up with the *Morning News*, simply run out of wind. Among the shrinking bright spots was "Joe Bob Goes to the Drive-In," which might have been the best-read feature in either paper. The *Times Herald* didn't simply tolerate Joe Bob. It put his name on billboards. It sold baseball caps that said "JOE BOB BRIGGS SEZ CHECK IT OUT" and T-shirts that said "JOE BOB BRIGGS IS A CLOSE PERSONAL FRIEND OF MINE."

The Baptists had been the first to complain. When it comes to objecting to offenses against public order and morality in Texas, they

are rarely beaten to the punch. Southern Baptists are well represented in Dallas — the First Baptist Church, led by the Reverend
W. A. Criswell, is the largest Baptist congregation in the entire
country — but the first serious complaint from Baptists about Joe
Bob Briggs came from a minister in Tyler, who said that Joe Bob's
preoccupation with sex and violence revealed a sick mind. The
Baptists were not alone. Joe Bob offended gays with some of his
San Francisco jokes, and he offended feminists with his Miss Custom Body Contest. Joe Bob offended so many different people
that the sheer variety of those he had outraged became part of the
standard defense of his column: Joe Bob's admirers said that he
was "an equal-opportunity offender." Joe Bob's response to complaints or criticism can be judged from an opinion survey he con-
ducted after a San Francisco film critic named Peter Stack differed
with him on whether a movie called *Basket Case* was an inept and
disgusting splatter flick or the single best movie of 1982. Inviting
the readers to settle the question democratically, Joe Bob provided
a ballot that said, "Question: In your opinion, is the french-fry-
head San Francisco writer named Peter Stack a wimp or not?"
Stack did not come out well in the balloting.

Despite Joe Bob's habit of referring to all females as bimbos and
his ubiquitous breast count and his celebration of movies that featured the dismemberment of women ("I'm telling you these
bimbos get hacked up until it's chop suey city") and his sponsor-
ship of the Miss Custom Body Contest ("All contestants must be
able to count to the number seven, and may not use such a demonstration as their 'talent' "), the first strong attack from feminists
didn't come until Joe Bob had been appearing for two years. A lot
of women who read the *Times Herald* — including a lot of women
who considered themselves feminists — thought Joe Bob was
funny. A number of them thought that he served to demonstrate
just how ludicrous Texas he-men were. In fact, before it became
general knowledge that Joe Bob was a creature of John Bloom,
Molly Ivins, who is widely known as a strong feminist, was regularly accused of being the author of "Joe Bob Goes to the Drive-
In."

When the attack came, it was led by Charlotte Taft, who runs an abortion clinic called the Routh Street Women's Clinic. At the time, she had been feeling vaguely guilty about not organizing a protest against the local showing of *Pieces*, a movie that had been picketed by feminists elsewhere because of its concentration on hideous violence against women. Someone who runs an abortion clinic in Dallas — where right-to-lifers seem to attack in endless waves, like Chinese regulars pouring over the 38th Parallel — can't always get around to the side issues. Then she came across a capsule review of the movie in the *Times Herald*. The *Weekend* section had got into the habit of running capsules by both of its movie reviewers, distinguishing them only by the initials at the end. Between reviews by JB of *The Osterman Weekend* (one star) and *The Right Stuff* (a star and a half), JBB's capsule review of *Pieces* said, "Best chainsaw flick since the original 'Saw,' about a gonzo geek pervert who goes around a college campus cutting up coeds into itty bitty pieces. Two heads roll. Arms roll. Legs roll. Something else rolls. Nine living breasts, two dead breasts. No motor vehicle chases. Gratuitous kung fu. Eight corpses. One beast with a chainsaw. Four gallons of blood. Not much talking. Splatter City. Joe Bob says check it out." The review included Joe Bob's rating: four stars.

Casting around for allies, Charlotte Taft found support from an old adversary — William Murchison, a conservative columnist on the *Morning News*. Murchison wrote that the celebration of a movie like *Pieces* was not simply a feminist issue but a humanity issue — a reminder that people who make movies seem to take no notice of someone like Mother Teresa but think nothing of turning out a movie that "devalues the human species." The reply in Joe Bob's column was headlined "JOE BOB ATTACKED BY COMMUNIST FRIEND OF MOTHER TERESA." In it Joe Bob said, "Last week this royal jerkola with a bad haircut named William Murchison wrote a column called 'Chain-Sawing Our Culture.' He wrote it on the *editorial* page of the Dallas Morning Snooze . . . It has this itty bitty picture of Willie Murchison with his lips mashed together like the zombie-monster in 'Dr. Tarr's Torture Garden,' and his eyes look exactly like the guy in 'I Drink Your Blood.' He also has a little resemblance to the woman-carver in 'I Dismember Mama,' but I'm sure that's just a coincidence." A couple of weeks later, Joe Bob finally got down to the issues at hand: "*Numero uno:* I have enormous respect for women. Especially when they have garbanzas the size of Cleveland. *Numero two-o:* I am violently opposed to the use of chainsaws, power drills, tire tools, rubber hoses, brass knuckles, bob wire, hypodermics, embalming needles or poleaxes against women, unless it is *necessary* to the plot. *Numero three-o:* I don't believe in slapping women around, unless they want it. *Numero four-o:* I would like to settle this matter in the easiest way possible, so I hereby challenge Charlotte Taft to a nude mud-wrestling match . . ."

Charlotte Taft decided that a better way to settle it was to organize a letter-writing campaign to the *Times Herald*. It was based on the same argument she had made in her letter to the editor — that men in Dallas still seemed to think it was all right to make jokes about violence against women, decades after a supposedly responsible newspaper would dare find anything funny about, say, ridiculing black people. Eventually, though, the feminists decided that their efforts were going nowhere. The editors of the *Times Herald* seemed uninterested. The feminists themselves were by no means unanimous in condemning Joe Bob. Molly Ivins, for one, said that the complaints were "displaced anger." Interviewed for a feature on Joe Bob by KERA, the local public television station, she said that what should be protested was "the vicious and degrading pornography" of exploitation movies, not someone who was "making brilliant fun of the kind of people who go to watch those movies." Charlotte Taft was never won over to that point of view. "John Bloom wanted to have it both ways — some readers taking it at face value and some taking it as satire," she has said. "But part of satire is to instruct, not to wallow in the fun of saying what's not supposed to be said. If there's an Archie Bunker, there has to be a Meathead. What I saw in it was self-indulgence — the self-indulgence of someone who wants to tell a racist joke and pretends to be making fun of someone telling a racist joke. It was indulging in an adult the humor of a seventh-grader — a seventh-grade boy."

She had decided, though, that all she was doing in her protest was providing material for Joe Bob, who wrote a lot about the high sheriffs' being pressured by what he always referred to as the National Organization for Bimbos.

John Bloom agreed that protest was just playing into Joe Bob's hands. On the KERA program, he was interviewed as Joe Bob's closest friend, and he said of the attacks by feminists, "One thing Joe Bob's critics should learn is that you should never attack an anarchist. He has nothing to lose." Using criticism as material for making fun of the critic was among the characteristics that, after two years, had been established firmly enough to be an unvarying part of Joe Bob's character. He could be counted on to reoffend the offended, just as he could be counted on to refer to women as bimbos, and to persist in trying to sneak in words that the high sheriffs considered inappropriate. John Bloom and Ron Smith and the other people at the *Times Herald* who dealt with Joe Bob, all of whom spoke of him in the third person even among themselves, still had the power to arrange for his Toronado to spin out on the interstate, of course. But as long as Joe Bob existed, he was, in certain ways, on his own.

"He's *gone* to all these movies," Charlotte Taft has said. "I find that kind of scary." Even those who didn't find it eerie that an honors graduate of Vanderbilt could thrive on a steady diet of splatter flicks might have wondered just how many chainsaw dismemberments and kung fu battles anyone could sit through without becoming too bored even to maintain an accurate body count. As it turned out, though, John Bloom got tired of movie reviewing before Joe Bob did. In 1984, Bloom gave up reviewing to become the paper's Metro columnist, responsible for three columns a week. Writing the Metro column was considered a full-time job, but once a week Bloom continued to turn into Joe Bob Briggs. In January of 1985, that became twice a week. Blackie Sherrod, one of the most popular sportswriters in Dallas, had jumped to the *Morning News*, and the *Times Herald* countered with a new sportswriter of its own — Joe Bob Briggs. Bloom had actually started out in newspapers writing sports for the *Arkansas Democrat* while he was still in high school; he went through Vanderbilt on a Grantland Rice Scholarship, awarded by the Thoroughbred Racing Associations. Will Jarrett has said that he saw the sports column, "Jock Talk with Joe Bob," as more than simply a counter to Sherrod. "I thought of it as Phase Two," he said. "The bimbo thing was kind of played out. He was depending a lot on ethnic humor. There was a lot of material in sports. John knew the field. It was a way to ride his popularity and get rid of some of the problem areas." Even writing about sports, of course, Joe Bob did not avoid the problem areas completely. In one of the first "Jock Talk" columns, he managed to make up a Boston Celtics theme song called "Attack of the Stupid White People" and to refer to Tony Nathan of the Miami Dolphins as "the only slow Negro in the NFL."

Will Jarrett had been off editing the *Denver Post* during most of the time Joe Bob was steadily dismantling many of the barriers against tastelessness the high sheriffs had erected, and he says that when he returned to Dallas, in 1984, he was surprised to see what Joe Bob was getting away with. There were occasional flareups from offended readers — there were complaints from members of Mothers Against Drunk Driving (MADD), for instance, when Joe Bob organized a group called Drunks Against Mad Mothers (DAMM) — but Jarrett got the impression that a lot of readers had been following Joe Bob Briggs long enough to shrug off most of what he said as just the sort of thing Joe Bob would say. *Times Herald* editors had never truly lost their nervousness about running the column, though, and some people around the newsroom were, in fact, troubled by what they saw as an increasing reliance on ethnic cracks. Reviewing a movie called *Breakin'*, for instance, Joe Bob managed to mention not simply "Negro Dancing" but also "Meskins," the perils he saw in Vietnamese immigration ("Pretty soon you can't go in 7-Eleven without wondering whether those guys are putting dog meat in the frozen burritos"), and a character "whose idea of a good time is to go sit on the beach with guys from the chorus line and talk about their Liberace record collections, if you know what I mean and I think you do" — all in the course of saying that he had been shown the path from racism by his friend Bobo Rodriguez: "I never did ask Bobo what race he was, but I'm pretty sure he was a Negro. His skin was the color of Taster's Choice Decaffeinated, which means he could go either way, but one time he tried to change his name to Bobo al-Salaam, and when he did that everybody started calling him 'Al' because they thought he was saying 'Al Sloan.' "

Although some of Joe Bob's fans around the *Times Herald* may have fallen away, he was publicly more popular than ever. His column was being syndicated to fifty papers or so, making him a figure of renown even in San Francisco — a place he normally referred to as "Wimp Capital of the World" or "Geek City, U.S.A." He was so popular in Cleveland that when the editors of the *Plain Dealer* decided to drop his column for tastelessness an avalanche of reader mail persuaded them to put it back. In some film circles, he was a sort of cult figure — someone who could attract Stephen King to the Third Annual World Drive-In Movie Festival and Custom Car Rally. There were those, though, who thought that Joe Bob's national popularity was his undoing. They thought that "the golden age of Joe Bob" had been in the early months of the column, when Jo Bob could be understood in a local context and could spice up his column with local stunts, like organizing a letter-writing campaign to the public official he held responsible for the removal of the drive-in-movie screens at Texas Stadium ("Dear French-fry Head Mayor of Irving . . ."). There were those who thought Joe Bob's undoing was that Bloom was spreading himself too thin by writing five columns a week. Theories about Joe Bob's undoing were widely discussed and closely analyzed in the spring of 1985, because on one April Friday the worst fears that *Times Herald* high sheriffs had entertained about the Joe Bob Briggs column finally materialized.

The offending column, published a couple of months after rock stars gathered in California to record a song for African famine relief called "We Are the World," was headlined ''JOE BOB, DRIVE-IN ARTISTS JOIN FORCES FOR MINORITIES WITH

'WE ARE THE WEIRD.'" Joe Bob said that the best-known drive-in artists in the world had gathered together to sing the song: "They all stood there, swaying from side to side, arms linked (except for The Mutant, who don't have arms) and singing their little hearts out." Although Joe Bob's song does not lend itself to summary — it's never precisely clear who's singing about exactly what — the first chorus was representative of its tone:

> We are the weird.
> We are the starvin,
> We are the scum of the filthy earth,
> So let's start scarfin . . .
> There's a goat-head bakin
> We're calling it their food,
> If the Meskins can eat it,
> They can eat it, too.

The drive-in stars' recording was, Joe Bob wrote, "for the benefit of minority groups in Africa and the United Negro College Fund in the United States, cause I think we should be sending as many Negroes to college as we can, specially the stupid Negroes."

It wasn't immediately clear how such a column found its way into the *Times Herald* and the distribution network of the Los Angeles Times Syndicate. The copy editors apparently had not flagged an assistant managing editor. According to one rather ornate theory, Joe Bob had for months been trying to sneak the word "twat" past the two copy editors, and they were concentrating so hard on spotting it — examining each syllable in the name of any town Joe Bob invented, searching any new organization for contraband acronyms — that they weren't paying enough attention to the content of the column. According to another theory, the copy editors, after a few years of reading Joe Bobbian copy, had grown desensitized, as some people are said to get after prolonged exposure to pornography. Bloom has always insisted that a managing editor who happened to walk by his desk and glance at the column on his computer monitor read the entire song, laughed, and said, "Great stuff!"

There were plenty of readers around Dallas who were as accustomed to Joe Bob's ways as the copy editors were, but not many of these readers were black. Even though the black community regarded the *Times Herald* as the newspaper sympathetic to its interests, "Joe Bob Goes to the Drive-In" had never attracted a wide black readership. The first Joe Bob column that a lot of black people in Dallas read was the column that included a famine-relief song with verses like:

> Send em a heart so they'll know that someone cares
> And a lung, and an elbow, and three big toes.
> As the Big Guy told us, we should always clean our plate,
> Cause then all the Africans' stomachs won't look gross.

"After a while, you get sort of used to Joe Bob," Ron Smith has said. "But if you read that thing flat cold it'll send chills up your spine. And that's the way a lot of black people read it."

Willis Johnson, who runs a morning talk show on KKDA, Dallas's leading black radio station, was not in the habit of reading Joe Bob's column, but he got a call from a listener — a reporter for the *Morning News*, as it happened — who told him he would do well to make an exception in this case. Johnson, who was outraged by the column, read it over the air, and the mounting rage soon monopolized his program. The *Times Herald* was also having serious trouble within its own building. Black *Times Herald* employees from a number of departments were furious about the column, and a meeting at which Bloom tried to explain himself only made things worse. By then, it was obvious that the outrage over the "We Are the Weird" column was of another order than the customary Joe Bob controversies that always blew over after some angry letters and a few Joe Bobbian jokes at the complainants' expense. One of Willis Johnson's callers had been John Wiley Price, a black county commissioner. Price is among a small group of militant black officeholders in Dallas who have tried to ease aside the black ministers whose style of leadership flowed from the old accommodation with the white business community. On the air, Price and Johnson agreed to go downtown on Tuesday afternoon, right after a weekly black-leadership lunch, and demand to know why the *Times Herald*, the newspaper that supposedly represented fair treatment for minorities in Dallas, had on its staff someone who used phrases like "stupid Negroes" and found it humorous to ridicule starving people in Africa. When they arrived that Tuesday afternoon, they found that they had been joined by several hundred other people. In a city that had basically skipped the public confrontations of the civil rights struggle, the presence of a large crowd of black people marching into a white institution in an angry mood was virtually unprecedented.

Jarrett and two other editors met with as many of the protesters as could be jammed into a small auditorium. The room was hot, and got even hotter when television lights were turned on. The people in the audience were fanning themselves with whatever was at hand. The three editors, surrounded by protesters, were sweating. That morning's edition had already printed an apology of a completeness that Will Jarrett called unique in his years of newspaper experience: "Joe Bob Briggs' column that appeared in Friday's *Times Herald* offended many readers. The *Times Herald* deeply regrets that the column was published. It was a misdirected attempt at satire. A great deal of insensitivity was reflected in the column. We apologize." But the crowd did not seem satisfied with an apology, however abject. "One apology in one postage-stamp-size corner of the front page is not enough," a black attorney said. "This column needs to be gone." Jarrett started out by saying that the question of whether "Joe Bob Goes to the Drive-In" would be run in the next Friday's paper was still being considered, but after a number of angry speeches he finally said, "I'm deeply concerned about it. I'm deeply concerned about the reaction. I'm deeply concerned about the staff reaction to it. So the Joe Bob Briggs column, the *Weekend* column, the drive-in-movie column, is dead." In a much smaller, more conventional meeting a few days later, the *Times Herald* pledged that twelve of the next twenty-two editorial positions filled would be filled by members of a minority. But for most of the black people of Dallas nothing could quite match the exhilaration of that public capitulation in the steamy auditorium, right there in front of the television cameras. Above the cheers that followed Jarrett's announcement the voice of a woman in the first few rows could be heard shouting, in triumph and amazement, "We did it! We did it!"

John Bloom was a hundred and fifty miles away from Dallas that afternoon, delivering a speech at Texas A & M. Will Jarrett drove out to Dallas–Fort Worth Airport to meet Bloom's return flight, but the plane had arrived early; Bloom was already on his way back to the city. It was days before they finally met again. Bloom wouldn't talk to Jarrett on the telephone. He was hurt and angry. He saw the front-page apology as a writer being "publicly disavowed by his own newspaper, not for any factual error or misrepresentation, but purely because his opinion is unpopular." He considered the way that Jarrett had canceled the column — publicly, without telling the columnist — basically unforgivable. Jarrett, who had brought Bloom to Dallas and remained close to him in the years that followed, was astonished that Bloom wouldn't come to the phone. "What I was worried about was John Bloom," he has said. "I realized that Joe Bob was more important to him than John Bloom was. John Bloom wouldn't talk to his editor for three days, even though Joe Bob had done the damage. I didn't fire John Bloom. I fired a mythical character John Bloom had always said he didn't agree with. Why was he mad at me?"

Jarrett had hoped that Bloom would continue writing his own column, and maybe even the "Jock Talk with Joe Bob" column. But John Bloom decided to resign from the *Times Herald*. In a final Metro column, which Jarrett declined to print, Bloom wrote that the real issue was not racism but the fact that some subjects, like African famine relief, had been put off limits for satire because "they are too close to our subconscious fears and guilts," and he reminded Jarrett of the newsroom sign that had said, "THE ONLY SACRED COW HERE IS HAMBURGER." He didn't discuss the offending column except to say that on the question of who the "we" was in lines like "We are the scum of the filthy earth" — the question that some *Times Herald* people referred to as Joe Bob's pronoun problem — "I realize I'm the person who should know the answer to this question, but I'm afraid I was too busy laughing to worry about Joe Bob's illogic." By the time Bloom resigned, there couldn't have been many people left in Dallas who were still unaware of the true authorship of the "Joe Bob Goes to the Drive-In" column — all pretense had been dropped in the barrage of news coverage of the controversy — but Bloom said he was resigning in sympathy with Joe Bob.

No one else at the *Times Herald* showed much sympathy, even though a lot of *Times Herald* reporters — and a lot of other Dallas reporters — were horrified at what seemed to be a capitulation under pressure in the *Times Herald* auditorium. "It created a precedent that's dangerous," Molly Ivins has said. "I know that Reverend Criswell could have five thousand people there about me at the drop of a hat." But that didn't translate into newsroom support for Joe Bob. In fact, most of the people in the newsroom had, in the first days of the controversy, signed a bulletin-board statement demanding that Joe Bob's column be more closely edited in the future. *Times Herald* reporters did not see what had happened as a case of one of their own being crushed by management. They didn't consider John Bloom one of their own. Not many of them really knew him, and some of them may have resented him with the special resentment reporters reserve for someone who seems to be getting away with the sort of writing that would be routinely edited out of their own copy. Some of them, particularly the younger ones, had long felt that it was dishonest for a newspaper to keep up the pretense that a fictional columnist existed. Also, as Jim Schutze has put it, "they were the ones who answered the phone when people started calling in and saying, 'The trouble is these colored people don't know good say-tire when they see it.' "

Even more important, a lot of the reporters simply hated the "We Are the Weird" column. They didn't know who the "we" in the song was, either — figuring out how the humor worked in the column required an almost scholarly knowledge of Joe Bobbian context — but, unlike Bloom, they weren't too busy laughing to care. Satire is obviously most offensive when the reader's first response isn't laughter; it lies there, waiting to be analyzed. Those in the newsroom who thought Joe Bob's problem was more in his delivery than in his subject matter pointed out that the rock stars' African-relief effort was not, in fact, a sacred cow; a number of political cartoonists and columnists had already taken a crack at it. But the column's subject matter was at the heart of the opposition. "Satire is a weapon you use against the powerful," Molly Ivins, who was not on Joe Bob's side this time, has said. "You don't use satire against the weak." Bloom's position seemed to be that a truly liberal society wouldn't recognize any subject as off-limits: now that black people are equal partners in modern, postsegregationist America, it would be patronizing not to subject them equally to the occasional satiric knock. What people like Molly Ivins found wrong with that was the assumption that black people are now equal partners in modern America. Presumably, most people at the *Times Herald* would have agreed with Bloom that these days a newspaper columnist is a lot less likely to get away with a joke about starving Africans or "stupid Negroes" than with a joke about the President, but not many of them seemed to think it followed that such jokes had to be made.

"For forty-eight hours, I thought, Well, it's over. It's gone up in flames. And it's kind of an ignominious end," Bloom has said. "Then I started getting these letters. A large number of responsible editors and reporters had been saying, 'The guy got what he deserved,' but the readers were saying, 'You can't let them do this.' Joe Bob was always responsive to readers." The column had been dropped by the Los Angeles Times Syndicate as well as by the *Times Herald*, but, without missing a week, Joe Bob signed with the Universal Press Syndicate, which has some experience with controversy as the distributor of Garry Trudeau's "Doonesbury." The first Universal column dealt, of course, with the *Times Herald* decision to kill the column — or with the assassination of Joe Bob in Dallas, as Bloom saw it.

"November 22, 1963. April 16, 1985," the column began. "They said it couldn't happen again.

"I guess I'll always remember where I was when they killed me on national TV, right after the Maybelline commercial. I guess we all will. Who couldn't remember the look on the High Sheriff's

face when he said, 'Joe Bob's dead!' ... Even though the High
Sheriff was arrested at the scene by TV reporters with bad hair,
there were immediate rumors of an international communist conspiracy, the 'three-gun theory,' the 'act of God theory,' the bizarre
'one-garbanza theory,' and the 'What would happen if you
dropped Joe Bob Briggs off a seven-story building and watched
him splatter all over the pavement?' theory." After some Joe Bobbian talk about the protest and a list of astonishing coincidences
("Lincoln and Kennedy were both assassinated on a Friday. Joe
Bob was assassinated on a Tuesday. Makes you think"), Joe Bob
found space for a quick summary of a movie called *Lust in the
Dust*: "Four breasts. Fifteen dead bodies. One riot. One brawl.
One gang rape, with midget. Two quarts blood. One beast (Divine).
Thigh crushing. Bullwhip fu. Nekkid bimbo-wrestling ..." It
would have been uncharacteristic, of course, for Joe Bob to acknowledge any regrets about the "We Are the Weird" column or
apologize to those it might have offended, and Bloom, when asked
about an apology, tends to say something like "Apologize for
what? There's not a single fact in the column. They say it's insensitive and in poor taste. Well, Joe Bob is insensitive and in poor taste.
I'll admit that."

The decision of the *Times Herald* to kill the Joe Bob drive-in column, which John Bloom seems to have heard as a decision to kill
Joe Bob, served to make Joe Bob a much larger part of John
Bloom's life. Bloom continued to write under his own name —
eventually, he began doing a monthly piece for Dallas's city magazine, *D*, and he started a book on Route 66 — but in the free-lance
market Joe Bob Briggs was likely to get more assignments than
John Bloom. For one thing, he was much better known, particularly after the "We Are the Weird" controversy. John Bloom is one
of a number of talented young Texas writers. Joe Bob Briggs is a
writer who can provide a unique way for *Film Comment* to deal
with exploitation movies or for *Rolling Stone* to deal with the end
of the Texas boom. Writing under his own name, Bloom had difficulty finding a publisher for a serious nonfiction book he and an-

other *Texas Monthly* writer, Jim Atkinson, wrote about a Texas murder; it was finally published by the Texas Monthly Press. As Joe Bob Briggs, he had assumed, correctly, that there were big-shot publishers in New York interested in getting filthy rich off his books.

The change was more than Joe Bob's simply easing out of the three-hours-a-week compartment Bloom had kept him in. A couple of months after Bloom left the *Times Herald*, his agent got a call from someone in Cleveland who offered to set up a speaking engagement for Joe Bob Briggs. Bloom, who had not even officially admitted writing the Joe Bob column until the "We Are the Weird" controversy erupted, decided to accept the date as Joe Bob. In a high school just outside Cleveland, he did a sort of one-man show, costumed in a cowboy hat and a more pronounced drawl. After that, those who phoned Bloom's agent with lecture inquiries were asked whether they were interested in John Bloom or Joe Bob Briggs. Joe Bob's rates were higher.

Bloom has said that in those first months of being on his own he was intent on keeping Joe Bob alive, partly because he was convinced that the high sheriffs' intentions toward Joe Bob continued to be murderous. Their weapon was a copyright. Although no objection had been raised to the Universal Press Syndicate's distribution of "Joe Bob Goes to the Drive-In," the *Times Herald* warned Dell, which was about to publish a collection of Joe Bobbiana, that John Bloom owned neither the name Joe Bob Briggs nor the rights to the material that had appeared in the *Times Herald*. The argument over rights exacerbated a hostility that already carried the special bitterness of a disagreement between people who had once been close. In his stage appearances as Joe Bob, Bloom had taken to referring to his old employer as the *Slimes Herald* and singing a song about how he'd like to make "editor fondue" out of the high sheriff who fired him — a high sheriff who happened to be John Bloom's old friend and mentor, Will Jarrett. ("A heart attack would do it, or trampled by a mob, or eaten by a giant bumblebee.")

Bloom claimed that the paper wanted to prevent the publication of Joe Bob's books out of spite. The high sheriffs of the *Times Herald* and the Times Mirror Company were indeed furious about the "We Are the Weird" incident — some of them saw it as one horrifying column destroying a position with the minority community that had taken years to establish — and they were apparently wounded by Joe Bob's insults. At one point, the paper offered to release the material under conditions that included a promise not to ridicule the *Times Herald* or its executives. The proposed agreement would also have given the paper control over which columns appeared in a book. Jarrett has said that the main issue was whether the *Times Herald* could acquiesce in the republication of the "We Are the Weird" column: "We'd be in the position of saying, 'Right, this is awful, it should never have been printed, we're going to kill the column,' and then turning around and saying, 'Sure, go ahead and publish it in a book, make a lot of money.' The black people would have said we were hypocrites." Bloom rejected the proposed agreement, and after months of meetings and lawyers' letters and phone calls he filed legal papers against the *Times Herald* in an attempt to liberate Joe Bob Briggs.

A little more than a year after the cancellation of the column, Bloom's lawyer won a declaratory judgment on one of the two questions at issue — the question of who had a right to use the name Joe Bob Briggs — and a date was set to hear arguments on whether Bloom had the right to reprint the columns that had appeared in the *Times Herald*. Outside the courtroom, the blood-feud aspect of the disagreement had begun to dissipate. Will Jarrett had already left the paper, in a purge that also claimed some executives on the business side. Not long after the declaratory judgment, the Times Mirror Company, in what the *New York Times* story called "an apparent acknowledgment that it was unable to win the heated Dallas newspaper war," announced that it was selling the *Times Herald*. The buyer was a young, Texas-born newspaper magnate who said he was moving the headquarters of his enterprises from New Jersey to Dallas and intended to become active in "the Dallas leadership community." The Joe Bob suit was specifically excluded from the assets and liabilities passed on to the new owner, and it was assumed that the sale had completed the transformation of the Joe Bob controversy from a serious altercation into the sort of loose end that a large corporation likes to have tied up before it leaves town. Times Mirror and John Bloom quickly settled their differences, and Dell made plans to publish the collection in the form Bloom wanted. Joe Bob, in effect, belonged to John Bloom.

A lot of Bloom's old colleagues do not think he won a great asset. "What bothers me is that John Bloom is a significant talent who can endure, and Joe Bob is an ephemeral kind of thing," one of them has said. "If John thinks no one else can kill Joe Bob, fine. Then at some point he should kill Joe Bob himself." The syndicated Joe Bob column is in fact a marginal operation. It appears in a few dozen newspapers, but a lot of them are college papers or alternative weeklies. The pattern, Bloom says, is that the feature editor buys the column, it runs once, and the executive editor cancels it. It's a difficult column to sell. The reason is partly the traditional cautiousness of newspapers — Bloom has always maintained that the only reason Joe Bob appears outrageous is that the material surrounding him is so bland — but it is also partly that the "We Are the Weird" controversy gave Joe Bob a reputation not simply for controversy but also for racism.

Joe Bob's one-man show has been polished considerably since its rather shaky start in Cleveland. He has even put out a video, called "Joe Bob Briggs Dead in Concert." Like a lot of shy people who have to transform themselves into public characters, Bloom uses hats in the stage show — a cowboy hat, a feed hat, one of those caps that have horns extending from the sides. Joe Bob tells stories about bimbos and Baptists and a county where the major industry is dirt. He sings songs like "Dirt Mine Blues" and "We Are the Weird" (with the words significantly toned down). This fall, he used his column to recruit a troupe of seriously overweight young women, and in a Dallas appearance on the weekend of the Texas-Oklahoma game he worked them into the act as the Dancing Bovina Sisters, doing dances like the Frito Stomp. People who know

John Bloom tend to be surprised that he's as fluid as he is onstage, but the act has received mixed reviews. One of the problems of Joe Bob's coming to life was pointed out a couple of years ago by Bloom himself, when he was explaining to Dennis Holder, in the *Washington Journalism Review*, why Joe Bob could never be on television: "This thing is so fragile that the last thing you'd want is to remove the mystery and magic through the cold reality of a camera. If you ever gave Joe Bob a specific face, or even a voice, some of the power would be lost." Onstage, Bloom plays a redneck who tells stories, but that may disappoint people who hope to see the real Joe Bob. A headline in the *San Francisco Chronicle* after Joe Bob's appearance in the Wimp Capital of the World said, "JOE BOB 'LIVE' IS A PUSSYCAT." Molly Ivins says that even without having seen the act she knows that Bloom can't be very persuasive as Joe Bob Briggs: "For one thing, he's too good-looking. If he could act, he'd play the young Byron."

"I'm bothered that he's given up serious journalism for a cardboard cowboy," Will Jarrett has said. In general, Bloom's former colleagues tend to talk about him the way a bunch of medievalists would talk about one of their number who had gone off to write potboilers. Their theories of just why Bloom is hanging on so hard to Joe Bob depend a bit on what they thought of him in the first place. Some people think it's just pure stubbornness. Some think that under Bloom's shy exterior was always a lust for show business; they point out that he became pals with some Hollywood types during his regular movie-reviewing days, and that he has appeared in a scene (later cut) in the sequel to *The Texas Chainsaw Massacre*. Some people think that Bloom sees Joe Bob as a ticket to fame and fortune, and some people think that Bloom sat through so many splatter movies "his brain got fried." Some people think that John Bloom, no matter how enlightened and how educated, simply had a wild, racist redneck inside him, and that the redneck finally surfaced; they tend to say, "John Bloom has become Joe Bob Briggs." Bloom himself says that he'll kill off Joe Bob when he gets tired of him. "Maybe I'll do it until I find the heart of Joe Bob, find out what about him disturbs people," he says. "When you see what a threat Joe Bob is to people, the issue becomes the integrity of Joe Bob."

Joe Bob Briggs is no longer much of a presence in Dallas. His column appears in a weekly paper, *The Observer*, and there are still plenty of hard-core Joe Bob fans. But the day is past when all Friday-morning talk seemed to center on what Joe Bob had gone and said now. These days, on Friday morning or any other morning, the talk in Dallas's shiny new office buildings is likely to be about how many square feet of the building remain unleased; the people driving into the city in pickups are likely to be concerned about whether a job will still be there when they arrive. When Joe Bob's mentioned, it's often in the past tense. "The trouble with the character was that he had to push it further and further," Molly Ivins has said. "The poor bastard just outlived his time."

The talk in Dallas about the incident that brought an end to Joe Bob's column sounds a bit like the talk that could be heard in some other American cities twenty years ago — some white people saying that militant blacks were simply looking for an issue, and militant blacks saying that *of course* they were looking for an issue. For a while, people like Willis Johnson thought that the success in galvanizing people around the issue of Joe Bob Briggs might awaken what was sometimes referred to as the sleeping giant of the Dallas black community. They thought that the victory in the *Times Herald* auditorium might serve as an impetus for a more confrontational approach in dealing with the white business community. But sooner or later there was a widespread feeling that the giant stretched and then went back to sleep. Johnson says that he and John Wiley Price have been subjected to some criticism among the traditional leadership for not trying to settle differences with the *Times Herald* in a quieter way. Charlotte Taft is still at the Routh Street Women's Clinic. One crowd of fundamentalists shows up to picket on Wednesday, another crowd pickets on Saturday, and the Catholics have set up next door in one of those operations whose advertising and name seem designed to attract young women who think they're going to an abortion clinic but find themselves in a place dedicated to talking them out of it. Sometimes Charlotte Taft gets discouraged. When she ponders the difficulty of financing her operation through the usual fundraising events, she sometimes says with a smile, it occurs to her that she might have been too quick in rejecting Joe Bob's nude-mud-wrestling challenge.

The *Times Herald* now has the same problem every other daily newspaper has in figuring out how to cover trashy movies. The paper is under new management, and there has been a lot of turnover in staff. Some people on and off the paper say that the controversy over Joe Bob was what finally pushed the Times Mirror Company into giving up on the Dallas newspaper war. There were, of course, solid business reasons for selling the *Times Herald*, which had just dipped into the red after fifteen years of considerable profits. The Dallas boom had fizzled. The war with the *Morning News* had been lost. The resources of the Times Mirror Company could presumably be better invested elsewhere. Those who say that the Joe Bob episode was the last straw for Times Mirror — the experience that soured it forever on Dallas — seem to mean that more symbolically or spiritually than literally. In the words of Ron Smith, one of the people who brought Joe Bob into the world, dealing with the "We Are the Weird" controversy was for the Times Mirror Company "like biting into a bad clam."

The advertising campaign of the new management features a picture of the new editor saying, "Nobody wants to read a wimp newspaper." It is said that the use of a Joe Bobbian word is a coincidence, but there is a temptation to see some connection between the strong anti-wimp statement and the fact that the capitulation in the auditorium left some lingering taint of wimpiness in the building. It also left a new verb in Dallas — "to Joe Bob," meaning to march on an institution with an intimidating number of citizens and hope to buffalo that institution into changing some policy. When Jim Schutze wrote a column critical of one of the black ministers in Dallas, for instance, the response of one of the minister's supporters was the threat "We're going to come down there and Joe Bob your ass." Some people on the *Times Herald* resent the part played by both John Bloom and management in creating the situation that led to the verb's existence, and some of the same people miss the excitement of those Friday mornings when everyone turned to *Weekend* to see who had been called a communist french-fry head this week. Talking about the career of Joe Bob Briggs at the *Dallas Times Herald*, Ron Smith said that Shelby Coffey III, who was the editor of the paper at the time the Times Mirror Company sold it, once turned down an idea for a satirical feature by remarking, "This paper has a sorry history on satire" — an allusion, of course, to Joe Bob Briggs. "I took exception to that," Smith said. "I don't think it was sorry. I think it was a noble experiment that went awry."

1986

RUMORS
AROUND TOWN

THE FIRST HEADLINE in the *Junction City Daily Union* —
"EMPORIA MAN FATALLY SHOT" — seemed to describe
one of those incidents which can cause a peaceful citizen to shake
his head and mumble something about how it's getting so nobody
is safe anywhere. The Emporia man was Martin Anderson, a peaceful citizen who had a responsible job and a commission in the
Army Reserve and a wife and four little girls. Early on a November
evening in 1983, he was murdered by the side of State Highway
177, which cuts south from Manhattan through the rolling cattle-
grazing land that people in Kansas call the Flint Hills. According to
the newspaper story, the authorities had been told that Anderson
was killed during a struggle with an unidentified robber. At the
time of the murder, Anderson was on his way back to Emporia
from Fort Riley, the infantry base that lies between Junction City
and Manhattan. Apparently, the trip had been meant to combine
some errands at the fort with an autumn drive through the Flint
Hills. His wife was with him, and so were the little girls.

There is a special jolt to the headline "EMPORIA MAN FA-
TALLY SHOT." For many Americans, Emporia, Kansas, conjures
up the vision of a typical American town in the era when people
didn't have to think about violent men bent on robbery — a town
where neighbors drank lemonade on the front porch and kidded
one another about their performances in the Fourth of July soft-

ball game. The vision grew out of the writings of William Allen White, the Sage of Emporia, who, as owner and editor of the *Emporia Gazette*, was widely thought of during the first forty years of this century as the national spokesman for the unadorned values of the American Midwest. The residents of Emporia in those days may have thought of their town as even more tranquil than its national reputation. What White had been looking for when he set out to buy a small-town newspaper, in 1895, was not a typical town but a college town — a place where his editorials could be understood and appreciated by "a considerable dependable minority of intelligent people, intellectually upper-middle class." Emporia, the seat of Lyon County and a division point for the Sante Fe Railway and a trading center for the surrounding farmland, had two colleges — Kansas State Normal School and a small Presbyterian liberal-arts school called the College of Emporia. During the years that people across the country thought of Emporia as a typical Midwestern town, its boosters sometimes spoke of it as the Educational Center of the West, or even the Athens of Kansas.

In some ways, Emporia didn't change much after William Allen White passed from the scene. The White family continued to own the *Gazette*. Even now, Mrs. William L. White — the widow of the Sage's son, who was an author and a foreign correspondent known into his seventies around Emporia as Young Bill — comes in every day. Commercial Street still has the look of the main trading street in a Kansas farm town — two-story buildings separated by a slab of asphalt wide enough to accommodate angle parking on both sides and four lanes of traffic. The College of Emporia folded some years ago, though; its campus is now owned by a religious cult called The Way. Although the Santa Fe's operation has been shrinking in recent years, Emporia has, on the whole, become more of what was called in White's day a lunch-bucket town. The construction of the Wolf Creek nuclear power plant, forty miles to the southeast, brought a few thousand construction workers to the area, and some of them remained after the plant was completed. Although Kansas State Normal expanded as it evolved first into Kansas State Teachers' College and then into Emporia Kansas State

College and then into Emporia State University, the largest employer in town these days is not a college but a big meat-packing plant, most of whose employees are not the sort of citizens who spend a lot of their time perusing the editorial page. There is less talk than there once was about Emporia's being the Athens of Kansas.

Still, a lot of people in Emporia lead an updated version of the peaceful front-porch life that White portrayed — a life revolving around family and church and school and service club and neighbors. The Andersons seemed to lead that sort of life. When they walked into Faith Lutheran Church every Sunday, the little girls wearing immaculate dresses that Lorna Anderson had made herself, they presented the picture of a wholesome, attractive American family which a lot of people still have in mind when they think of Emporia. Marty Anderson, a medical technologist, ran the laboratory at Newman Memorial County Hospital. He was on the board of directors of the Optimist Club. His wife was working part time as the secretary of Faith Lutheran. She was a member of a social and service sorority called Beta Sigma Phi, which used its annual Valentine's Day dance as a benefit for the local hospitals. The Andersons were among the young couples who saw one another at Optimist basketball games or church fellowship meetings or Beta Sigma Phi socials — people who tended to recall dates by saying something like "Let's see, that was the year Jenny started nursery school" or "I remember I was pregnant with Bobby."

Faith Lutheran Church is dominated by such families. It's a young church, in a former Assembly of God building on the West Side of Emporia — an area filled with split-level houses along blocks so recently developed that most of the trees are still not much higher than the basketball goals. Faith Lutheran was founded in 1982, when the one Missouri Synod Lutheran church in Emporia, Messiah Lutheran, decided that the way to expand was to ask for volunteers to form what was thought of as a "daughter congregation" on the West Side. Faith Lutheran grew so quickly that in October of 1982, just eight months after its founding, it was chartered as a separate congregation. The church — a pale brick building on a corner lot across the street from a school — turned out to have been well placed, but the congregation had other advantages besides a fortunate location. The people who had volunteered to move from Messiah tended to be active young families with a strong interest in a range of church activities — what was sometimes called at Messiah "the early-service crowd." Thomas Bird, the minister who had been called from Arkansas to Messiah to lead the new undertaking, turned out to be a dynamic young pastor who fitted right in with his congregation. Tom Bird had been a long-distance runner at the University of Arkansas. He was married to his high school sweetheart, an astonishingly energetic young woman who had a master's degree in mathematics and managed to combine the responsibilities of a pastor's wife with some teaching at Emporia State. Like a lot of couples in the congregation, they had three small children and a small split-level and a swing set in the back yard.

The Missouri Synod is a particularly conservative branch of American Lutheranism. Tom Bird thought of himself as conservative in doctrinal and liturgical matters but flexible in dealing with the concerns of his congregation. Distinguishing Faith Lutheran from Missouri Synod churches more set in their ways — Messiah, for instance — he has said that he wanted his church to be more interested in people than in policies. Faith Lutheran lacked the stern, Germanic atmosphere sometimes associated with Missouri Synod churches. The attachment of some of the young West Side couples who soon joined the founders from Messiah was more demographic than liturgical. A lot of them were attracted by a friendly, almost familial bond among contemporaries who tended to be interested in the church volleyball team as well as the Bible classes. The Andersons, who had been active at First Presbyterian, were introduced to Faith when Lorna Anderson decided that its preschool, the Lord's Lambs, might be a convenient place for their two youngest children, twin girls. Eventually, Martin and Lorna Anderson found Faith Lutheran a comfortable place for the entire family. Lorna Anderson went to work half days as the church secretary. Marty Anderson put the pastor up for the Optimists.

A memorial service for Marty Anderson was held at Faith Lutheran. Tom Bird, Lorna Anderson's boss and friend as well as her pastor, was by her side. He could have been assumed to have sad cause for empathy. Only four months before, his own wife had died — killed, from what the authorities could ascertain by reconstructing the event, when her car missed a nasty curve next to the Rocky Ford Bridge, southeast of town, and plunged over an embankment into the Cottonwood River. On the day of Martin Anderson's memorial service, the sanctuary of Faith Lutheran Church was full. Tom Bird delivered the eulogy. The Optimists sat in the front rows.

The day before the memorial service, Susan Ewert, a friend of Lorna Anderson's from the Andersons' days at First Presbyterian, walked into the office of the *Emporia Gazette* first thing in the morning with an angry complaint. She said that the *Gazette* article reporting Martin Anderson's murder — a short Saturday-afternoon item that had been written near deadline on the strength of telephone conversations — implied that Lorna Anderson wasn't telling the truth about what had happened. The *Gazette*'s implication, according to Mrs. Ewert, had so disturbed Mrs. Anderson that her pastor, who was trying to console her, had found her nearly suicidal. The managing editor of the *Gazette*, Ray Call, said that the paper would be happy to give Mrs. Anderson the opportunity to tell her story in detail, and when the *Gazette* came out that afternoon it carried a story headlined "MURDERED EMPORIAN'S WIFE RECALLS TERROR ON HIGHWAY."

Lorna Anderson's story was this: She was at the wheel of the family's van as it headed down 177 from Manhattan toward Emporia that evening. Apparently having eaten something in Manhattan that disagreed with her, she felt that she was about to be ill, so she stopped the car. As she got out, she took the keys with her — her husband had always insisted that she remove the keys any time she left the van — and then accidentally dropped them in the field at the side of the road. When her husband came out to help her look for them, he told her to return to the van and shine the headlights in his direction. While she was doing that, she heard someone say, "Where's your wallet?" She turned to see her husband hand his wallet to a masked man, who started shooting. Her husband fell to the ground. Then the man grabbed her, held the gun to her head, and pulled the trigger. The gun failed to fire. He fled into the darkness.

The story presented some problems. Would someone who was about to be ill really pull the keys out of a car parked on a deserted stretch of highway when her husband was sitting right in the front seat? What were the odds against a bandit's being on that stretch of highway when the Andersons' van stopped? The original item in the *Gazette* — an item that followed Lorna Anderson's account with the sentence "Officers are investigating the story" — had, in fact, reflected the skepticism of the Geary County officers who listened to the account the night of the murder. The implication of that skepticism was clear in a headline run by the *Junction City Daily Union* the next day: "VICTIM'S WIFE AMONG SUSPECTS IN KILLING." The *Emporia Gazette* was not as blunt, but that didn't mean an absence of suspicion in Emporia. There were a lot of rumors around town.

Emporia, with a population of twenty-five thousand, is about the right size for rumors. In a tiny town, people are likely to know firsthand what is true and what isn't. In a large city, most of the population won't have any connection at all with the people under discussion. In a place the size of Emporia, though, people tend to have an uncle who knows the cousin of someone through the Kiwanis, or a next-door neighbor who has the word through a lawyer who has a kid in the same Boy Scout troop. The Andersons had been in Emporia for only seven years — Marty Anderson was from a small town south of Wichita, and his wife had grown up in Hutchinson — but a lot of people knew someone who knew them. Just about everybody had something to say about them.

Marty Anderson sounded like a person who had been both easy to like and easy not to like. "He could be very aggravating, and the next minute he could get you laughing," a fellow Optimist has said. The way Anderson tried to get people laughing was usually through needling or practical jokes, and in both forms he occasionally passed over the line from funny to mean. Sometimes the object of the needling was his wife. He was a big man, more than six feet tall, and not the sort of big man who slowed up coming into second base for fear of bowling over a smaller player. At Newman Hospital he sometimes employed an army-sergeant manner that irritated people in other departments, but the technologists who worked for him considered him an essentially fair man who tried to run a meticulous laboratory. Basically, they liked him. Outside the hospital he was known as a man who after quite a bit too much to drink at a party might decide to play a prank that turned out not to have been such a good idea after all. His wife was given to tearful recitals of how miserable life with Martin Anderson could be, and some of the people who tried to be of comfort were told that he beat her.

"Everybody was always comforting Lorna," a female associate of Martin Anderson's has said, putting a little twist on the word "comforting." Lorna Anderson cried easily. Until a couple of years before her husband's death, she had often phoned him at the lab, distraught and tearful, but she was better known for seeking her comfort elsewhere. The Emporians of William Allen White's day could have described her with one sentence: She had a reputation. A trim, dark-haired, pleasant-looking woman of about thirty, she did not have the appearance of the town bombshell. But there were women in Emporia — women who worked at the hospital or were members of Beta Sigma Phi — who said that they avoided parties where the Andersons were likely to be present because they knew that before the evening was out Lorna Anderson would make a play for their husband. There were people in Emporia who said that a police investigation that included scrutiny of the Andersons' marriage had the potential of embarrassing any number of prominent business and professional men — men who had met Lorna Anderson when she worked at one of the banks or men who knew her through her work as local fundraiser for the American Heart Association or men who had simply run into her late in the evening at a place like the Continental Club of the Ramada Inn. Some people in Emporia — people who, say, worked with someone who knew someone connected with Faith Lutheran Church — were saying that Lorna Anderson's latest catch was Pastor Tom Bird. "Just after we got home from Marty's funeral, the phone rang," a colleague of Martin Anderson's has said. "The person calling said there was a rumor that Lorna and Tom Bird had something to do with Marty's death."

Pastor Bird had been one of the people who were always comforting Lorna. Almost from the time she began working at the church, in early 1983, there were whispers in the congregation about the possibility that the pastor and his secretary had grown too close. After Sandra Bird's death, in July of 1983, Lorna Anderson was just one of a number of women from the congregation who concentrated on providing whatever support they could for the young pastor, but she was the only one whose relationship with Tom Bird continued to cause uneasiness in the congregation. The pastor of Messiah had spoken confidentially to Bird about what people were saying, and so had Faith's lay ministers — the equivalent of church elders in some Lutheran congregations. At one point, the lay ministers, intent on avoiding even the appearance of impropriety by the pastor, considered asking Lorna Anderson to resign. Finally, it was agreed that she would remain church secretary but would limit her presence at the church to the hours that her job called for. Bird had assured the lay ministers that there was in fact no impropriety in his relationship with his secretary. She had a troubled marriage and a tendency to "spiral down," he told them, and he was only doing his best to counsel and support her. He continued to stand by her after Martin Anderson's death and after suspicion was cast on her. He continued to stand by her when, only a couple of weeks after Anderson's death, Daniel Carter, an Emporia man who had been picked up by the Geary County authorities on a tip, said she had given him five thousand dollars to see that her husband was killed. Pastor Bird's support did not waver even when, shortly after Carter's arrest, Lorna Anderson herself was arrested for conspiracy to commit first-degree murder.

Lorna Anderson said she was innocent. Daniel Carter said he was guilty. He agreed to cooperate with the authorities investigating the role of Lorna Anderson and others in the plot.

"Do you recall when it was you first had occasion to meet her?" Steven Opat, the Geary County attorney, asked during one of the times Carter testified in court.

"Yes," Carter said. "I used to cut her hair."

That was at Mr. & Ms., on Commercial Street, in 1981. The relationship was strictly business for about a year, Carter testified, and then there was an affair, which lasted a few months, and then, in August of 1983, Lorna Anderson asked him to find someone to get rid of her husband. By that time, Carter was working on the construction crew at Wolf Creek, where he presumably had a better chance of finding a hit man among his co-workers than he would have had at the hairdresser's. The Geary County authorities didn't claim that Carter had concocted a scheme that actually resulted in the death of Martin Anderson. As they pieced the story together, Carter took five thousand dollars from Lorna Anderson and passed it on to Gregory Curry, his supervisor at Wolf Creek, who passed it on to a third man, in Mississippi, who, perhaps realizing that nobody was in a position to make a stink about having the money returned if services weren't rendered, didn't do anything.

That left the mystery of who killed Martin Anderson, which meant that a number of investigators from the Geary County Sheriff's Office and the Lyon County Sheriff's Office and the Kansas Bureau of Investigation were still asking questions around Emporia — scaring up a covey of rumors with each interview. When the next arrest came, though, it was not for murder but for another plot, which nobody claimed had gone any further than talk. On March 21, 1984, four and a half months after Martin Anderson's death, the Lyon County attorney, Rodney H. Symmonds, filed charges against Thomas Bird for criminal solicitation to commit first-degree murder. In an affidavit filed at the same time, a KBI agent said that the prosecution was acting largely on information it had received from an Emporia housebuilder named Darrel Carter, Daniel Carter's older brother. Shortly after the arrest of Daniel Carter, the affidavit said, Darrel Carter had gone to the authorities to inform them that in May of 1983, three months before the plot his brother had described, he, too, had been asked to help get rid of Martin Anderson. According to the affidavit, Darrel Carter had gone to Faith Lutheran Church one weekday morning at Lorna Anderson's request, and there had been asked by Tom Bird if he would help in a murder scheme that was already worked out. After Martin Anderson's death, the affidavit said, Darrel Carter had got word that Tom Bird wanted to meet with him again in order to "reaffirm their trust," but this time Carter had shown up wearing a hidden transmitter provided by the Kansas Bureau of Investigation.

"Who would have thought that little old Emporia would have *two* hit men?" a professor at Emporia State University has said. Even to people in Emporia who had spent the months since Martin Anderson's death savoring the ironies or embellishing the rumors, though, the idea of a minister plotting a murder scheme right in his own church was shocking. There was an accompanying shock in what the affidavit said about one of the possible murder plans that Bird was accused of presenting to Darrel Carter: "Bird told Carter he found a place with a bend in a road and a bridge outside of Emporia, which had an approximately fifty-foot drop-off to the river and that a person could just miss the curve, especially if the person were drunk, and go off down the embankment. Bird told Carter they were going to drug Marty, take him out there, and run the car off into the river."

Anyone who might have missed the implication of that could see it spelled out in the *Gazette*'s coverage of Bird's arrest. "On July 17, Sandra Bird, Mr. Bird's wife, was found dead near the wreckage of her car that went off the road at the Rocky Ford Bridge southeast of Emporia," the *Gazette* said. "According to the accident report, Mrs. Bird had been driving northbound on the county road when the car apparently went off the roadway at the approach to the bridge and down a 65-foot embankment.

"An autopsy concluded that Mrs. Bird's death was accidental, caused by severe abdominal and chest injuries.

"Mr. Symmonds declined to comment on whether he considered Mrs. Bird's death to be accidental.

" 'Whenever a person dies, it's always subject to further investigation,' he said."

· · ·

Members of Faith Lutheran offered to post Tom Bird's bond. The church's attitude was summed up by the *Wichita Eagle* with the headline "CONGREGATION RALLIES AROUND PASTOR." There were people in the congregation who had been put out at Tom Bird at one time or another — he was known as someone who could be strong-willed about having things done his own way — but in general he was a popular figure. To people who might have expected a Missouri Synod Lutheran pastor to be a severe man on the lookout for sin, Tom Bird had always seemed accessible and informal and concerned. "We're going to stand behind him all the way," one young woman in the congregation told the reporter from Wichita. Faith Lutheran people spoke of Christian love and the American principle that a man is innocent until proved guilty. A lot of them considered the charge against Tom Bird a horrible mistake that would be straightened out at his first hearing. There were some people in the congregation, however, who believed that it would be inappropriate for Bird to continue in his pastoral duties as if nothing had happened, and there were a few who thought he should resign. Bird said that he had no intention of resigning or asking for a leave of absence. In a congregational meeting, a compromise was reached: it was decided that as a way of easing the pressure on Pastor Bird while he dealt with his defense, he could be relieved of preparing and delivering sermons while retaining his other pastoral duties. That arrangement was supposed to last until Bird's preliminary hearing. When the hearing was postponed for some weeks, Bird said that he would prefer to take the pulpit again, and the lay ministers, to the irritation of a few members who were outspokenly opposed to Pastor Bird's continued presence, agreed. On the Sunday that he preached his first sermon after his arrest, the worshippers emerging from the church after the service were greeted not only by their pastor but also by a couple of television crews and some out-of-town reporters.

In Bird's view, the presence of the press that Sunday effectively ended his ministry at Faith Lutheran by making it clear that the church would be no sanctuary from temporal concerns as long as Thomas Bird was its pastor. With or without television cameras at Sunday services, it was a hard time for Faith Lutheran. The atmosphere of relaxed fellowship that had attracted so many young families had turned tense. The effort of most members to withhold judgment meant that no one was quite certain of where anyone else stood. A few families had dropped out of the congregation, and some people came to church less often. "I didn't feel comfortable going to church," a member who was a strong supporter of Pastor Bird has said. "I felt people judging us as well as judging Tom." Faith members also felt some pressure from outside the church. The questions and remarks they heard from outsiders often seemed to carry the implication that the attitude of the congregation toward its pastor was naive or silly. In the view of one Faith Lutheran member, "it got to be socially unacceptable to go to our church." In the days after Bird's return to the pulpit, it was clear from the pressure within the church not simply that he would no longer deliver sermons on Sundays but that he would have to resign. He delayed the announcement by several weeks in order to avoid going into his preliminary hearing carrying the burden of having resigned under pressure.

Bird had often expressed gratitude for the congregation's support, but even before his arrest he had written in a church newsletter that his reputation was being "sullied by the local gossips." Some of the people who thought the congregation had not been strong enough in its support believed that in the strained atmosphere that followed his arrest the pastor had reason to feel "unwelcome and unloved" in his own church. When he finally resigned, two months after his arrest, his farewell speech to the congregation was partly about such subjects as authentic Christian love and the purposes of the church, but it also included some rather bitter remarks about his treatment. "When I remained silent, I was judged to be unfair for not informing people; when I have spoken, I was judged to be defensive," he said. "When I looked depressed, I was judged to be full of self-pity; when I smiled and looked strong, I was judged to be failing to take matters seriously. When I acted timid, I was judged to be weak; when I acted boldly, I was judged to be manipulating. When I was indecisive, I was judged to have lost my leadership capacity; when I acted decisively, I was judged to be using my position to railroad matters. To multiply the anguish of my predicament, I only hear these judgments second or third hand, so that I cannot share directly what is in my heart and my intentions to my accusers within the congregation."

By the time of Tom Bird's resignation, a folklorist at Emporia State who is interested in the sorts of jokes people tell was collecting Tom-and-Lorna jokes. The folklorist, Thomas Isern, believes that the range of humor in the mass media these days has forced folk humor to be scurrilous in order to remain folk humor, and scurrilous jokes flowed easily from a situation that included a couple of stock folklore characters — the preacher and the loose woman. The relationship between Tom Bird and Lorna Anderson was not the only subject of intense speculation in Emporia. A lot of people were talking about whether Sandra Bird's death had really been an accident. A couple of months after Bird's arrest, the *Gazette* reported that Sandra Bird's family, in Arkansas, had asked a Little Rock lawyer to supervise an investigation into the circumstances of her death. Once some doubt about the incident was made public, it became apparent that a number of people had at the time entertained doubts about whether Sandra Bird had simply missed a curve. A lot of people — neighbors, for instance, and people at Emporia State — had driven out to the Rocky Ford Bridge to have a look at the scene. What had given them pause was not any suspicion of Tom Bird but a feeling that the physical evidence didn't make sense. If Sandra Bird liked to take late-night drives by herself to unwind, as her husband had reported, why would she drive on the distinctly unrelaxing gravel road that approached the Rocky Ford Bridge? If the car was going so fast that it missed the curve at the bridge, which is the second half of an S curve, how did it negotiate the first half? If the car was going that fast, how come it wasn't more seriously damaged? It turned out that there were people in Emporia who for months had not actually believed the official version of how Sandra Bird died. They thought that she might have committed suicide or that she might have been abducted in the parking lot at Emporia State, where she sometimes went late at night to use the computers, and murdered by her abductor.

By far the most popular topic for speculation, though, was what people in Emporia began to call simply the list. The prosecution, it was said, had a list of Emporia men who had been involved with Lorna Anderson. In some versions of the story, the *Gazette* had the list. In some versions, it was not a list but a black book. In some versions, the men who were on a list of potential witnesses for Lorna Anderson's trial had been informed of that by the prosecution so that they could break the news to their families themselves. The version of the list story some of the reporters on the *Gazette* liked best turned into one of the jokes that could be collected by Tom Isern:

A prominent businessman calls an acquaintance on the *Gazette* news staff and says nervously, "I have to know — does the *Gazette* have a list?"

"No," the *Gazette* reporter says, in a soothing voice. "But we're compiling one."

Those people in Emporia who were counting on Lorna Anderson's trial to end the suspense were in for a long wait. The case against her got tangled in any number of delays and legal complications. As it turned out, the first person to come to trial for plotting to murder Martin Anderson was Tom Bird. The defense asked for a change of venue, providing the court with the results of a survey indicating that an overwhelming majority of Emporia residents were familiar with the case. The motion was denied. In Kansas, there is a strong tradition against granting changes of venue even when there is wide community awareness of a case, and, as it happened, the survey indicated that a relatively small percentage of those who were familiar with the charges and the rumors had already made up their minds. But among the ones who had, there was a strong indication of how Emporia opinion was running: out of thirty-nine people with firm opinions, thirty-two thought Tom Bird was guilty.

Bird's mother and his father, who is also a Lutheran minister, came up from Arkansas for the trial. So did Sandra Bird's father and mother and stepfather — who, it was noted around town, seemed to keep their distance from their former son-in-law during the proceedings. Reporters and television crews from Wichita and Topeka were in town; despite objections from the defense, a fixed television camera was permitted in the courtroom for the first time in Lyon County. There were members of Faith Lutheran who had come to testify for the defense and members who had come to testify for the prosecution and members who had come merely because, like most residents of Emporia, they were attracted by the prospect of seeing witnesses under oath clear up — or perhaps improve on — the rumors that had been going around town for eight months. The courtroom was jammed every day. "I've never been to anything like this before," one of the spectators told the *Gazette*. "I feel like I know them all; I've heard their names so many times."

The prosecution's case was based on the assumption that Tom Bird and Lorna Anderson had been lovers. According to the prosecutor, they wanted Marty Anderson out of the way, and they weren't interested in a less violent means of accomplishing that — divorce, for instance — because they also wanted the four hundred thousand dollars his death would bring in insurance money. The prosecution's witnesses included the Andersons' insurance agent — he turned out to be the president of the Optimist Club — and a babysitter, who said that she once heard Lorna Anderson say on the telephone, "I cannot wait for Marty to die; I can't wait to count the green stuff." There was testimony from Faith Lutheran people who had been concerned that the pastor and his secretary were growing too close. "I saw a sparkle in their eyes when they talked to each other," said the preschool teacher, a young woman who under cross-examination acknowledged that she herself had wrestled with a crush on the pastor. "I felt electricity in the air." There was testimony from a development director of the Heart Association, who reduced the talk of electricity and eye-sparkling to more direct language; according to her testimony, Lorna Anderson had told her about having an affair with the pastor and had said that she was using Heart Association business as a cover for trysts in out-of-town motels. The Andersons' nine-year-old daughter, Lori, testified that she had seen her mother and Tom Bird hugging; Marty Anderson's brother and a KBI agent both testified that what Lori had said when she was first questioned was that she had seen her mother and Tom Bird kissing.

The prosecution's star witness was, of course, Darrel Carter. He testified that the meeting at the church in the spring of 1983 was not the first time Lorna Anderson had asked his help in killing her husband. She had first asked him a year or so before that, he said, at a time when the Andersons and the Carters knew each other casually from Beta Sigma Phi functions. "I was really kind of shocked to think that she would ask me that," Carter testified, " 'cause Martin Anderson was a friend of mine." According to Carter's testimony, that friendship hadn't prevented him from having his own fling with Lorna some months later. To back up Carter's story of the meeting at Faith Lutheran, the prosecution called a couple of people he had mentioned the scheme to at the time. "I was doing a little work there one evening in my garage on an old Corvette that I'm restoring," one of them, a neighbor of Carter's, said, in testimony that summoned up the traditional vision of summertime in Emporia. "We visited about several things, which I can't tell you all they were, but the one that sticks in my mind right now is that he told me that someone had contacted him about killing someone."

What the defense asked the jury to do was to view Darrel Carter's testimony not as a story he had finally come forward with after his brother's arrest but as a story he had concocted in order to win some leniency for his brother — who had, in fact, been given probation, while Gregory Curry, his confederate in the scheme, was sentenced to prison. From that angle, the details that Darrel Carter knew could be seen as coming from police reports available to the defense in his brother's case. The similarity of the murder plan to the circumstances of Sandra Bird's death could be explained by the fact that when Carter concocted the story he knew how Sandra Bird had died. The meeting at Faith Lutheran had indeed taken place, the defense said; its purpose was not to plot murder, though, but to explore the possibility of Faith youth-group members' working at Carter's fireworks stand in order to raise money for a trip to see the Passion play in Eureka Springs, Arkansas. After Marty Anderson's death, Bird had indeed let it be known that he wanted to talk to Carter, the defense said, but that was because Susan Ewert, Lorna Anderson's friend, had told Bird that Carter was spreading rumors about him, and Bird wanted to put a stop to that. "I've heard enough rumors for sure," Bird could be heard saying to Carter on the tape. "Rumors are rampant."

During that conversation with Carter, in a bowling alley parking lot, Bird made what the prosecution presented as incriminating remarks about the meeting at his church ("I just wanted to touch the bases and make sure that we just talked about possibly my youth group sellin' firecrackers for you") and about the murder of Martin Anderson ("Well, maybe we ought to be glad that we didn't follow through") and about how he felt about Anderson's death ("I ain't celebratin', but I ain't mournin', either"). Still, nothing on the tape was absolutely explicit, and Bird took the stand to provide a benign explanation for every remark — mostly based on the contention that what he and Carter hadn't followed through on was a plan to refer Lorna Anderson to an agency that assists battered wives. When the prosecution managed to bring into evidence two notes from Tom Bird that the police said they had found in Lorna Anderson's lingerie drawer, Bird said that they were meant simply to buck up Lorna's spirits and that such sentiments as "I love you so very much and that's forever" were expressions not of romantic attachment but of "authentic Christian love."

In describing his efforts to counsel Lorna Anderson, Bird admitted that, emotionally drained by his wife's death, he might have used bad judgment in providing the gossips with even the appearance of something worth gossiping about. In explaining why he had arranged the parking lot meeting through a go-between, a woman he knew from an inquiry she had made about the Lord's Lambs preschool, he admitted a pressure tactic that some jurors might have considered un-Christian: he happened to know that the woman and Darrel Carter were having an affair, he testified, and he figured that making Carter aware of that knowledge might send "the message that everybody is capable of being a victim of rumors." But that was about all he admitted. Bird said that people who saw him hugging Lorna Anderson while comforting her might not have understood that standing across the room with consoling words would not have been "full communication." She had a "self-esteem problem" that required a lot of comforting, he said, and he had provided it as her pastor and her employer and her friend but not as her lover.

"If only he had admitted the affair," a remarkable number of people in Emporia said when talking about Tom Bird's trial for criminal solicitation. The defense had insisted that the case amounted to a simple choice of whether to believe Tom Bird or Darrel Carter. In some ways, it was an unequal contest. Darrel Carter was nobody's idea of a model citizen. He did not claim that his response to having been asked to help murder a friend of his had included outrage or a telephone call to the authorities. He acknowledged — boasted about, the defense might have said — two affairs with married women while he was married himself. Someone who had hired him to build a house took the stand to say that he was "the biggest liar in ten counties." In contrast, several character witnesses testified that Tom Bird was a trustworthy, God-fearing man. "He is very conscious of the Word of God," the chairman of Faith Lutheran's board of lay ministers said, "and he is very deliberate in his close attention and following of the Word of God."

But practically nobody in Emporia believed Tom Bird when he said he had not had an affair with Lorna Anderson. If only he had admitted the affair, people in Emporia said, the jury might have believed the rest of the story — or might at least have been understanding about what passion could have led him to do. The defense that Emporia people thought might have worked for Tom Bird amounted to a sort of Garden of Eden defense — a tragic twist on the jokes about the preacher and the loose woman. To some people in Emporia, it seemed that Tom Bird could have been presented as a vulnerable man who, at a particularly stressful time in his life, had been led by his passion for a temptress to do some things he came to regret, but who would never have conspired to break God's commandment against murder. A lot of people in Emporia, in other words, thought that Tom Bird's only hope was to repent. The people from Faith Lutheran who continued to believe in Pastor Bird right through the trial found that approach enraging. He could not repent, they said, for the simple reason that he had done nothing that required repentance. That, apparently, was not the view of the jury. Bird was found guilty of soliciting murder. He was sentenced to a term of two and a half to seven years in the Kansas State Penitentiary.

"Like most Emporians, we love a bit of juicy gossip now and then," an editorial in the *Gazette* said a month or so after Tom Bird's conviction. "But in recent weeks here, the saturation point for rumors has been reached and innocent people are being hurt." The *Gazette* mentioned some rumors about the possibility that "the defendant in a recent sensational trial had remarried." There were also further rumors about Lorna Anderson, who had moved back to Hutchinson, and about what might be revealed in her trial. Time had swollen accounts of the list. "At first the list was said to contain 20 names," the *Gazette* said. "Now the number has grown to 110 and includes 'bankers, lawyers and other professional men.' This is a case of gross exaggeration." The *Gazette* thought it necessary to inform its readers that a professional man who had recently left town had not in fact fled because he was on the list and feared exposure.

The *Gazette* had begun a campaign to have the rumors surrounding Sandra Bird's death tested in a court of law. "Was it only coincidence that Mr. Bird's wife died in the manner and in the place that the minister had suggested for the murder of Mr. Anderson?" its editorial on the verdict in Tom Bird's trial asked. Two *Gazette* reporters, Roberta Birk and Nancy Horst, pounded away at the Sandra Bird case with stories carrying headlines like "CIRCUMSTANCES OF DEATH RAISE SUSPICIONS" and "TROOPER THOUGHT DEATH NOT ACCIDENT." The *Gazette* made a reward fund available for information on the case and ran a series of stories about contributions to the fund from Sandra Bird's friends and family. In a sheriff's election that November, the *Gazette* editorialized against the incumbent partly on the ground that he had bungled the original investigation of Sandra Bird's death, and he was defeated. Eventually, Sandra Bird's body was exhumed, a second autopsy was performed, and a grand jury began investigating the case. In February of 1985, the grand jury handed up an indictment against Tom Bird for the murder of his wife.

The *Gazette*'s campaign angered the people in Emporia who continued to believe in Bird's innocence. In the months since the headline "CONGREGATION RALLIES AROUND PASTOR," of course, their ranks had suffered serious attrition. Some supporters had dropped away as they heard more and more about the relationship between Tom Bird and Lorna Anderson. A lot more had defected after the revelations of the trial or after the guilty verdict. But there remained people in the Faith Lutheran congregation who believed that the verdict was just wrong — a result of Darrel Carter's perfidy and the judge's perverse refusal to move the trial out of a community that had convicted Tom Bird before any witnesses took the stand. The Bird supporters who remained could point out inconsistencies in prosecution testimony. But basically they believed Bird was innocent partly because they thought he was incapable of the deeds he was accused of and partly because he said he was innocent. "He told me that he swears before God he's innocent," one of the lay ministers has said. "I have to believe him. I don't think he would say that if he were guilty."

Almost everybody else in Emporia tended to believe that Bird was guilty not only of plotting to kill Martin Anderson but also of murdering his own wife. According to a survey taken for Bird's lawyer to support a motion to move his murder trial out of Emporia, virtually everyone in town was familiar with the case, and more than ninety percent of those who had made up their minds about it believed that he was guilty. The motion was denied. In July of 1985, the familiar cast of characters gathered once again in Lyon County District Court — Tom Bird and his parents, the family of Sandra Bird, the small band of Faith Lutheran members who remained loyal to Bird, County Attorney Rodney H. Symmonds, Darrel Carter, the TV crews from Topeka and Wichita. As the trial got under way, though, what most Emporia residents seemed to be discussing was not any revelation from the witness stand but news

from Hutchinson that Lorna Anderson, whose trial was finally
scheduled to begin later in the summer, had remarried. The bride-
groom was a Hutchinson man named Randy Eldridge, someone
she had known for years. In answer to reporters' questions, Eldridge said he believed that his new wife was innocent. She said
that he was "a wonderful, Christian person" — someone who, it
turned out, was a member of a gospel-singing sextet in his spare
time. That fact and the rumors that both Eldridges were quite active in an Assembly of God church in Hutchinson had some people
in Emporia concerned. It looked as if Lorna Anderson Eldridge
might be planning to come to court as an upstanding Christian wife
and mother who couldn't have had anything to do with plotting
murder — and presumably the prosecution might attempt to destroy that picture of probity by calling to the stand any number of
men from the list.

In Tom Bird's trial for murder, there was even more testimony
about his relationship with his secretary than there had been in the
previous trial. The prosecution called witnesses, Sandra Bird's
mother among them, who testified that the pastor's wife had been
so distraught over the relationship that she had been unable to eat.
But a lot of the testimony was rather technical — testimony from
pathologists and accident-reconstruction specialists — and there
were days when finding a seat in the spectators' section was no
problem. The prosecution called expert witnesses to testify that
neither the injuries to Sandra Bird nor the damage to the car was
consistent with an accident; the defense called expert witnesses to
testify the opposite. By pointing out inconsistencies in Tom Bird's
account of that evening and presenting some physical evidence,
such as the presence of bloodstains on the bridge, the prosecutor
suggested that Bird had beaten his wife, thrown her off the Rocky
Ford Bridge, run their car off the embankment, and dragged her
body over to it in order to create the appearance of an accident.
The defense argued that inconsistencies were to be expected from
a man who had been up half the night worrying about where his
wife was and had had to start the day by telling his children that
their mother was dead. Tom Bird was on trial not for how he ran

his personal life, his lawyer said, but for the crime of murder, and "there's no evidence that a crime of any kind was committed." The testimony required twelve days. After that, the jury deliberated for six hours and found Tom Bird guilty of first-degree murder. He was sentenced to life in prison.

"Even a lot of people who thought he was guilty didn't think the trial proved it," a supporter of Bird's said after it was over. It is true, at least, that the prosecutor was not able to provide an eye-witness, as he had done in the criminal-solicitation case. It is also true that he went into the trial holding the advantage of Bird's conviction for plotting Martin Anderson's murder. Among people familiar with the case, it is taken for granted that without the earlier conviction Bird would never have been brought to trial for his wife's murder. Discussing the astonishing chain of events that transformed Tom Bird from a popular young minister to a lifer convicted of killing his wife, a lot of people in Emporia continue to say, "If only he had admitted the affair."

A month after Bird's second conviction, Lorna Anderson Eldridge sat in the same courtroom — neatly dressed, composed, almost cheerful — and said, "I believe it was in June, 1983, Thomas Bird and I met with Darrel Carter at the Faith Lutheran Church. During that meeting we discussed various ways of murdering my husband, Martin Anderson." In a last-minute plea bargain, she had agreed to plead guilty to two counts of criminal solicitation to commit first-degree murder and to tell the authorities anything she knew about a case that had presumably already been decided — the death of Sandra Bird. In her plea, she said that Tom Bird had also been involved later in trying to hire a hit man through Danny Carter, and had, in fact, furnished the five thousand dollars. Lorna Eldridge's lawyer said she wanted to purge her soul. A month later, she was sentenced to a term of five and a half to eighteen years in state prison.

Her plea was a blow to those who had continued to believe in Tom Bird, but it did not significantly reduce their ranks. At one point, one of them has said, Bird had told his supporters, "There are very few left. They are falling away. And sooner or later you, too, will be gone." As it turned out, the people who had stuck with Tom Bird even through the murder trial did not fall away just because Lorna Anderson stated in open court that what the prosecution said about Tom Bird was true. They figured that she might be lying because she thought a plea bargain was in her best interests, or that she might be lying simply because she liked to lie. They continue to believe that someday something — a large criminal operation like a drug ring, perhaps — will come to light to explain events that the state has explained with accusations against Tom Bird. At times, they sound like early Christians who manage to shake off constant challenges to their faith. "Questions come up," one of them has said. "And I stop and think. But I always work it out." Tom Bird, when asked by a visitor to the Kansas State Penitentiary about the loyalty of his supporters, also explained their support in religious terms — as the action of Christians who understand that we are all sinners and that it is not our role to judge others. "They've grown in their faith," he said.

It is possible that the challenges to their faith in Tom Bird are not at an end. It is not known yet precisely what, if anything, Lorna Anderson Eldridge had to tell the prosecutors about the death of Sandra Bird. So far, nobody has been charged with the murder of Martin Anderson. In Geary County, though, investigators believe that they have made considerable progress. Presumably acting on information provided by Lorna Anderson Eldridge, the Geary County Sheriff's Office drained several farm ponds and eventually found the gun it believes was used in the killing. It is said that the gun belonged to Martin Anderson. Shortly after the sheriff began draining farm ponds, Tom Bird was taken to Junction City from prison to answer questions. Each step in the investigation in Geary County set off ripples of speculation in Lyon County. Will Tom Bird be charged with another murder? Had one of the murder schemes already uncovered by the authorities resulted in Anderson's death after all? Or could it be that little old Emporia had *three* hit men?

·   ·   ·

To some extent, Lorna Anderson Eldridge's guilty plea meant that William Allen White's home town could get back to normal. Faith Lutheran Church, which had absorbed a fearful blow, has begun to recover. Nobody claims that it has regained the momentum of its early days, but the new pastor — another athletic and personable man with several children — believes that the church has come through its crisis into a period of consolidation. The Lord's Lambs preschool is back to its routine. So are the Optimist basketball games and the laboratory at Newman Hospital and the front page of the *Gazette*. Presumably, Mrs. Eldridge's guilty pleas brought a great sense of relief to those residents of Emporia who had reason to look with some trepidation on the prospect of her coming to trial. There was now less danger that what the *Gazette* called "the most sordid case in Emporia's history" would extend to sworn testimony about the sexual escapades of prominent citizens.

One change in Emporia is that two families are no longer there. The adults are dead or imprisoned, the children living in other cities. (The Anderson children have been adopted by Randy Eldridge; the Bird children are living in Arkansas with Tom Bird's parents, who are in the midst of a custody suit brought by the family of Sandra Bird.) Also, there are some people who believe that what happened to the Birds and the Andersons has to have changed what Emporians think of their town and their neighbors. People who have long taken the guilt of Tom Bird and Lorna Anderson for granted are still left with questions about how they could have brought themselves to do such awful deeds. Was Lorna Anderson a temptress who merely used Tom Bird to help get rid of her husband? Or did the death of Sandra Bird — perhaps caused by her husband in some fit of rage — lead inevitably to the death of Martin Anderson? If Tom Bird and Lorna Anderson were bound together, were they bound together by love or by guilty knowledge? Lately, there has been more talk in Emporia about the possibility that what happened can be explained through some sort of mental illness. In a 1984 story about the background of the Birds, Dana Mullin of the *Topeka Capital-Journal* reported that Tom Bird was once hospitalized with a severe heat stroke after a six-mile run in Arkansas and that such heat strokes have been known to cause brain damage. Putting that information together with some of the bizarre behavior attributed to Lorna Anderson even before her husband's death, some people in Emporia have theorized that perhaps Tom Bird and his secretary, who seemed so much like their neighbors, had mental difficulties that somehow meshed to result in deeds their neighbors consider unthinkable.

What was sordid about Emporia's most sordid case, of course, was not simply the crimes but the lives they revealed — lives full of hatred and maybe wife-beating and certainly casual, apparently joyless liaisons. (When Daniel Carter testified that his affair with Lorna Anderson had ended because she seemed to want more from him than he was willing to offer, the prosecutor asked what he had been willing to offer. "Nothing," Carter said.) Although the *Gazette* may have criticized rumors about a hundred-and-ten-man list as "a gross exaggeration," the prosecutors have never denied that a list, perhaps of more modest size, existed — assembled, it is assumed, in case the state of the Andersons' marriage became an issue. A jury had concluded that an Emporia minister beat his wife until she was unconscious or dead and threw her body off a bridge. A church secretary acknowledged involvement in plans to get rid of her husband, who was murdered virtually in front of their own children. What now seems remarkable about the outrageous rumors that gripped Emporia for so long is that so many of them turned out to be true.

1986

A COUPLE OF
ECCENTRIC GUYS

I WAS IN A CHINESE RESTAURANT in Philadelphia asking
Wier Chrisemer about the origins of the Othmar Schoeck Memorial Society for the Preservation of Unusual and Disgusting
Music. Chrisemer is the man to talk to about Othmar Schoeck. It
was Chrisemer, after all, who brought Schoeck's name to the attention of the general public, at least the general public of a portion
of western Massachusetts. This was in 1970, when Chrisemer,
then an Amherst College music major, was browsing in the record
collection of the college radio station and came across an album of
Schoeck's music called "Lebendig Begraben," or "Buried Alive."
Of such seemingly chance encounters, I reminded Chrisemer, is
history made.

Listening to the album back then, Chrisemer had a strong suspicion why the music of Othmar Schoeck, a Swiss composer who
died in 1957, was not familiar to him. "It was awful," he told me.
"It had no redeeming merit." Chrisemer was also struck by the fact
that Othmar Schoeck, whose picture was on the front of the
album, could have been picked out of a large crowd as a Swiss
composer of music that made you long for intermission: "He was
in the standard pose of the composer leaning on his hand, but he
had a rather fleshy face, and some of the flesh was hanging over the
tops of his fingers." Thus doubly inspired, Chrisemer decided that

it would be appropriate to try to build Othmar Schoeck a cult following. When I was in college, I could have seen the logic in that myself. I think I can still see the logic in that.

Chrisemer figured that the core of Schoeck's celebration would be two or three concerts a year at Amherst sponsored by the Othmar Schoeck Memorial Society for the Preservation of Unusual and Disgusting Music. The concerts did not go so far as to include any works by Othmar Schoeck. The pieces performed tended to be what Chrisemer describes as "arrangements of standard classical chestnuts for different instruments" — Beethoven's Ninth for electric piano, prepared piano, saxophones, trash-can lids, recorders, electric bass guitar, nose flute, slide whistle, and chorus of four, for instance, or a Sousa march for a Baroque ensemble of recorder, harpsichord, cello continuo, and krummhorn. Chrisemer was serious about music — he abhorred the notion of basing humor on wrong notes — and eyewitnesses to Othmar Schoeck concerts have assured me that the most astonishing aspect of the arrangements was that they could strike a sympathetic ear as not simply funny but, somehow, just right.

In all but musical terms, the concerts were strongly Schoeckian. The program bore the logo of the Society, featuring a coffin to represent Schoeck's death in an avalanche — the circumstances of the composer's demise having been one of the embellishments Chrisemer contributed to a life that seemed a bit conventional for a cult hero. The program also included the Society's motto — a German poem that went *"Sehen wir Haufen von Hundedreck, wir denken an dir, Othmar Schoeck,"* which Chrisemer translates as "Wherever we see piles of doggie-doo, O Othmar Schoeck, we think of you." Chrisemer even went to the trouble of picking up a knockwurst at the Amherst dining hall before the first concert, keeping it in a drawer for longer than anyone has a right to keep a knockwurst in a drawer, and declaring it the Othmar Schoeck Memorial Knockwurst. At concerts, it was displayed in a separate room, resting in a custom-built case and guarded by a man who wore what looked very much like the uniform of an officer in the United States Coast Guard.

"In fact, I still have the Othmar Schoeck Memorial Knock-wurst," Chrisemer said that evening at dinner.

I calculated that the knockwurst would be about eighteen years old. "How does it look?" I asked.

"About the same," Chrisemer said.

Running along with the musical numbers in an Othmar Schoeck concert were various "bits of business" — often, Chrisemer cheerfully admits, based on jokes that were not immediately comprehensible to most of those in the audience. In the final year of the concerts, when Chrisemer had graduated and was working in a stereo store in nearby Greenfield, Massachusetts, the bits included an extremely tall teenager riding across the stage on a unicycle as part of Chrisemer's interpretation of "The Battle Hymn of the Republic." The unicyclist was someone Chrisemer had met at the stereo store — a recent graduate of Greenfield High School named Penn Jillette, who had completed his higher education at the Ringling Bros. and Barnum & Bailey Clown College. Jillette also participated in the playing of "The Star-Spangled Banner" by juggling some balls above a large bass drum and letting one drop onto the drum on the appropriate beat: "Oh, say can you see [boom] by the dawn's early light [boom] . . ."

One of the people who had helped with the staging of that concert was a close Amherst friend of Chrisemer's who was by then teaching high school Latin in New Jersey. Even as a college magician doing a silent and rather arty act at fraternity parties, he had taken to using only his last name — Teller. (The act was silent partly as a means of deflecting hecklers and partly as a means of increasing its artiness.) In the lobby at intermission, the silent Teller, outfitted with a cane and dark glasses, sold Othmar Schoeck pencils.

It was the presence of Penn Jillette and Teller that had piqued my curiosity about the Othmar Schoeck concerts. Eventually, the two of them teamed up with Wier Chrisemer to form "The Asparagus Valley Cultural Society," a show that blended Teller's magic tricks and Jillette's juggling and Chrisemer's odd musical arrangements into an evening of neo-Schoeckian humor. Eventually, "The Asparagus Valley Cultural Society" transformed itself, without Chris-

emer, into a theatrical performance called "Penn & Teller," which
had successful runs Off Broadway and on. It's a performance that
critics find so difficult to describe that the Obie it won when it was
Off Broadway was given to Penn and Teller for "whatever it is they
do." Trying to describe a show that somehow presents carnival
stunts and magic tricks in a way that is funny and menacing at the
same time, critics often fall back on the description of the principals which Penn himself offers at the beginning of the evening —
"a couple of eccentric guys who have learned to do a few cool
things." Toward the end of the evening, Penn only adds to the con-
fusion by saying, "The question we want you to ask yourself is not
how we do these tricks but why we do them." But the question
that I wanted to ask — and the reason I was talking history with
Wier Chrisemer in a Chinese restaurant in Philadelphia — was neither of those. It was "How did you guys get that way?"

Like most occasional Off Broadway ticket buyers, I am not drawn
to magic acts. Until I ran across Penn and Teller, my only experience with magicians in some years had been a brief sidewalk encounter during which I asked Harry Blackstone, Jr., to turn my
younger daughter, Sarah, who was then twelve or thirteen, into an
elephant. One spring afternoon, we happened to be standing in
front of our house when a taxi stopped and Harry Blackstone, Jr.,
emerged. He was visiting a neighbor of ours named Charles
Reynolds, who is a producer of magic effects, a scholar of magic,
and a consultant on magic to productions ranging from Broadway
musicals to touring rock acts. Charles, who had come out to greet
his guest, introduced us. Even without being a close follower
of the magic game, I knew that Harry Blackstone, Jr., is regarded
as one of the finest magicians in the country — the leading ex-
emplar of the formal tradition of grand illusion — so it seemed
natural to ask him for a real stunner. Blackstone declined to turn
Sarah into an elephant — "Either he couldn't or he wouldn't,"
I've always said in my carefully balanced account of the incident
— but he declined with great aplomb, pointing out to me that an
elephant is one of the few beasts that require more upkeep than a
teenager.

I admire the skill of a first-rank magician like Blackstone, but in general I'm not someone who is entertained by being astounded. Also, a lot of magicians have in common with a lot of people in children's theater the habit of performing with the sort of broad gesture that seems based on the assumption that the entire audience is one rather slow-witted person in the back row. When "Penn & Teller" first opened in New York, in 1985, at a small Off Broadway house called the Westside Arts, I didn't rush right over. I had heard vaguely that Penn and Teller were magicians, and I had further heard that one of them didn't speak — a report leaving open the dread possibility that he was a mime. It's no secret by now that I would subject myself to a thousand hours of American Legion Hall magicians rather than endure ten minutes in the presence of the world's most accomplished mime. In my less restrained moments, I have gone so far as to suggest that people performing mime in public be subject to citizen's arrest, on the theory that the normal First Amendment protection of free speech has in effect been waived by someone who has formally adopted a policy of not speaking.

I was finally lured to the Westside Arts by the reviews — a collection of all-out raves. Some of the critics mentioned the dark, and even terrifying, side of the show. It begins with Teller suspended upside down in a straitjacket over a bed of spikes; it ends up with Penn on a darkened stage eating fire and talking about how at the Franklin County Fair he always felt himself drawn into the sideshow tent to see the freaks and fire-eaters while his high school buddies waited outside. But what attracted me was the general agreement that Penn and Teller were terribly funny. In my experience, a funny magician is so rare that an innovative entrepreneur might be able to attract a crowd simply by announcing that he had one on the premises, in the way those roadside zoos next to filling stations along Route 66 used to put out signs saying "SEE ALBINO RACCOON."

Like most people seeing Penn and Teller for the first time, I was struck by their appearance. Both of them were dressed in gray business suits and red ties. Penn is six feet six, nearly a foot taller than his partner, and happens to be that rare person to whom the word "shambling" can be appropriately applied — although he also crosses the stage at times in a style of locomotion he describes, quite accurately, as grooving. His hairdo included a sort of frizzy ponytail and another fistful of hair tumbling over his forehead. He wore clear polish on all but one fingernail, and that one was painted red. Penn referred to neither his hair nor his fingernail during the act, but when the subject of his being asked to cut his hair for a movie role came up a year or so later — in an interview with Kevin Kelly of the *Boston Globe* — he offered a comment on his appearance that I think of as typical of his showier offstage remarks: "Hey! All I care about is my hair and fingernails! Everything else is just affectation." A couple of years after that, I happened to be standing next to Penn while he was chatting with members of the audience during intermission — chatting with the audience during intermission is routine for Penn and Teller, as is hawking T-shirts in the lobby after the show — and a man who appeared to be just a shade over five feet tall asked him directly what the significance of having one red fingernail was. Penn looked down at the man and said, in the same cheerful voice he had used to answer other inquiries, "It means I once killed a man for asking personal questions."

After I saw that first performance, it occurred to me that Penn's fingernail was one of the few subjects he didn't get around to onstage. The words just poured out of him — a constant, aggressive, consciously hip, often overbearing, occasionally hostile flow that sometimes sounded like the language of a man on the street corner up to no good and sometimes like the language of the world's leading academic authority on Run D.M.C. Teller, on the other hand, said virtually nothing except what he said behind his hand as the voice of a creature called MOFO, the Psychic Gorilla. But he was no mime. He was simply a subtly expressive man who didn't seem to feel the need to say anything. He was definitely a magician. In one elegant number, unlike anything I'd ever seen, he silently dismantled a rose by cutting away at the shadow cast on a screen behind it. In another number, he swallowed a hundred embroidery needles, a few dozen at a time, topped them off with some thread, and then pulled out of his mouth a thread glistening with needles. The swallowing of each batch of needles produced a series of squirms and grimaces that I can describe only as high peristaltic drama. For me, the expression signaling that the needles had reached their destination — an expression part triumph, part blissful relief — was the high point of the show. I have seen Teller swallow needles any number of times since, and I have laughed out loud at that expression every single time.

The show also included numbers that were built on such magic effects as levitating a volunteer from the audience and guessing the card that someone had chosen from the deck, but it didn't feel like a magic show — and not simply because Penn announced explicitly at the beginning of the evening that the audience would not be seeing the sort of magic associated with "some greasy guy in a tux with a lot of birds." For one thing, the show avoided the "make-believe," as magicians sometimes call it, that what was taking place was magical — the make-believe advanced by the magician who ends each trick by drawing attention to the miraculously empty cage or the miraculously unsawed-up assistant with what Penn sometimes calls "Vanna White hand gestures." Explaining toward the end of the evening that everything in the show is a trick, Penn said, "That woman we had floating up in the air, she wasn't hypnotized. You want to try that at home, get a couple of chairs, clear your mind, study Zen, and *you'll break your ass!*" Penn's version of "Abracadabra!" was a muttered "Now I give the cards another false cut." He referred to magic effects not as wonders but as cons or swindles. Early in the show, he and Teller did the traditional cups-and-balls trick with clear plastic cups and a running commentary on precisely how the trick was being done — although after seeing that demonstration several times, about all I know about the cups-and-balls trick is that I wouldn't have the manual dexterity to do it.

Penn and Teller had a relationship with the audience that seemed to me less characteristic of magicians than of street performers, which they both once were. They treated the crowd with the cheeky familiarity of some itinerant juggler who shares with those gathered around him the unspoken understanding that at the end of the act he will not only ask for donations but also make fun of them for not donating enough. Street performers tend to include the crowd in a commentary on the performance that becomes a central part of the performance. Carrying that attitude to the Westside Arts meant that the Penn and Teller show was partly about being at a show. "Is it your birthday or anniversary or anything?" Penn asked one volunteer from the audience, who had already testified that he knew nobody connected to the show. "What I'm getting at, Joe, is there any reason that one of your wacky, wild, zippy, zany friends — and I know you've got 'em, Joe — any reason why them friends would have hired two hundred and forty-three unemployed Equity actors to sit in these seats and *act* like they're watching a show just to blow your mind, freak you out, mess with that gray matter? Is it possible you're the only one here that bought a ticket and everyone else is *cast*? No wonder we're always sold out, Joe: it's *one ticket*!"

A few months after I saw "Penn & Teller" at the Westside Arts, I had occasion to meet both Penn and Teller. They became involved in an educational film that my wife co-produced. Offstage, they seemed more or less consistent with their roles in the show. Teller talked, of course — lucidly, but not at length. Penn talked at great length, and sometimes lucidly. They were both analytical; it was obvious that their act, which seemed so freewheeling, had been thought through to the tiniest detail. The educational film was about how artists create the illusion of depth on a flat surface, and Teller came up with a remarkable number of entertaining ways to demonstrate that phenomenon. Sarah met Penn and Teller and thought they were both cool, although Penn made it clear that he found her taste in rock music a bit tame.

Before going any further, I'm afraid I have to report that Penn was once caught deflating his résumé. It's not an infraction you come across much these days, but Penn is an unusual sort of guy. This came about because of the great pleasure Penn takes in describing the total rebel he was as a high school student — a walking disruption who was a lot more interested in playing punk-rock music and flaunting his long hair than he was in handing in the assigned homework. Describing his teenage years to Kevin Kelly, of the *Globe*, in 1986, Penn said that he had been kicked out of Greenfield High School. Kelly phoned Edward Jones, the principal of Greenfield High School, who told him that Penn had graduated at the normal time with good marks. Penn just shook his head when I reminded him of the incident. "It was the greatest day in Ed Jones's life," he said. "He got his name in the *Globe* and he got to call me a liar at the same time."

Penn is not exactly a liar, but he is not absolutely wed to the facts of a story if they interfere with the general theme. The general theme of stories he tells about life in Greenfield is his rebelliousness, and he likes to begin those stories with phrases like "If I happened to be wearing eye make-up to school that day . . ." He is also attached to the allied theme of being uneducated in the formal sense, particularly compared with the erudite Teller — and, in "Asparagus Valley" days, with the equally erudite Wier Chrisemer. In 1977, when John Corr, of the *Philadelphia Inquirer*, paid a visit to an old mansion in Lambertville, New Jersey, that seemed to be serving as home for just about everybody with any connection to the "Asparagus" troupe except Chrisemer ("I have a limited tolerance for squalor"), Penn told him, "I'm the only one of the group who is not overqualified." Onstage in the "Asparagus Valley" show, Penn not only identified Chrisemer as a magna cum laude graduate of Amherst but mentioned his SAT scores. Penn says that when he and his partners formed "Asparagus Valley," in 1975, they made a pact prohibiting any jobs outside show business — a pact he now sees as "my way of pulling them down to my level: I was the only one who had no other skills."

Chrisemer told me that it was not exactly a pact and not exactly a prohibition, but Penn is not a man who has much use for qualifying phrases. Although he speaks admiringly of few performers, if he does admire someone — the comedian Bobcat Goldthwait, for instance, who also happens to be a favorite of Sarah's — he tends to express that admiration by saying simply, "Bobcat Goldthwait is a god." Penn also has a penchant for praising performances that you wouldn't think were his sort of thing — the nightclub act of Dean Martin, say, or the launching of a NASA space probe. I was once with Penn when the name of Liberace came up. Several of us were standing in a hall at NBC, waiting for a taping of "Late Night with David Letterman" to begin. After the Westside Arts run, Penn and Teller became frequent guests on "Letterman" and "Saturday Night Live," and they made their biggest television splash by emancipating a small bag of cockroaches on Letterman's desk. At the taping we were waiting for, they were hoping to outdo that with a little trick involving bloodsucking leeches.

"I loved Liberace," Penn said. "He was doing what the Rolling Stones tried to do, but he was doing it right."

A couple of people nodded slowly. Someone muttered, "In a manner of speaking."

Even Edward Jones has acknowledged that Penn was a character in high school. Penn remembers having the second-longest hair in the school. The longest hair, he has always been willing to admit, was on the head of Marc Garland, who now presides over props and other backstage matters for "Penn & Teller" — a position identified in the program as Director of Covert Activities. Penn's admission does not in any way mean that he cedes Garland any leadership in the bad-attitude department. ("I was a troublemaker and he wasn't.") So far, Garland has been spared the experience of hearing his SAT scores discussed from the stage, but in telling the audience the enormous contribution the Director of Covert Activities makes to the show Penn has been known to work in the information that Garland was elected president of the senior class. Penn says they became close only after the election. "He would never have been elected senior-class president if he had been my friend then," Penn once told me, with some pride. Garland bears other marks of overt respectability. He acknowledges being a college graduate, for instance, and he is the son of a doctor. Penn insists that his association with Garland is the only way folks in Greenfield can explain the success of a rebellious cutup like Penn Jillette: "This talentless lump of flesh has been dragged to stardom by Marc Garland."

"Penn was just outrageous," Garland says now, recalling high school days in Greenfield. "He had all this creative energy. He was out of his mind with ideas — maybe not even ideas, but ideas that he wanted to have ideas — and here he was stuck in this very straight, for him oppressive atmosphere. So he was the crazy: too loud, too much energy, too crazily dressed." Even his choice of a sympathetic grownup to talk to was unusual — John Norton, who sold ice cream bars out of a decorated truck called the Ding Dong Cart. An educated man who had worked as a parole officer, Norton answered Penn's questions about books and discussed any subject Penn wanted to discuss and never mentioned Penn's appearance. That must have taken some doing. As Norton remembers his first glimpse of Penn, "I saw this tall, gawky, frightwig-hair sort of kid riding a unicycle and juggling. Which caught my eye."

Penn had never been in much danger of becoming the typical American boy. He was an ungainly child, taller than his teachers before he got out of grade school. His parents were considerably older than those of his classmates; his only sibling, a sister, was twenty-three when he was born. His father worked for some years as a guard at the Franklin County jail but quit at fifty-five to devote full time to trading in coins. When I met him, in Boston — it was opening night of the national tour of "Penn & Teller" — he gave me a business card that said "Why Don't 'Jillette' Me Have Your Coin Business?" If I had any coin business, I would. Almost everyone who meets the elder Jillette and his wife seems to use the same phrase to describe them — "the salt of the earth." Penn's life toward the end of grade school was covered in a high school essay he wrote in the third person for a sympathetic English teacher named Beverly Adler Lucey, who became a close friend: "He smiled a lot and was called 'goofy,' walked kinda funny and was called 'Froggy' (affectionately of course) and was rotten at sports, so he had for friends a kid who longed to play kickball but had 30 pound braces

on his legs, a curly-haired kid who never knew why he hung around
with Penn, and anyone else who could be conned into sitting out a
kickball game. He had 47 strikes against him from the beginning
— the major one of which was not being aware he had all these
strikes against him."

If Edward Jones had been a truly vengeful sort of high school
principal, he could have said something about Penn even more embarrassing than the fact that he had graduated in good standing
with his class: he was never in any serious trouble. John Norton,
the Ding Dong man, remembers him as "a lamb in wolf's clothing."
According to Marc Garland, "Penn would hang out with all the
guys who did drugs and were very harmful to themselves, and then
he never did any of it. He was always under control." Penn might
maintain that he was too much of a weirdo to have hung out with
anybody, but he wouldn't deny having always had an abhorrence
of drugs. He says that he decided at the age of twelve or thirteen
never to drink or take drugs. At the time, he recalls, Frank Zappa,
someone whose music and antics Penn admired, was talking
against drugs "from a condescending point of view rather than
from a goody-goody point of view." At that age, Penn also blamed
drugs for killing his one true hero, Lenny Bruce — although,
he acknowledges, "I blame every other addict for his own problems."

Penn has also publicly confessed a deep affection for his parents.
Teller, too, dotes on *his* parents. "It's such a wild thing they do," I
was once told by Teller's mother, who actually doesn't know quite
how wild it is, since she can't bear to keep her eyes open during the
dangerous parts of the show. "You'd think they'd be hardboiled.
But they're not — not toward their parents." Readers of a *Playboy*
interview with Penn and Teller in 1987 must have been surprised to
find that it ended with Penn saying, "*Please* let us say something
nice about how wonderful our parents are" — just as fans who ask
what a manic talker like Penn could be on are surprised to be told
that he is on Diet Coke. In fact, Penn and Teller treat all older people with great respect. After the opening night of the show in
Boston — an event that drew some rather exotic punk fans as well

as a number of older people, many of whom had come on a chartered bus trip from Greenfield organized by Marc Garland's mother — Penn confessed to me, "I like both kinds of people with blue hair." In a way, I suppose, the most surprising thing about Penn and Teller — performers who once called themselves "The Bad Boys of Magic" and have been called by others hip and cynical and nihilistic, and even sadomasochistic — is that they are, in some old-fashioned ways, pretty good boys.

Teller has never even claimed to have been a rebellious teenager, but he'll bow to no one when it comes to having been an outsider. Teller was an accomplished magician by the time he got to high school — which, as Penn once said about skill in juggling, is another way of saying, "I have a terrible social life. I'm not normal. I spend all my time practicing." By his own account, Teller spent a lot of time alone in his room. "He always seemed to isolate himself," Teller's mother has said. The family lived in a row house in center-city Philadelphia. Teller was an only child, a late arrival to people who had reached the age at which they assumed they would be childless. Teller's parents had met at art school in Philadelphia; his father eventually found work doing lettering for advertisements. Teller thinks of them both as bohemians who worked hard at doing what parents in conventional families do — father building a puppet stage for his son's show, mother ordering a little magic set from "Howdy Doody" when her son displayed an interest in magic. The magic set was obtained when Teller was five. "From then on," his mother has said, "his whole life was in terms of magic. Even *he* is a mystery to us."

Teller was interested in Edgar Allan Poe rather than Lenny Bruce. He went to Central High School, a legendary high-aptitude public school, and it never occurred to him not to go to college. He didn't show up at Central High in the sort of clothing and haircut that would make him notorious. In fact, he was the sort of quiet, slight, rather shy young man who doesn't make much of an impression on his classmates at all. What he did have in common with Penn, in addition to a high tolerance for practice, was an outsider's instinct for finding an adult to talk to — in Teller's case, an English teacher named David Rosenbaum, who ran the dramatic society. Rosenbaum, a magician himself, believes that a properly structured magic act is "a tiny drama reporting something that can't happen," but he and Teller often talked about principles that Rosenbaum could apply to any sort of dramatic performance. They still do. Rosenbaum is a strong believer in a theory of dramatic structure propounded by Aristotle and tinkered with a bit by Nietzsche — the tragic rhythm of mimesis praxeos (prologue), agon (conflict), mimesis peripeteias (reversal), pathos sparagmos (suffering and dismemberment), and epiphany. He has no trouble at all doing a close textual analysis of, say, "The Asparagus Valley Cultural Society" according to the theory — seeing a "two-level epiphany" in the combination of a knife-throwing parody and a rendition of Khachaturian's "Sabre Dance" that included Penn juggling plumbers' plungers.

Rosenbaum is retired now, but he still goes into Central on Wednesday afternoons to meet with the magic club. He lives right across the street from the school, in an apartment that includes, in no discernible order, a nonreversing mirror and a clock that runs counterclockwise and a spittoon and a lot of pasteboard boxes and a heavy layer of dust. ("I'm allergic to dust, so rather than stir it up I leave it on the floor and walk quietly.") He does some writing, and he works on his magic act, which he performs annually for the Lombard Swimming Club. After some years of discussion, Teller persuaded him to change the character in the act from a cheeky Irish teenager — the character that already existed when Rosenbaum got the act, many years ago, from a cheeky Irish teenager — to a Scottish magician whose body has been inhabited by the Devil. Apparently, Rosenbaum always had a certain resemblance to the common notion of what Satan looks like, and, with the trim of a goatee here and the addition of a devilish waistcoat there, he began trying to heighten the resemblance. At this point, he looks enough like the Prince of Darkness to throw a scare into people who might have once made some rash promises they'd just as soon forget.

Even in college, where Teller spent a lot of time working on his magic act, he saw his future life as something like the life lived by David Rosenbaum — high school teaching, with some performing on the side. By chance, Penn says that he, too, saw the life of his grownup friend as a model: Penn could see himself making a living by doing something that didn't take a lot of concentration, such as selling ice cream from a truck, and spending the rest of his time writing stories that were heavily influenced by Lenny Bruce. In fact, Penn eventually did drive his own Ding Dong Cart, but not for long. Teller, though, taught Latin for four years, with very little performing on the side. Having just been given tenure, he resisted Penn's pestering before he finally agreed, in 1975, to take a one-year leave of absence to do magic, starting with a Renaissance festival in Minnesota. Teller thinks that without the push from Penn he might still be teaching Latin. Rosenbaum thinks that might be true — partly because Teller's aspirations in magic went so far beyond being a run-of-the-mill magician. "Teller saw himself — and, I think, justifiably — as among the greats," Rosenbaum told me. "The single name has something to do with that: there was a great magician named Heller and a great magician named Kellar. The kind of success that Teller's vision insisted upon seems too grandiose to be possible. It looks like a fantasy. You need gall to think you can do it." It isn't clear that Teller had that kind of gall. Fortunately for him, Penn had gall enough for two.

I would describe Teller now as more of a grownup — more of a grownup, that is, than Penn. Teller has bought himself a house in Westchester. He lives there with a friend, and he enjoys, say, building a stone wall next to the garden. He often listens to music composed by people who are dead — and not as a result of a drug overdose. He almost never goes to more than one movie a day. All those are what I think of as grownup characteristics. Teller is seven years older than Penn, of course, but then these matters are not always strictly chronological. It may be that Penn will be more like Teller in seven years, but I rather doubt it.

Penn's offstage life is easy to imagine. Think of what would happen if an exceedingly smart teenager were suddenly told that from now on he's going to have no school, a lot of disposable income, and a job that leaves him free all day. You've got it. Penn goes to a lot of movies. He has a rock band. When I spent some time with him in New York just before "Penn & Teller" began its national tour, he was romantically involved (if that phrase can be applied to Penn) with an actress who happened to be off in California pursuing her own career, so he spent a lot of time hanging out with the guys. He and the guys would sometimes drop into record stores or the Times Square porn emporiums. Mostly, they went to the movies.

Penn and his friends may go to a movie any day of the week, but when he's in New York he always goes to a Times Square movie house at midnight on Friday. It's more than a habit; it's a ritual. The ritual is called Movie Night. It begins at the Howard Johnson's in Times Square at ten-thirty. Penn is partial to the Times Square Howard Johnson's. That may be partly because he once washed dishes at a HoJo's. It may be partly because eating at Howard Johnson's sets him apart from the sort of people who go to restaurants that serve whole-grain bread — the sort of people he suspects of believing in the healing power of crystals and of not appreciating the wonders wrought by the National Aeronautics and Space Administration. It may be partly because when he and Marc Garland first went to Howard Johnson's in Times Square at ten-thirty, after a Westside Arts performance, the service was so bad that the timing worked out perfectly for a midnight movie.

No announcements are made about Movie Night. Anybody who wants to participate simply shows up at the Times Square Howard Johnson's at ten-thirty. The night I went, there were a dozen or so people — Penn, Marc Garland, some film students from NYU, a young woman who had done a piece for *Rolling Stone* on the movie Penn and Teller have made, and a comedy writer named Eddie Gorodetsky, who collaborated with Penn and Teller on a sort of how-to video called "Penn & Teller's Cruel Tricks for Dear Friends." A lot of the dinner-table discussion was about movies — particularly *Leonard: Part VI*, which the Movie Night regulars found so bad that they saw it three Fridays in a row. Everyone at the table seemed excited to be there. "Actually, Movie Night is too big a part of my life," one of the students said to the table at large. "It's because the rest of my life sucks."

The rules surrounding Movie Night are strict. Joining the gang at HoJo's for a late supper of fried clams and then skipping the movie is not done. "It's called *Movie* Night," Penn reminded me when I said that I wasn't sure I was up to going to a movie that starts at midnight. When the Motion Picture Association rating symbol flashes on the screen to indicate that a preview is about to be shown, all Movie Night patrons always say "Yessss." (That custom started as a simple expression of anticipation, I was told by Penn, who added, "The fact that previews are better than movies is so obvious it's not even an observation.") If the title of the movie is mentioned in the movie, it is always greeted by Movie Night people with polite applause. I'm still not clear as to how that custom began, but I do know that it leads to a lot of applause in a movie like *Wall Street*. Perhaps the most important rule is that Movie Night people always sit in the first row. Penn told me that the Movie Night gang once arrived to find a young man sitting in the first row. Somebody explained to him that he was certainly welcome to stay as long as he understood that certain Movie Night rules would be observed around him, and that he'd be expected to help pass the candy that gets handed back and forth so constantly at Movie Night that its presence is practically another rule. He decided to stay, and became a regular.

Neither the drawn-out affirmative that greets previews or the applause at the mention of the title draws any attention from the rest of the audience. You'd have to do a lot more than that to be noticed at a Friday-night midnight show in Times Square. The patrons are not shy. Some of them play their beat boxes right up to the time the lights are lowered. A lot of them comment freely on the movie while it's going on. Hooting is a common form of response to whatever's happening on the screen. Just before the movie starts, the theater looks and sounds a bit like the subway station underneath it — people milling around, radios playing, an occasional argument breaking out. I'm told that every so often, just before the lights dim, Eddie Gorodetsky leaps up from his front-row seat, turns around to face the audience, and, in his best film-festival manner, delivers a film analysis that starts with something like "Tonight's film is a delightful comedy romp . . ." Apparently, the Movie Night gang loves it, partly because nobody else pays the slightest attention.

I agree with Penn that building an act on extraordinary skill at what he sometimes calls "cheap circus schlock" — juggling, acrobatics, clowning, magic, sword-swallowing, fire-eating — is an outsider's game. The homecoming queen and the president of the student council simply have better things to do. Penn spent a lot of his childhood practicing. He has often said that he did nothing but practice juggling from the age of twelve to the age of fifteen, at which point he discovered that it wasn't cool. Then, apparently, he spent only most of his time practicing juggling, leaving some time to practice the unicycle. In Greenfield, Penn happened to live next door to brothers named Colin and Michael Moschen, and in high school the three boys had a juggling act that played the occasional nursing-home date or school assembly. Michael Moschen is now a renowned juggler who has been called by the *Times* "a sculptor in motion." Although it's not easy to imagine Penn as the partner of someone whose act is so rarefied that he is sometimes described as a "movement artist" rather than as a juggler, the two of them once spent months in a cheap East Village apartment trying to perfect an act highlighted by the passing of nine clubs between them. "We had heard that no jugglers had ever done that before," Penn told me, "so we figured that as soon as we passed nine clubs the world would beat a path to our door." Eventually, they did pass nine clubs between them, and, as it turned out, nobody much cared. Penn took that as an early lesson in the ways of show business.

Moschen and Penn ended up doing their act at Great Adventure, in New Jersey, and then Penn worked on the street in Philadelphia as a single. By all accounts, Penn's street act — which featured the juggling of knives the size of smallish broadswords — was spectac-ular. In 1977, when he was performing next to a hot-dog stand in the Newmarket shopping area of Philadelphia, a piece in the *Inquirer* said that he was "the best thing to hit the scene since hot mustard." It also said that he drew crowds because "he is too obnoxiously loud to be ignored," and that he spent money "as fast as he makes it on movies." According to Teller, Penn had a perfectly structured street act — "the tightest and most magnificent twelve minutes that anyone had ever seen on the street." Penn was loud and he was funny and he was good at the delicate game of separating spectators from their money at the end of the act. "Remember," he'd say as he passed the hat, "I'm six-six, I have three very sharp knives, and I have an excellent memory."

Penn no longer juggles at all in "Penn & Teller." His last juggling number was cut between the Westside Arts run and Broadway. "My father hates that," Penn told me when I mentioned the absence of juggling. "He thinks everyone will think that I can't do anything except talk." I suspect that Penn has some lingering sympathy for that viewpoint himself — although he and Teller are dismayed when they're mentioned as part of the New Vaudeville, a group of performers who tend to base their acts on mastering the traditional carnival skills. (Teller once dismissed the New Vaudeville as "a bunch of aging hippies looking at old pictures of W. C. Fields.") From childhood, he and Teller, both obsessive practicers and incurable perfectionists, seem to have operated in the belief that any performance rests on an extraordinary level of pure skill. Just before the national tour of "Penn & Teller" opened in Boston, Penn mentioned to me that Teller was now better at the needle trick than he had been when I last saw the show — on the opening night of the Broadway run. I said that was hard to believe. Teller has been doing the needle trick since college. One statement in Penn's monologue that might have been literally true is that seeing Teller do the needle trick fourteen years before was what convinced him that he absolutely had to work with Teller. Even before Broadway, Penn had seen Teller do the needle trick a couple of thousand times. "It's better," Penn insisted. "Teller manages to get more across with subtler moves. He's been working on it."

•　　•　　•

It's natural for street performers to extract humor from the fact that whatever skill they have managed to master in those years of practicing is not generally considered worth anybody's time. Even now, about the nicest thing that Penn ever says about juggling or magic or ventriloquism or acrobatics is that they are "intrinsically boring." Penn's juggling act always included a harsh view of where juggling stood among the minor theatrical arts, and a harsh view of those who did it in public. When he did his trademark knife-juggling number in "Asparagus Valley," he used to say, "What I think about when I'm watching a routine like this is what kind of mental or physical inadequacies would force a person to take up such a self-destructive, exhibitionist form of overcompensation." In fact, the relationship that street performers strike up with their audience is based partly on the assumption that everyone involved is hip enough to realize that in the great scheme of things light entertainment of any kind is not of earthshaking importance. At one point in the version of "Penn & Teller" that opened on Broadway, Teller's insistence on staying submerged in a water tank until Penn is able to divine the proper card seems to have led to his drowning, and Penn says that you have to admire "the little creep" for being willing "to die for a principle he believed in, albeit an insignificant card trick."

Now that magic has supplanted Penn's juggling and Chrisemer's performance on the pipe organ and the xylophone as the foundation the show is built on, all of Penn's disdain for the intrinsically boring skills has been channeled into an attitude toward magic that is often expressed by the description of "Penn & Teller" as "the magic show for people who hate magic." In the show and in interviews, Penn goes out of his way to make fun of magicians like Doug Henning and David Copperfield; he once said in a *Penthouse* interview that for the past forty or fifty years magic in this country had been "controlled by retards." It makes sense commercially, of course, for Penn and Teller to put some distance between themselves and the greasy guy in a tux with a lot of birds. One thing that Richard Frankel, the producer who brought "Penn & Teller" to New York, insisted on was that they drop the sobriquet "The Bad

Boys of Magic"; he considered the very word "magic" box-office poison. As it happens, though, Teller does believe that conventional American magicians are mired in a style of magic that was fresh and interesting only around the time it was invented — in the mid-nineteenth century, by the French magician Robert-Houdin, who revolutionized magic by discarding the magician's traditional flowing robes and mysteries-of-the-East presentation in favor of modern devices and the same sort of evening clothes that the gentlemen in the audience were wearing. Penn and Teller see their style as rejecting the assumption that "the people in the audience are ignorant savages who will fall at our feet and worship us for performing supernatural miracles." Penn may enjoy describing the "Penn & Teller" approach to magic as tipping the gaff; Teller can also describe it as the same sort of departure that was made by Robert-Houdin.

Before Penn and Teller perform the cups-and-balls trick with clear plastic cups, Penn talks about an enraged magician ("some guy who works cruise ships") who confronted them in the lobby one night and accused them of betraying their colleagues by revealing tricks. I asked Charles Reynolds if some magicians were genuinely upset by such revelations — we were having lunch so that I could exploit the rare privilege of having an authority right in the neighborhood — and he said that they were indeed. He later sent me a two-issue interview on the subject in a newsletter called *Stan Allen's Inside Magic*. In the interchange, Penn and Teller maintained that they actually gave away virtually nothing that the audience didn't already know. ("If anybody is performing magic thinking that when they handle a deck of cards people think they're handling them in a completely fair and normal way, they're just kidding themselves," Penn said. "If you don't know that anyone else knows where Argentina is, that's *your* problem"). Some readers maintained that Penn and Teller were, among other things, "insulting, egotistical, stuckup geeks." Charles himself believes that Penn and Teller are an overall benefit to the trade, since they send audiences away from a magic show in a happy state. He thinks that many magicians of the first rank share that belief, even if they sometimes find the constant magician-bashing tiresome. In Charles's view, the magicians who become furious when Penn explains how a card is "forced" or how a cup is "loaded" have an outsized notion of how much people in the audience learn from having a trick explained to them, and how much they care.

From what Charles told me, I gather that anybody willing to read enough books can find out how most magic tricks are done — which still leaves the problem of doing them, of course. According to Charles, virtually all magic acts lean heavily on the same dozen or so basic effects — what varies is simply what magicians call the presentation — and almost all those effects were being produced in Victorian times. It's rare for a magician simply to invent an effect, Charles told me, but Teller apparently invented the effect in which he destroys a rose by cutting into its shadow. ("I can recall some night when I was probably sixteen or seventeen," Teller told me when I asked him about the origin of the trick he calls Shadows. "I was doing the sort of thing that I used to do in those days, which was sitting around alone by melodramatic candlelight. I had this set of Playskool blocks, and when I piled the blocks up I noticed that the candlelight was casting a shadow on the wall, and the idea just occurred to me to go up and touch the shadow and flick the blocks at the same time, so the blocks would tumble down. And they clattered down with this wonderfully skeletal sound. And I thought, God! There's got to be something to do with this!") Charles believes that Teller's Shadows and Harry Blackstone's Floating Light Bulb are the two outstanding moments in American magic.

The needles trick is not unique, Charles told me, but Teller is the first magician to give it national prominence since Houdini used it as one of the featured effects of his show at the Hippodrome in 1918. (On what was then the largest stage in the world, Houdini said he would perform both the largest and the smallest feats of magic; the other featured trick was the vanishing of an elephant.) In a book Charles wrote with Doug Henning he said that there is some dispute about where Houdini got the needles trick. Houdini himself once said he got it from a couple of Hindu conjurers at the

1893 World's Fair, in Chicago; others have concluded that he picked it up from a sideshow entertainer called Maxie the Needle King. Since Houdini's time, some magicians have done the trick with razor blades, on the theory that razor blades would be easier than needles for the audience to see — a variation that David Rosenbaum finds less satisfying, since the "story" of needles appearing on a thread is much more satisfying. A magician named Marvin Roy does the trick with tiny light bulbs, which emerge lighted on a wire. Charles says that the secret of Houdini's needles trick has been explained in any number of magic books; in 1898 Houdini's own magic book offered it for five dollars. Apparently, though, Teller figured out a better way to do the trick, and, according to David Rosenbaum, if Houdini saw Teller perform it now he wouldn't know how it was done. As Penn said in Boston, Teller has been working on that trick.

The needles trick is not actually one of Charles's favorite effects — he sometimes refers to it as "oral magic" — but he admires Teller's presentation of it. In fact, he has great admiration in general for Teller as a serious magician. Penn, of course, also sees Teller as an extraordinary magician — the sort of magician who can invent Shadows because he begins by thinking of what he wants to do and then works backward to figure out how to do it. "Shadows is a pure statement of Teller's taste," Penn once told me. "Fire-eating is a clear statement of me. And they're back to back in the show. The fact that his is better I've been able to put aside." When I mentioned to Penn one day that Charles Reynolds thinks of Teller as among the finest half-dozen magicians now working, Penn said, "Teller's one of the three best magic minds alive today, and the two others don't have taste."

"We were very grandiose," Penn said. "Wier was intellectually grandiose, Teller was artistically grandiose, and I was just grandiose."

Penn, Eddie Gorodetsky, my wife, and I were at Sylvia's Restaurant in Harlem the afternoon after I attended Movie Night. The plan was to have lunch, then drop Penn and Gorodetsky in Times

Square on the way home so that they could go to another movie. Penn was recalling the days when "The Asparagus Valley Cultural Society" was formed. "I had unbounded energy and unfounded confidence," he went on.

"And unprofessional make-up," Gorodetsky said.

At Chrisemer's suggestion, Penn had looked up Teller in New Jersey, and they had taken to having dinner together whenever Teller came into New York — long, necessarily cheap dinners that revolved around acid analyses of whatever was being offered up in the way of entertainment in New York. The assumption that they could do better than the performances they were discussing was an unspoken premise of the dinner-table conversation, and by the time Penn and Teller drove out to the Renaissance festival in Minnesota it was understood that in addition to doing their separate acts they would be working together on writing a show. The show's name came from a stretch of land along the Connecticut River in western Massachusetts that got its sobriquet in the days before absolutely everything was grown in California — the Asparagus Valley.

I finally went to a Renaissance festival, after years of hearing them described as a triumph of American packaging. The one I attended, which is organized as a benefit for the Kansas City Art Institute, runs seven weekends every fall on some land next to the Agricultural Hall of Fame, fifteen miles from Kansas City. It turned out to be much more elaborate than I had expected. What appeared to be three-quarter-scale ersatz-timbered buildings held dozens of booths serving "feasts fit for ye kings" and the Budweiser and Coke that in Renaissance festivals come under the category of "drynke." There was an outdoor arena for jousts that took place twice a day. There were a hundred and thirty crafts vendors, with names like Ye Olde Wood Turnery and Ye Olde Bellsmith. The entertainment included acts like Simpkin the Foole (Ballad Monger), Seymoure (Churlish Loute), and what is often spoken of as the most successful act on the Renaissance-festival circuit — a couple of antic Shakespearean duelers called, I'm afraid, Puke & Snot. Businessmen in Friar Tuck costumes sold peanuts for a Kiwanis Club project. A lot of young people who were costumed as Shakespearean fools or members of Robin Hood's band roamed the grounds making smart-aleck remarks in vaguely English accents. A sign just outside the entrance said, "BE YE WARY OF LIGHT-FINGERED VARLOTS IN THE PRESSE OF THE CROWDE." The weekend I was there, the paid attendance was twenty-four thousand three hundred and six.

Like most of the places where Penn and Teller worked on the street, Renaissance festivals provide a protected environment for street performers, so that a juggler can concentrate on the clubs rather than keeping one eye on the lookout for cops or for the three acrobats who seem to think the corner belongs to them. The strollers are there to be entertained, and they can even find a schedule of entertainment in a program. Turning a sword-swallower or an acrobat into a Renaissance sword-swallower or a Renaissance acrobat is just a matter of a leather vest here and a rope belt there. In fact, Teller, who was still in his grandiosely arty phase, was already accustomed to working in a more or less Renaissance costume — black tights, a black turtleneck, and leather boots. (Penn and Teller have never been able to decide who had the more pretentious act in those days, although Penn claims that Teller's silence skews the comparison: "He could be redoing parts of the *Iliad* in his linking-ring routine, and because he didn't speak, it didn't come across well enough for him to get busted on it.") Penn made an easy transition to Renaissance-festival patter. "Basically, it's just anachronism jokes," he once told me. "A Renaissance festival is nothing but 'ye olde Michael Jackson.' "

As "The Asparagus Valley Cultural Society" was struggling to establish itself — scrambling for small theaters, trying to get on the college circuit — Renaissance festivals became the fallback occupation of choice for Penn and Teller. Even Wier Chrisemer appeared for a while in a Renaissance festival. Just how he managed to give a Renaissance twist to the xylophone is lost to history; he claims to have forgotten. At a Renaissance festival, top acts are paid by the management as well as by the crowd, and an effective street performer can prosper. Eventually, Penn and Teller were taking in several thousand dollars a weekend — more, Teller thinks, than any other act on the circuit except, of course, the nonpareils, Puke & Snot.

Getting "The Asparagus Valley Cultural Society" on the boards for the first time proved relatively easy. Some friends of Teller's had access to a tiny theater in Princeton, and "Asparagus" played a two-weekend engagement there in November of 1975. In the hope of attracting some press attention, Penn, who had been put in charge of publicity, concocted an appropriately grandiose stunt that was a parody of the spectacular jumps then bringing a lot of notoriety to Evel Knievel, the daredevil motorcyclist. Penn's stunt was called Asparagus Penn's Unicycle Jump for Life and was described as an attempt to jump over five Volkswagen Rabbits on a rocket-propelled unicycle. "I had a lot of phony figures on what would happen when the rockets kicked in when the unicycle hit thirty-five miles an hour," Penn told us at lunch that day at Sylvia's. Chrisemer had composed some ersatz aphorisms like "One Man One Wheel." Apparently, the irony of all this was lost on the people who showed up to watch Asparagus Penn's Unicycle Jump for Life — and there turned out to be a lot more of them than anyone could have predicted. The organizers of Asparagus Penn's Unicycle Jump for Life sometimes estimate the crowd as having been in the thousands, but they all would probably acknowledge that the memories of disaster survivors are not completely trustworthy. According to Chrisemer, "everyone in the world was there to see Penn spill his blood, and they were greatly disappointed when he didn't." The Volkswagen dealer who had lent the Rabbits was also disappointed, since the crowd took out some of its own disappointment on his cars. Penn remembers falling off the ramp, being surrounded by angry drunks who were kicking him and spitting on him, and being rescued by an ambulance team that had been asked to the event strictly for reasons of verisimilitude. Penn told us that Teller offered the best analysis of Asparagus Penn's Unicycle Jump for Life only a day or so after the event: "Well, we wanted to see how far deadpan humor could go, and we found out."

You'd think that Asparagus Penn's Unicycle Jump for Life might have ended Penn's career as a press agent, but he savors a story about how he went about trying to get "Asparagus" reviewed a year after the Jump, when it opened in a hundred-seat house called Theatre Five, upstairs in the Walnut Street Theatre complex, in Philadelphia. Theatre Five was the show's first extended booking. There was even an opening-night party, featuring cookies baked by Teller's mother. Penn says that, having no idea how reviewers happened to show up at openings, he looked in the *Inquirer* for a byline on a review, came across a review signed by William Collins, who was and is the *Inquirer*'s first-string drama critic, and simply walked into the office and demanded to see him. (A person who is less protective of the general theme of a story than Penn is might point out that the meeting actually took place on a return engagement of "Asparagus" in Philadelphia two years later, when Penn's experience with reviews already included two or three reviews of the show by second-string *Inquirer* critics, but Penn might suggest that such a person's wild, wacky friends could have gone to the trouble of planting earlier reviews in the morgue of the *Inquirer* just to mess with his gray matter.) According to the story, Collins came out of his office to meet Penn — who was dressed in his usual costume of black leather jacket, jeans, and motorcycle boots — and, after being told about "Asparagus," asked why he should review it. Penn responded by picking up one of the spikes that newspapermen sometimes keep on their desks as a sort of old-fashioned vertical file, jamming it up his nose ("It's like the old carny trick of driving a nail up your nose — not a trick, really, just a skill"), and spinning it around by the papers at its base. Collins decided to review the show.

"Well, I do think I'd remember it, because that would certainly have been the most unusual approach anybody has ever made," Collins said when I asked him about the spike story one day. Not being one of those Ed Jones types who can make their day by calling Penn a liar, Collins added, "I'm not saying it couldn't have happened." Collins does remember writing a rave review of the show. He also remembers that when he returned to "Asparagus" one evening with his entire family, Penn, giving no indication that Collins had been spotted in the audience, began talking about how helpful the review had been, and then said, "I hate to tell you how much we had to pay for it."

The fact that the "Asparagus" players "had absolutely no respect for any institution" — or any theater critic, for that matter — impressed Collins. He was also impressed by the odd combination of characters onstage. Chrisemer, who came across as what Collins called "the starchy one," spent a good part of the evening sitting rather stiffly at his keyboard. Teller was wearing the black Renaissance costume of the arty magician. (Teller, rather than Penn, was the one with long hair in those days. In a later version of "Asparagus," Penn at one point flips up the back of Teller's hairdo and says, "Hey, Teller, the sixties are over, and we lost.") Penn was almost as voluble as he is in the current show, but much less overbearing and cynical. His costume — cut-off shorts, a T-shirt, and mismatched sneakers — reflected his role as a prankish but almost naive schoolboy. "There was something extremely unsettling psychologically about the combination of people," Collins told me. "That's what stopped me in my tracks. It had a kind of Pinteresque subtext."

The effect was not accidental. When I asked Teller what he thought "Asparagus Valley" was about, he said, " 'Asparagus Valley' had more to do with living with the idea of being different and enjoying that idea. The three of us dressed in complete contradiction to one another, and didn't acknowledge that at all. The fact that these were three people you wouldn't invite to the same party was always strongly commented on in reviews. And the fact that they were working apparently smoothly together, exploiting what were obviously their freakish individual natures, was, I think, really one of the central themes of it." Teller also believes that "Asparagus Valley" had "the formal elements of a religious ceremony." There was organ music, of course, and Chrisemer, the son of a Lutheran minister, delivered one monologue that always struck Teller as sounding very much like a sermon. The finale of "The Asparagus Valley Cultural Society" featured Penn — costumed, as Chrisemer puts it, "as a simple stalk of asparagus" — leading the audience in a song that was sung to the tune of the hymn "He Leadeth Me!" and had as its only lyric, repeated over and over, the word "asparagus."

"Asparagus" was "a play about theatrical risk," according to James Freydberg, the producer who took it to San Francisco after seeing it in Philadelphia. "What it said was that all entertainment is a risk — playing a violin concerto on the xylophone as much as swallowing fire," he told me. "It was also about how what you see is not really what's happening. It was a brilliant play. And if you didn't get it on that level it was simply enormously entertaining." Enormously entertaining was enough for most people who saw "Asparagus." The word "goofy" was often applied to it, in a nice way, and so was the word "zany." I've watched a videotape of "Asparagus," made in San Francisco, where the version produced by Freydberg ran for two and a half years. It's a jolly evening. One of my favorite moments is in a number called the Mystery of the Peking Snow Duck. Chrisemer, dressed in a Chinese costume, shows the audience a rabbit, which he identifies as a Peking snow duck. (Penn, of course, says, "That's no duck.") As Chrisemer covers the rabbit with a cloth, Penn says, "You as audience members have only one responsibility — "

Suddenly, in the back of the house, Teller appears, wearing a gorilla mask — a mask that many years later was recycled as the head of MOFO, the Psychic Gorilla — and banging cymbals together. When the audience turns to look at Teller, Chrisemer calmly picks up the rabbit, walks offstage, and returns with a balloon that he places under the cloth. As the suckers turn back to the stage, realizing that they've been tricked with a gross example of what magicians call misdirection, Penn finishes what he was saying about the audience's only responsibility: "At no time allow your eyes to wander."

The Mystery of the Peking Snow Duck is about as close as "Asparagus" gets to a "Penn & Teller" theme that Teller describes as "using your head in a world full of flimflam." There's no talk of cons or swindles in "Asparagus." Nobody seems in danger of being stabbed or drowned. There are, as Freydberg points out, plenty of risks, but they seem daredevil rather than menacing. There's a straitjacket number, but those trying to escape are not suspended over a bed of spikes. In "Asparagus," Penn does virtually the same monologue with his fire-eating number that he does in "Penn & Teller" — talking about being attracted to the sideshow tent, and about how carnival fire-eaters gradually and knowingly make themselves sick through the accumulation of the tiny amount of lighter fluid that is invariably swallowed in each performance — but the number is done on a lighted stage and the show does not close with it but with Penn at his goofiest leading everyone in the "Asparagus" anthem. One number in "Asparagus," based on translating "Somewhere Over the Rainbow" into German and back into English, does include a long, uncomfortable scene that begins with Penn taunting Chrisemer for being a spoiled college boy — a scene that both participants apparently found easier and easier to play as frictions surfaced toward the end of the run. In general, though, there was something jovial about "The Asparagus Valley Cultural Society." It had some of the collegiate tone of the Othmar Schoeck concerts — what Chrisemer calls "a wide-eyed innocent craziness." In attempting to describe "Penn & Teller" as it finally evolved for Broadway, critics have reached for a lot of adjectives, but I doubt if anybody has ever called it innocent.

As the San Francisco audience for "Asparagus" began to thin out, toward the end of 1981, Freydberg wanted to try bringing it to New York. Chrisemer was willing. Penn and Teller were not. They were leaving the show to do a sort of play they had written, "Mrs. Lonsberry's Evening of Horror," but doing the play was a way of leaving Chrisemer. When I asked Teller what caused the split, he said, "Wier wanted a life. He wanted at some point to go home to his girlfriend and try out a new dish from Julia Child. He wasn't as crazy as we were." Chrisemer, who was more interested in concocting musical numbers than in being a virtuoso of the keyboard, did not seem monomaniacally concerned with working on the details of the show — at least not when compared with people who had spent great chunks of their childhood alone in their room

practicing. The way Chrisemer might have put it is that he didn't
subscribe to the proposition that practicing was the one true path
to enlightenment. According to Freydberg, when it became apparent that the show needed some help he and Chrisemer wanted to
bring in a director to have a look at it; Penn and Teller wanted to
practice more. In Freydberg's view, Penn wanted Chrisemer to have
not simply the same commitment to perfectionism that he had but
the same style of life — an impossibility for Chrisemer, who made
no effort to hide his distaste for punk-rock music and Howard
Johnson's cuisine. Penn and Teller both say that they were getting
restless, unsatisfied with "Asparagus" and itching to write a play.
Their instincts were to try something both harsher and more outrageous. Even while they were doing "Asparagus Valley," Chrisemer
had begun to feel a pressure from his partners to turn toward
darker material — material that he found "theatrically uninterest-
ing." When it came to subject matter and language, there was a serious problem between Chrisemer and his two partners that
sounds rather old-fashioned these days — a problem of religion.
Chrisemer is not only the son of a Lutheran pastor but a regular
churchgoer and a choir leader. Both Penn and Teller have an active
dislike of religion. In conversation they tend to lump it with spiri-
tualism and psychic spoon-bending and a belief in channeling —
all of which they dismiss as scams whose supposed miracles are easily explained tricks. "Religion was not only all bunk to them but
they made no distinctions," Chrisemer has told me. "To them, Fal-
well and Bonhoeffer are all the same."

When the San Francisco run of "Asparagus Valley" closed, after
nearly a thousand performances, Chrisemer wandered around for a
while. He eventually settled not far from the house in New Jersey
where he had gone to join Penn and Teller and Marc Garland in
putting together the original "Asparagus." He now works for
AT&T, answering questions that customers have about computers.
Although he sometimes says that in the long run the breakup was
probably for the best, he also says, "I still smart sometimes." Penn
had told me that Wier Chrisemer was the funniest person he had
ever known — I suppose even Bobcat Goldthwait was included in

that, since Penn never qualifies — and I found him to have a quick, dry wit. He hasn't talked to either Penn or Teller in some years, and he has never seen their show — even though, by chance, he was in San Francisco recently while "Penn & Teller" was there on national tour.

"My wife was out there at the same time," I told Chrisemer one day on the telephone. "In fact, she ran into Penn in the lobby of her hotel. He was looking for someplace to get a manicure."

"A manicure?" Wier asked, sounding puzzled.

"He has one red fingernail," I explained.

Chrisemer paused a beat, and then said, "Is it supposed to get better?"

"Penn told me that he's the worst director in the history of the world," I told Teller one day when we were discussing "Mrs. Lonsberry's Evening of Horror," Penn's first and last directorial effort.

"Oh, I wouldn't say that," Teller said. He paused to give the matter some thought. "Surely there are people who directed Whoopi Goldberg movies who are worse than Penn."

"Now that I think of it, I saw a Whoopi Goldberg movie called *Jumpin' Jack Flash* on an airplane once, and you may be right," I said. "And I speak as someone who didn't see 'Mrs. Lonsberry's Evening of Horror.'"

Apparently, Penn was bad enough. Apparently, it was not a standout evening for Teller, either. He appeared (and spoke) as Julian Lonsberry, the son of a woman who gives séances for suckers — who are played, more or less, by the audience. Teller now says that "Lonsberry" was "a difficult, excessively cerebral show," and that's about the best thing anybody has ever said about it. Freydberg says that he considered it simply an extension of the dispute Penn and Teller were having with Wier Chrisemer about the theatrical value of horror and blasphemy. ("They got carried away with taking a shot at him.") The *San Francisco Chronicle*, comparing "Mrs. Lonsberry's Evening of Horror" unfavorably with the "bright and smudge-free" show that Penn and Teller and Chrisemer had presented in "Asparagus," said "Lonsberry" had been ensnared in "its own labored premises." It closed immediately — in Penn's words, "a dismal failure."

Teller now says that the disaster could have been worse. As producers, he and Penn had budgeted the show so that they could lose only what they actually had — basically, what they had saved during the long run of "Asparagus." But Penn was, by all accounts, devastated. In Teller's view, "it took him almost a year to recover." Much of the recuperation took place on the Renaissance-festival circuit.

"Minneapolis is where I understand us to have created the show," Teller has said. This was when Penn and Teller were back at the Minnesota Renaissance Festival, in the late summer of 1982. They were working as one act, called "Penn Jillette and/or Teller," rather than as two singles, but otherwise, despite the long run of "Asparagus" in San Francisco, they didn't seem much further along the show-business road than they had been when they drove out to Minnesota together seven years before. At a comedy club that happened to have an evening free, each of the two most popular acts at the festival — the other act, it almost goes without saying, was Puke & Snot — did a forty-five-minute segment. With forty-five minutes to fill instead of the twenty-five they ordinarily worked at a festival, Penn and Teller began to put together what eventually evolved into "Penn & Teller." They had a core of numbers from "Asparagus" — Teller's Shadows and his needles trick, Penn's knife-juggling and his fire-eating. They salvaged what they could from the wreckage of "Lonsberry" — some of the darker language, the levitation of someone chosen from the audience, a complicated psychic trick that produces the Bible verse some volunteers had seemed to arrive at randomly. Without Chrisemer — without his antic musical numbers and his starchy presence on the stage and his neo-Schoeckian taste in material — the "cheap circus schlock" of "Asparagus" became colored more by Teller's lifelong interest in menace and Penn's growing interest in using your head in a world full of flimflam. The dominant voice was no longer that of a man of precise diction sitting at a pipe organ but that of a smart-aleck street performer holding some very large knives. As the tone evolved, it was as if Lenny Bruce and Edgar Allan Poe had formed a vaudeville act and one of them could juggle.

Penn and Teller polished their act in Minneapolis and in Toronto and in Texas. Then there was a sudden opening at the L.A. Stage Company, a theater in Los Angeles where Marc Garland had sought shelter as a technical director after the "Lonsberry" debacle. "Penn Jillette and/or Teller" was booked, and shortened to "Penn & Teller." After a moderately successful run at the L.A. Stage Company, Penn and Teller played over a disco, with the beat coming up through the floor. In a theater in Westwood, they sometimes played before audiences so small that the same volunteer might have to be called to the stage for more than one trick. They supplemented their income by doing séances for rich people's dinner parties — announcing beforehand that everything was a trick, and then astonishing those present with revelations about their personal lives and connections with their dear departed. Eventually, though, Penn and Teller established themselves in Los Angeles as an evening in the theater. They became sufficiently well known to do a PBS special, during which Penn said that he thought of the typical public television show as "a mime piece called 'The Birth of a Baby Dove in the Ghetto.' "

In fact, Richard Frankel told me, there were long and heated negotiations before Penn and Teller would agree to his terms for producing the show in New York — terms that included bringing in a director. Penn later told him that any time he negotiated over the phone with Frankel he stood naked under a Nazi flag. Why? Because he had read somewhere that when you negotiate you should know something that your opponent doesn't know. Penn knew that he was standing naked under a Nazi flag, and Frankel didn't. Furthermore, I suppose, it wasn't the sort of thing Frankel might tumble to with a lucky guess.

"Do you think he was really standing naked under a Nazi flag?" I asked Frankel.

He shrugged. "You know Penn," he said.

·   ·   ·

The show that I saw in Boston might strike the casual theatergoer as more or less the show Penn and Teller brought from Los Angeles to the Westside Arts. Penn and Teller, of course, think of it as something that has changed considerably. Although Teller can say, "At long last, we have a show that I'm very happy with," they treat it as a machine that is in constant need of tuning and adjustment. Is there a line in the MOFO number that is not needed? During their dangerous version of what Penn calls a "wimpy card trick," is he irritating enough to give the audience a split second of guilty satisfaction when he seems to have been stabbed in the hand by the partner he was irritating?

Teller can still analyze the show in terms of the Greek tragic rhythms he learned from David Rosenbaum at Central High School. To him, the first number is the prologue. Penn announces that he will read "Casey at the Bat" while sitting in a chair, and will then leap up to receive his accustomed applause, at which point Teller either will be out of the straitjacket attached to the pulley that is tied to the chair or will be dropped head first onto a bed of huge and obviously authentic spikes. From that number, Teller told me one morning in Boston, "you learn that one guy's going to talk and one guy's not going to talk. You learn that these guys can do things — that there's talk interlocked with action, and that it's action that takes place in the present, in the apparent reality of the theater. You learn in very plain terms that we don't see any difference between what's named poetry, albeit illustrated by a piece of doggerel, and daredevil, life-and-death stunts. And you learn that these two people absolutely trust each other, because night after night one person willingly and comfortably places himself in the position of being completely subject to the other person's reliability. One of the things this show is implicitly and constantly about is the nature of partnership and friendship."

Teller told me that he considers the remark that Penn makes before pulling out his copy of "Casey at the Bat" — the remark that the magic they're interested in is "the magic of fine poetry" — to be the "topic sentence" of the show. "What the audience learns from the straitjacket and 'Casey at the Bat' is, first, that they're going to see a show that is about poetry," he said. "Although we make fun of that idea again and again, I think that when people leave the theater at the end they leave with the sense of having seen a sort of poetic event."

"What do you mean by 'poetic'?" I asked.

Teller paused for a long time. Finally, he said, "I would like for people to have the experience I would like to have. Which is for a period of time I would like to have my attention compelled by something that moves me from one place to another, from one feeling to another, from one understanding to another — and hints at mysteries that somehow fit together. When I was a kid in my back yard, almost daily I used to build what I would call a fun house. It was really not very elaborate, but it was almost a compulsion. There were odd pieces of wood in my back yard — things like long planks with four-by-fours nailed to the ends of them so as to form a small table, and assorted things. And I loved to take those things and put them in sequences, so that at each step something surprising as far as I was concerned would happen — so, say, a plank would tip in a different direction. And then I would get kids who lived on my street to come in and walk through it. And I would be right there to catch them if they fell. If they fell down, they didn't usually get hurt. I got hurt wonderfully once. But in my head what was happening was they were going into a fun house in an amusement park — a haunted house that was pretty scary." He paused. His eyes had filled with tears. "And then they'd come out at the other end . . ." He paused again. "You start off at the beginning, and you come out and you feel like you've been someplace . . . I don't know why I get all weepy over that."

I was helping Penn and Teller block out an appearance on a Boston talk show. I played what Penn likes to refer to as "the meat puppet." It's a term he picked up from television cameramen, who invented it as a description of some of the beautiful but vacant people who recite the local news. Most of Penn and Teller's talk-show appearances revolve around making the meat puppet edgy, or even terrified. The plan this time was to engage him in a game of rodent

roulette, a game played on a lazy Susan on which Penn and Teller
had glued seven or eight huge rat traps. There is a short piece of
cord attached to the bar of each of the traps, so you can trip it
without worrying about its snapping shut — unless, Penn will explain to the host, you happen to trip the one whose cord has been
cut underneath the trap. That one will break your finger.

"Well, welcome to Boston," I said, in my assigned role as host. "I
hear your show is wacky, madcap fun. Are you going to do a trick
for us today?"

"Tell me," Penn says. "How's your show doing in this market?"

"Well, we're O.K., I guess."

"You creaming the competition?"

"Well, we don't say creaming, actually," I said, aware that I was
now the one answering the questions.

"What's next for you after this?" Penn asked, glancing around as
if looking for something to break.

"Well, actually, Peoria beckons if we're not careful here," I said.

Deciding that a host in my position must be on top of the world
and looking for new thrills, Penn suggested rodent roulette, explaining that we'd take turns putting our fingers into the traps. As
the routine works, Teller, taking his second turn, lets out a horrible
shriek as blood spurts from his finger onto Penn — the result of a
simple squirt-ring filled with stage blood. We did that part, with
plain water, twice, since Penn didn't seem to be hit squarely
enough in the eye the first time. As Penn was wiping his face after
the second squirting, he said, "What are we doing here?" and Teller
joined in for the ritual chorus: "We're earning a living."

The rodent roulette routine worked pretty well the next morning. The host turned out to be an amiable and relaxed young man
named Matt Lauer, who didn't panic even when Penn, working up
to the suggestion that any thrill-seeking instincts the host had be
channeled into the nearly harmless pastime of rodent roulette,
said, "I get this premonition of you being found dead in a hot tub
with a fourteen-year-old girl." Still, it was, I thought, a long way
from the tension and precision and polish of the "Penn & Teller"
performance. In general, I think of their television appearances as a

mixed bag. So do they — although Penn enjoyed the liberation of the cockroaches on David Letterman's desk, at least more than Letterman appeared to. Penn says that on television "you can only do the grossest strokes." Sometimes even the grossest strokes are not quite caught by the camera. Sometimes the audience doesn't seem to know quite what to make of Penn and Teller; they're out of context. A lot of the problem, I think, is that on television they can't lure the audience into a constant but ever-changing role in the swindle.

I think of Penn and Teller as two acts — the stage performance and everything else. By now, because of their appearances on "Letterman" and "Saturday Night Live," they are probably better known for everything else. The way show business is organized, of course, their success may be measured by how well they cross over into everything else. They may measure success that way themselves. They worked hard on their video; they've written a book. There are people in the trade who think Penn and Teller may be too specialized in tone to translate well into other areas of show business, and those people would cite as confirmation the troubles encountered by Penn and Teller's most ambitious breakout project — a movie called *Penn & Teller Get Killed* that they wrote and Arthur Penn directed. Months after its scheduled release, the movie had not appeared. Word from Hollywood was that studio executives were shocked by its ending and that the audience at its first test showing was distinctly unenchanted. Even after recutting, it lingered in what a friend of Penn and Teller's calls Hollywood Hell.

As it happens, Penn and Teller love the way the movie came out. The prospect that it may not be the mainstream triumph their supporters had looked forward to does not seem to horrify them. After all, they also measure success by infinitesimal degrees of improvement in the needles trick. In Chicago on the national tour, Penn is still hauling Teller up on a pulley eight performances a week and sitting down to read "Casey at the Bat." Teller says he sees the stage show continuing into the foreseeable future, although, of course, it will change. There might be less magic. Penn, Teller predicts, may get to the point at which he'll be able to admit from the stage that he didn't actually go into the sideshow tent at the Franklin County Fair, and will tell "that much more chilling story that he never did see the fire-eating, that it was so fascinating and so fearful from such a distance that he had to go do it instead." Teller says that he and Penn would like to try a stadium show someday, because they're fascinated by the problem "How do you do a theatrical event before an enormous number of people?" They even have a trick in mind, which Teller told me about one day in Boston. It starts with Penn announcing that they were allowed to bring only one prop to the show. At that point, he leaves, and Teller lies down, draping a towel over his chest. Penn reappears with the one prop — an eighteen-wheeler. He drives right over Teller and out of the stadium. "Then I get up and take a bow," Teller said.

"And there are tire marks on the towel?" I asked.

"Absolutely," Teller said. "Absolutely."

1989

COMPETITORS

REDUCED TO ITS ESSENTIALS, the dispute between Ben & Jerry's Homemade and Häagen-Dazs involved a simple case of what antitrust lawyers call market foreclosure, but nobody was ever tempted to reduce it to its essentials. The players were a lot more interesting than the game. The founder of Häagen-Dazs, Reuben Mattus, fits easily into the role of the prototypical immigrant entrepreneur — the plugger who overcomes his lack of education and connections and capital with tenacity and shrewdness and an enormous capacity for hard work and one simply brilliant idea. By just about any account, Reuben Mattus created the field that is now known by the appropriately excessive name of "super-premium ice cream," and he was appropriately rewarded: the Pillsbury Company bought his company for a price usually estimated at eighty million dollars. The president of Ben & Jerry's Homemade, Ben Cohen, makes a fine, shaggy-bearded prototype of what has come to be known as the hippie entrepreneur — one of the people who carried the style of the sixties into consumer businesses aimed at their contemporaries, and whose response to success is to express not gratitude for living in a land of opportunity but astonishment at a world so weird that people like themselves are considered respectable businessmen. When Ben Cohen and his partner, Jerry Greenfield, felt the need to complain that their ice cream was being denied access to the marketplace in violation of federal laws on fair competition, the forums they chose included not just federal district court but the classified advertisement section of *Rolling Stone*. They took an ad under the "Bumperstickers" heading. The ad asked readers to "help two Vermont hippies fight the giant Pillsbury corporation" by buying a bumper sticker that carried the war cry "WHAT'S THE DOUGHBOY AFRAID OF?" In fact, it was closer to one Vermont hippie. Jerry Greenfield, at the age of thirty-four, began spending most of his time in Arizona, in a condition somewhere between semiretired and dropped out — although he did bestir himself long enough to carry on a one-man picket line in front of Pillsbury headquarters, in Minneapolis. Semiretirement at thirty-four and picketing a competitor's headquarters are both subjects that can cause Reuben Mattus to shake his head in wonderment at how times have changed. When he tries to be gracious toward Ben and Jerry — and graciousness toward competitors is not a hallmark of the sort of ice cream business he has known for half a century — he will say, "They're very . . . unconventional."

There is no doubt that Ben and Jerry carry on in a way that nobody inside the corporate headquarters of Pillsbury would recognize as conventional behavior for executives. They must be, for instance, among the very few American executives who periodically perform an act in which one of them places a cinder block on his stomach and the other one shatters the cinder block with a sledgehammer. The act is a staple of an autumnal celebration — the Fall Down — that Ben & Jerry's has sometimes staged on the lawn of the First Congregational Church in Burlington, Vermont. Burlington was the site of Ben & Jerry's original corporate headquarters — if the phrase can be applied in this case. A typical Fall Down also includes an apple-peeling contest (longest unbroken peel), entertainment by Don Rose on his honky-tonk piano, a lip-synch contest, and a Ben and Jerry look-alike contest. The highlight, though, is what Ben & Jerry's normally advertises as "the Dramatic Sledgehammer Smashing of a cinder block on the bare stomach of the noted Indian mystic Habeeni Ben Coheeni." Ben appears in a sort of bare-midriff swami costume and warms up with what he calls "some metabolic chants." Then he suspends himself between two chairs, and a cinder block is placed on his stomach. Because Ben is beginning to show the effect of steady product sampling, he acknowledges, there has been a tendency in recent years for the cinder block to roll off his stomach unless volunteers stand by to hold it in place. Then Jerry Greenfield, wearing a pith helmet, is carried onto the scene by four bearers. The background music is "The Rubberband Man" by the Spinners. Jerry approaches Ben with a perfectly conventional sledgehammer, takes a mighty swing, and pulverizes the cinder block without harming his partner.

When Ben Cohen is asked about the origin of the Dramatic Sledgehammer Smashing, he says that Jerry happened to learn the trick when he took a half-credit course at Oberlin called Carnival Techniques. Ben conveys that information matter-of-factly — the way some businessmen might explain a partner's concentration on long-range financial planning by saying that finance was his specialty at Wharton. In commenting on such matters, Ben speaks as someone whose own brush with higher education included a semester or two studying pottery- and jewelry-making in an open-university program at Skidmore. The other trick Jerry learned in Carnival Techniques was the Flaming Tongue Transfer. In the Flaming Tongue Transfer, the performer, working alone, ignites a fire on his tongue with a flaming torch and then uses the fire to ignite a second torch. Jerry Greenfield has sometimes done the Flaming Tongue Transfer as well as the Dramatic Sledgehammer Smashing at the Fall Down, if the wind wasn't up. Reuben Mattus might well shake his head in wonderment at that. It is amazing enough that someone could study such subjects in a respectable American college. Who could have predicted that they would prove valuable in a business career?

Reuben Mattus — who remained chairman of Häagen-Dazs after it was sold to Pillsbury — studied neither finance at Wharton nor carnival techniques at Oberlin. He had to drop out of high school to help support his family. "We all came up the hard way," he often says. "Just like all the other immigrants." When Mattus was brought to Brooklyn from Poland by his widowed mother shortly after the First World War, one of his uncles was already in an early form of the ice cream business. In partnership with an Italian, Uncle Nathan peddled Italian lemon ice from a horse cart, after taking the precaution of teaching the horse, a rusticated cavalry nag, to understand Yiddish. The rules concerning fair and unfair competition which Reuben Mattus learned as a child from his mother's family were pretty straightforward. Because his mother was a widow with a family to support, it was fair for her brother, Reuben's Uncle Nathan, to become partners with her in establishing a noncompeting ice cream business in the Bronx. But another brother set up his ice cream business right across the street from uncle Nathan, and the two of them spent the rest of their lives trying to steal each other's customers.

When Reuben Mattus was growing up, Brooklyn and the Bronx had dozens of little ice cream companies, most of them run by immigrants, who competed with the ferocity of people who know that they have no capital to fall back on. The product changed steadily over the years. Starting out with lemon ice, the Mattus family gradually changed over to ice cream novelties like Popsicles and ice cream sandwiches, then began making bulk ice cream, and eventually was producing something called Ciro's Ice Cream in pint and quart containers. The battlefields changed almost as often as the product. For a while, the ice cream makers supplied mostly candy stores. Then it was grocery stores. Then it was supermarkets. After the advent of refrigeration, the independent companies that had fought for the New York–area business for years found themselves with more to fight than one another. Refrigeration transformed the ice cream business from a seasonal local occupation into something that could be carried on year-round by large companies distributing over vast areas. When the large companies first began providing grocery stores with refrigerated cabinets, Mattus has recalled, small operators tossed their novelties into the same cabinets, whereupon the large companies used their political muscle to pass state legislation making that illegal. The history of the ice cream business as Reuben Mattus tells it consists of one such crisis after another. There were times during the Second

World War when it seemed impossible to get ingredients. There was a time just after the war when the large corporations, armed with the capacity for paying supermarket chains thousands in what were euphemistically called advance rebates, seemed unstoppable in their efforts to purge the freezer case of independent local brands. Reuben Mattus fought on. He survived. When he talks about it, his survival seems almost miraculous. Mattus's tales of trying to make a living in the ice cream business during all those years sound a bit like what Odysseus might say about what a person has to go through just to get home from Troy.

Recalling the early days, Mattus figures that he survived partly by brute application of labor. He worked all the time; his wife, Rose, worked all the time. But he also believes that he managed to stay one jump ahead of the competition through an ability to innovate. Almost from the start, he thought of himself as an inventor of techniques — color-coding pint containers, for instance, or devising a display case called the Happy Cabinet. That sort of thing can just bring along another crisis, of course, since imitators were never far behind. "All my life, people copied me," he has said. "I would start something; they would copy it and undermine me." In the late fifties, when the business had become focused on mass-marketing ice cream through supermarkets, there came a time when Mattus thought his inventiveness had run out. He feared that the big companies were about to drive him out of business — mostly by economic muscle but partly, in his view, by using some marketing techniques that he himself had helped develop. "My people said, 'You got to come up with something new,' " he says. "I said, 'Whaddaya think I am — a magician? You don't come up with something new just like that.' " Then, in 1960, Reuben Mattus came up with something new just like that. He invented Häagen-Dazs.

Like a lot of people who have created entirely new ways of approaching something, Mattus had an idea that in retrospect seems simple, maybe even obvious. In the fifties, as supermarkets spread across the country and American housewives seemed to be judging foodstuffs purely on their cost and convenience, the entire ice cream industry was competing to produce the cheapest possible ice

cream in the largest possible containers. It was a competition that
small, independent ice cream companies were unlikely to survive.
Reuben Mattus's idea was, in its simplest form, to produce the best
possible ice cream instead of the cheapest possible ice cream. In
that endeavor, he figured, the size of his operation was actually an
advantage: he could maintain quality control that would be impossible for huge corporations with plants spread across the country.
Instead of mixing into his new product as much air as the law
allowed — government regulations prohibit manufacturers from
using the phrase "ice cream" to describe a product that is more
than fifty percent air — he would use very little air. Instead of
skimping on butterfat, he would produce an ice cream with a butterfat content of sixteen percent. Years before a significant number
of Americans had demonstrated any interest in making a distinction between artificial and natural ingredients, he would use only
natural ingredients. Years before a significant number of Americans
had indicated any willingness to spend a lot of money for what
came to be called gourmet foods, he would gamble on finding
enough people who didn't mind spending half again as much as
they had to on a pint of ice cream just because it happened to be
superior ice cream. After years of being knocked about in the un-
ruly procession of ice cream makers, Reuben Mattus just turned
around and marched smartly in the opposite direction.

Of course, Mattus had Simon Levowitz to help point the way.
Mattus thought of Simon Levowitz as a sort of mentor —
someone a person could turn to for advice, in the way people in the
old country might have turned to a particularly wise rebbe. Levowitz had once been in the ice cream business, but, unlike most
Brooklyn practitioners of that trade, he was an educated man —
so learned, Mattus says, that as a sideline he wrote sermons for
rabbis and ministers, and even Catholic priests. Levowitz had traveled in Europe — not the way most ice cream people had traveled
in Europe, from the shtetl to the dock, but as a businessman. He
was a man of wide business experience. He was a scholar. Most of
all, he was a talker. "He used to exhaust me with all the words he'd
throw at me," Mattus has said. "But sometimes a diamond would

come out." Mattus says that Levowitz talked constantly about the importance of quality and consistency. He often told the parable of the stale milk powder. During the war, when ingredients were hard to find, Levowitz had bought a large supply of milk powder that was usable but had a slightly stale taste. Once ingredients were available again, he replaced the milk powder, only to find himself beset by customers complaining that the taste of the ice cream had changed. Consistency!

Levowitz often spoke of the quality and consistency maintained by an ice cream operation in Copenhagen called Premier Is. When Mattus was searching for a European name to add some Continental cachet to his new brand, he naturally thought of Denmark. Premier was in Denmark. Denmark was a dairy country. For someone who had grown up in the immigrant neighborhoods of Brooklyn, Denmark had another advantage. "I figured there were people who hated the Irish, there were people who hated the Italians, there were people who hated the Poles, there were people who hated the Jews," Mattus has said. "But nobody hated the Danes." Mattus put a map of Scandinavia on his pint containers and settled on the ersatz Danish words "Häagen-Dazs" for a name. He figured that the strangeness of the phrase would be an advantage: slowing up shoppers for the split second required to register the words might be enough to cause some of them to take another look. At first, he was concerned that customers might feel awkward about trying to pronounce the words — words as foreign to a Dane as to anyone else — but then he realized that "the type of people we were looking for, if they mispronounced it they'd think they were right and any other way was wrong."

"The big companies could have crushed him in a minute," one of Reuben Mattus's competitors from Brooklyn has said. "They weren't paying any attention." Mattus had trouble getting distribution for Häagen-Dazs, not because the big companies were trying to shut him out of the market but because distributors didn't think anyone would buy astonishingly expensive ice cream. Mattus plugged away, though, and eventually American tastes caught up with his ice cream. The story of Mattus's invention of a product and his perhaps even more imaginative invention of a name became a sort of capitalist folktale, repeated in *Fortune* and *People*. During the strongest blast of publicity, in the early eighties, Mattus grew a beard: not a shaggy beard like Ben Cohen's but a neatly trimmed beard that made him look more — well, Continental. Even though the container with the map of Scandinavia on it had said from the start that Häagen-Dazs was made in the Bronx (or, in later years, in equally prosaic New Jersey), Mattus found in pre-beard days that people he met were disappointed to discover that the company had been created by "just an ordinary guy."

The other ordinary guys were right on his heels, of course. Sooner or later, a superpremium ice cream called Alpen Zauber appeared in the stores; sooner or later, a superpremium ice cream called Frusen Gladje appeared in the stores. What was particularly irritating to Mattus was that the people copying Häagen-Dazs were his old competitors from Brooklyn. One of the principals in the company that produces Frusen Gladje is Mattus's cousin, a son of one of the warring uncles. Gold Seal Riviera, the company that makes Alpen Zauber, is owned by the Kroll family, who were plumbers on Mattus's block in Brooklyn when he first arrived from Poland, but who went into the ice cream business early enough to battle Mattus and his family for customers at every turn. Mattus's views on Alpen Zauber can be expressed succinctly: "The Krolls have been knocking me off forever."

At one point, Mattus went to court in an attempt to stop the knockoffs. Häagen-Dazs tried, unsuccessfully, to stop the marketing of Frusen Gladje on the ground that the packaging was a trademark infringement on Häagen-Dazs's "unique Scandinavian marketing theme" — a position that the unkind took as basically a matter of Mattus's accusing someone of stealing his scam. Häagen-Dazs also tried to protect its market by imposing exclusive contracts on distributors. In 1981, the national sales director of Häagen-Dazs sent a letter to distributors and subdistributors spelling out a policy toward ice creams like Alpen Zauber and Frusen Gladje. "It would be potentially confusing to the public and inconsistent with the *proper* handling and marketing of Häagen-Dazs ice cream for a distributor or subdistributor to simultaneously sell Häagen-Dazs and the other ice cream brands," the letter said. "If a distributor in the exercise of his best independent business judgment elects to handle one of these other brands, it is our intention . . . not to supply him with Häagen-Dazs ice cream." (A few years later, in an interview with *USA Today*, Mattus expressed the same thought in a different way: "If you want to have a wife and a mistress, I don't blame you, but it's no good for the wife.") Alpen Zauber went to court for a preliminary injunction. In granting it, the judge was inspired to quote Gilbert and Sullivan ("Things are seldom what they seem / Skim milk masquerades as cream") as well as the phrase that Thomas Carlyle attributes to Charles V ("the iron hand in a velvet glove"). Then Reuben Mattus and Abe Kroll, of Gold Seal Riviera — two men who had known each other for sixty years or so — came to an out-of-court agreement. The lawyer for Alpen Zauber was Martin Kroll, a younger-generation member of the Gold Seal Riviera family. According to Kroll, he persuaded his Uncle Abe and Reuben Mattus to settle by reminding them how long they had known each other and by telling them the old shtetl tale about the two men who argued over the ownership of a cow — one pulling on the head, one pulling on the tail, and lawyers milking the beast the entire time. Alpen Zauber got access to the distributors. Reuben Mattus still had more than seventy percent of the cow.

When Ben & Jerry's began, in 1978, there was no mistaking it for a knockoff of Häagen-Dazs; it seemed more like a knockoff of Steve's, a homemade ice cream parlor in Somerville, Massachusetts, on the edge of Cambridge. In fact, what Ben Cohen and Jerry Greenfield, high school pals from Long Island, had in mind was to move to a relatively quiet college town and start some more or less entertaining business of the sort that had already proved itself in places like Cambridge and Berkeley and Ann Arbor. It didn't have to be ice cream. In fact, it is now an established part of the Ben & Jerry's startup story — a capitalist folktale that is rapidly becoming almost as well known as the one about Reuben Mattus — that Cohen and Greenfield were leaning toward a bagel operation before they discovered how much bagel-baking equipment cost. They simply figured that having a business together would be an improvement over what they had found themselves doing. Greenfield, who had not been able to get into medical school, was working as a lab technician in North Carolina. Cohen, whose academic aspirations had not extended much past the pottery-making and jewelry-making courses, was teaching pottery-making to emotionally disturbed children near Lake Champlain. Something like a homemade ice cream store, they thought, would be a way to have some independence and a way to live in a pleasant college town, and maybe even a way to have some fun. They raised eight thousand dollars for capital. They bought an old-fashioned rock-salt ice cream maker. They rented an abandoned gas station in Burlington, half a mile or so from the campus of the University of Vermont, and began fixing it up themselves. They read several books about homemade ice cream. Then they capped off their preparations by sending away to Pennsylvania State University for a five-dollar correspondence course in ice cream making — two-fifty apiece. Like a lot of people who were in college during the late sixties and early seventies, they had been educated to think small.

College-town ice cream parlors like Steve's seemed to be founded on the principle that the atmosphere of a retail business — at least a retail business selling homemade ice cream to young people — could be more or less the atmosphere one might expect to find in an Ugliest Man on Campus contest. In the original Steve's store — which still exists in roughly its original form, even though the business has changed hands and has been expanded into a franchise operation — there was an old-fashioned homemade ice cream maker in the window producing the store's entire ice cream supply. Steve's also provided a player piano, elaborate rules posted on the wall concerning which combinations of ice cream and toppings and mix-ins were allowed, a bulletin board for notices of yoga classes and rides to New York, and a trivia contest to pass the time spent standing in what always seemed to be a long line. That's the sort of operation Cohen and Greenfield opened in Burlington.

Greenfield made the homemade ice cream, which was popular from the start, and Cohen handled the hot food, which wasn't. On summer evenings, they showed free movies on the wall of a building next door. On cold winter days, they instituted an ice cream cone discount scheme they still call POPCDBZWE, pronounced the way it's spelled, which stands for "Penny Off Per Celsius Degree Below Zero Winter Extravaganza." On just about any day, customers were likely to be entertained by Don Rose on his honky-tonk piano. Rose was a volunteer, and his service to the cause earned him the rare distinction of being named a "Ben & Jerry's lifer": he is entitled to free ice cream for the rest of his life.

Ben & Jerry's drifted into the wholesale ice cream business partly because some local restaurants began to ask about being supplied and partly, Cohen always says, because meeting the salesmen who called on the ice cream parlor persuaded him that traveling around the state selling ice cream might be a pleasanter life than being stuck in front of a stove in a former filling station. Ben & Jerry's started to manufacture ice cream by the pint, with Jerry acting as production manager while Ben lived out his traveling-salesman dreams on the roads of Vermont. Their approach to presenting their wares did not have much in common with what Reuben Mattus had done at Häagen-Dazs. Instead of concocting an ersatz European name, they called their ice cream Ben & Jerry's Homemade — although Cohen likes to say that there was some consideration given to putting an umlaut over the "e" in Ben. The picture on the top of their pint container was not a map of Scandinavia but a photograph of the two of them, looking pretty much like two Vermont hippies. The description of the ingredients on the container was done in the sort of hand printing often used on menus that list a variety of herbal teas. The geographical connection Ben & Jerry's tried to project was not with the capitals of Europe but with rural Vermont. Times had changed. For the generation Ben and Jerry belonged to, the Continent had lost its cachet. Cachet had lost its cachet. Cohen and Greenfield were interested not simply in using natural ingredients but in being natural themselves.

They still speak of what they do as being "in our style." From antiftccgarturple-

the start, it was their style to be funky. It was their style to be slightly embarrassed at being in business at all. "We grew up in the sixties, when it wasn't cool to be businessmen," Greenfield once said to a trade magazine reporter while trying to explain why Ben & Jerry's has a policy of turning back part of its profits to the community. "Our whole motivation for doing business was never to get rich." It was their style to assume that part of the reason for going into business was to have fun. Their promotional style can be summed up by the fact that a trip to Florida offered as a prize in the Ben & Jerry's "Lick Winter" promotion included not just airfare and hotels but dinner with Jerry's parents, who are retired down there, and a day at Walt Disney World with Ben's uncle.

The two Vermont hippies set out to produce the sort of high-butterfat, low-air-content ice cream that Reuben Mattus had pioneered. Like Mattus, they used natural flavor, and they used plenty of it. (Jerry says that was because it took a strong dose of flavor to get any response from Ben, the sampler, who "doesn't have a real acute sense of taste.") When it came to marketing, though, Ben & Jerry's had practically nothing in common with Häagen-Dazs and Alpen Zauber and Frusen Gladje. Even the flavors were different. When Reuben Mattus began marketing Häagen-Dazs, he carried only vanilla, chocolate, and coffee; Ben & Jerry's seemed to specialize right away in flavors like Chocolate Heath Bar Crunch and White Russian and Dastardly Mash. (Even now, the two brands have only half a dozen flavor names in common.) When Cohen is asked to compare his ice cream with brands like Häagen-Dazs and Alpen Zauber and Frusen Gladje, he often says that Ben & Jerry's is "the only superpremium ice cream you can pronounce." In their strategy of positioning their ice cream in the market, Cohen and Greenfield had, in their own consciously small way, turned around and marched smartly in the opposite direction.

Their sixties sense of limitations was reflected in their motto, "Vermont's Finest All-Natural Ice Cream" — a motto that is, by the standards of ice cream business superlatives, almost pathologically modest. In the summer of 1981, a year after Ben & Jerry's started producing pints, *Time* ran a widely noticed cover story on the popularity of ice cream, and the writer, John Skow, commented on the inflation of ice cream bragging by routinely referring to just about every brand mentioned as the best ice cream in the world. The irony in the way the phrase was being used became clear before the end of the first paragraph, but in the opening sentence of the story the superlative still carried an impact. That sentence said, "What you must understand at the outset is that Ben & Jerry's, in Burlington, Vt., makes the best ice cream in the world."

The recognition by *Time* added momentum to what had been a steady expansion of the Ben & Jerry's wholesale operation. By 1983, Ben & Jerry's was selling well over a million dollars' worth of wholesale ice cream annually, even though the ice cream was being distributed almost entirely in Vermont and New Hampshire and Maine and upstate New York — states that are noted for per capita ice cream consumption but are not long on capita. (Cohen's explanation for the fact that New Englanders, who live in one of the coldest parts of the country, eat the most ice cream per capita rests on his theory that what makes people feel cold is not air temperature, as is commonly believed, but the difference between air temperature and body temperature — a difference that can be reduced by a steady intake of ice cream.) Some grownup business decisions had to be made. Should Ben & Jerry's reach toward the lucrative markets in lower New England? If so, how could enough ice cream be produced to meet a large market's demands? The Ben & Jerry's manufacturing operation consisted of a tiny staff of young people in a tiny galvanized-tin building that a Ford dealer had formerly used to repair trucks — a production setup that a succinct visitor might have described as five dropouts in a garage.

Jerry Greenfield had already made a business decision of his own — to move to Arizona. He eventually moved back to the East, but not to full-time participation in Ben & Jerry's. "It got to the point where it was too big for me," he said after his return. "It wasn't as personally rewarding. I was more comfortable in the filling station." As the partner who spent a lot of his time presiding over production, Greenfield found that quality control had put forty or fifty pounds on him. The young woman he lived with wanted to go back to graduate school at Arizona State. The obvious move was semiretirement. While he was in Arizona, he was asked what he did with his time, and he said, "I help out some at the public library." He also helped out some at Ben & Jerry's. He still owns ten percent of the company. Ordinarily, he has returned in the summer to pitch in with high-season production and to lend his talents, as the leaves begin to fall, to the shattering of a cinder block on Ben's stomach. It's a corporate stint that is done in the spirit of an ex-counselor coming back to camp at the end of the season to help put on the big show, and it makes Jerry neither uncomfortable nor fat.

What the remaining partner had decided was to test the Boston market and, if that augured well, to figure out how to finance a new plant. Once it was clear that Boston looked promising, the new plant was financed partly through a scheme that was well attuned to Ben and Jerry's style. An intrastate stock issue was floated; only bona fide Vermont residents were eligible. The relevant executives — Cohen and Greenfield and the new general manager, a young man named Fred (Chico) Lager — traveled from town to town all summer talking to potential stockholders in informational meetings that included a sample of something like Chocolate Oreo Mint but stopped short of the Dramatic Sledgehammer Smashing. Three quarters of a million dollars was raised in the stock offering, an urban-development grant and industrial revenue bonds were obtained, and in August ground was broken on a large plot along a country road that happens to run between two large ski areas. Chico Lager figured that the plant would sooner or later be the third-largest tourist attraction in Vermont, with a thriving company store, a guided tour, and a rustic atmosphere featuring his father-in-law's dairy cows grazing on the lawn.

Meanwhile, according to allegations made by Ben & Jerry's in a complaint filed in federal district court, the manufacturers of Häagen-Dazs had "engaged in a pattern of conduct designed to coerce and require distributors who handle both Häagen-Dazs and Ben & Jerry's superpremium ice cream to cease dealing with Ben &

Jerry's as a condition of such distributors continuing to function as distributors of Häagen-Dazs superpremium ice cream." All of which would, the complaint maintained, enable Häagen-Dazs to have "entrenched its dominant position in the marketplace, stifled competition, thwarted Ben & Jerry's entry into the Greater Boston and the Massachusetts and Connecticut geographic markets for superpremium ice cream, and illegally acquired and maintained a monopoly in such superpremium ice-cream markets." Or, as Chico Lager put it, "they were going for the throat."

Merely suing would not have been the Ben & Jerry's style. It wouldn't have been much fun. It wouldn't have sold much ice cream. Also, Cohen says he feared that in the absence of some public pressure a corporation the size of Pillsbury could keep a corporation the size of Ben & Jerry's Homemade in court long enough to run it out of money. Cohen says that the possibility of being shut out of Boston and Connecticut was also a genuine threat to the survival of Ben & Jerry's. The company was already deeply involved in putting together the complicated package of financing for the large new plant, whose existence had been predicated on an expanded market. "We were really scared," Chico Lager has said. "This was not a joke to us. How we responded was a lot of fun, but the matter itself was very serious."

But what fun! It was a marketing opportunity made for Ben & Jerry's. Although the lawsuit was filed against Häagen-Dazs, the publicity barrage was directed against the parent company, Pillsbury — the sort of huge, faceless corporation that makes a perfect foil for a company whose founders have their faces right on the pint container. Ben & Jerry's could play the hit-and-run guerrillas against the cumbersome regiments of Pillsbury's conventional army. It took some effort to come up with a war cry that encompassed the accusations against Pillsbury and the unevenness of the contest. "We were hung up for a long time on the word 'strangle,'" Chico Lager has said. Finally, during a long meeting at which the strategists agreed that it might be worth trying to use Pillsbury's corporate symbol in some way, Lager blurted it out: "What's the

Doughboy Afraid Of?" The slogan went up on bus signs in Boston. It was made into a bumper sticker. It got printed on T-shirts. A Doughboy Hot Line was set up, so that interested citizens could, by calling an 800 number, receive a Doughboy kit that explained the battle. The kit included two versions of a form letter that could be sent to W. H. Spoor, the chairman of Pillsbury, criticizing "the lack of ethics your company is showing in trying to keep Ben & Jerry's ice cream out of the market." One version began, "I've tasted Ben & Jerry's and I know what the Pillsbury Doughboy is afraid of." Both versions ended with "P.S. Why don't you pick on someone your own size?"

The campaign started slowly, but eventually thousands of people called the Doughboy Hot Line, and thousands of words appeared in the press about Ben & Jerry's. For Ben & Jerry's customers, it was almost as much fun as the Fall Down. Some of the letters people sent to Pillsbury or Häagen-Dazs were businesslike ("I would admonish you to adopt a policy of fair play"), but it was more typical for them to express outrage at "the desire to use the corporate heel to stamp out your competition" or to begin by saying "CORPORATIONS LIKE YOURS REALLY MAKE ME SICK!" A remarkable number of the letters of support received by Ben & Jerry's mentioned the writer's favorite flavor; some of them even mentioned the writer's favorite flavor of Häagen-Dazs. One of them was signed "Helene 'Dastardly Mash' Jones." Some of them were from outraged schoolchildren, who offered to help by, say, forming gangs of Doughboy Busters. Chico Lager sent a copy of one of those letters to W. H. Spoor at Pillsbury, along with a note that ended, "Why not think it over and repent?"

The lawyer hired by Cohen to handle the case that was going on at the same time is not a hippie. The Ben & Jerry's style doesn't go that far. After the Pillsbury legal department had more or less brushed aside a couple of letters from attorneys — one was from a lawyer who is on the board of Ben & Jerry's, the other was from a member of a Vermont firm — Cohen went to Ropes & Gray, a prominent Boston law firm whose reputation has been built partly on defending corporations like Pillsbury from antitrust actions launched by irritants like Ben & Jerry's Homemade. The partner who handled the case for Ropes & Gray, Howard Fuguet, began in May of 1984 by writing Pillsbury a ten-page letter that went into precedents in some detail and suggested that the cause of action was a straightforward matter of the sort not requiring protracted and expensive litigation — what he has called on other occasions a "garden-variety violation" of the Clayton Act. "It would be wishful thinking on the part of your subsidiary's officers to imagine that it can bully Ben & Jerry's, stifle its growth, and cause it to roll over," Fuguet wrote toward the end of the letter. "Ben & Jerry's is a classic entrepreneurial success, and its owners are aggressive. They like the taste of success and will fight for it." The Ben & Jerry's crowd liked Fuguet's style, even though he had stopped short of naming his favorite flavor. They also liked his knowledge of the precedents. Chico Lager said the letter was "inspiring."

Pillsbury was also impressed. By the time Fuguet was ready to file for a temporary restraining order, the Pillsbury lawyers were ready to go along with its terms. After that, the two sides began negotiating, although without the benefit of any old shtetl stories. Fuguet was confident that he could win in court and that Pillsbury's lawyers knew it. Exclusive contracts with distributors are not inherently illegal, but they are illegal if they have the effect of substantially reducing competition in the marketplace — if, for instance, there is a limited number of distributors and the manufacturer imposing the exclusive contract on them already has a dominant share of the market. In the early exchanges, the Pillsbury lawyers claimed that Häagen-Dazs had only a tiny share of the overall ice cream market. After nearly a year of negotiations, though, they agreed to an out-of-court settlement by which Häagen-Dazs promised to impose no exclusive contracts in the area for two years — presumably long enough for Ben & Jerry's to establish itself in the market. Fuguet, of course, had been prepared to demonstrate in court that Häagen-Dazs did have a dominant share because a special market exists in superpremium ice cream. Reuben Mattus had created it.

·   ·   ·

Mattus saw the entire episode as a publicity stunt. And it was a publicity stunt, although Ben Cohen says that he genuinely saw it as publicity to expose corporate bullying as well as publicity that might result in some ice cream sales. ("If we were going to go down this way, I was going to at least make sure people knew what was happening.") Ben and Jerry are among those creatures who are good copy even when they behave the way they would normally behave — or the way they would normally behave except for a little stronger dose of flavor. Jerry Greenfield thought picketing Pillsbury was fun; everybody at Ben & Jerry's thought that directing bales of letters in the direction of W. H. Spoor was fun. Mattus, a man who understands the value of publicity in marketing, couldn't help being impressed by the Doughboy campaign. ("These are sharp, creative guys — a little wild, but very sharp.") He was also irritated, however. He said that if Ben & Jerry's had really been interested in distribution rather than in publicity it would have simply found other distributors or distributed the product on its own — more or less what he had done in the early days of Häagen-Dazs. "They got P.R. and exposure they couldn't buy for millions," he has said. "What they did in a couple of years took me eighteen years to do. I did it the hard way."

Mattus says that sort of thing with a certain amount of pride in his voice. He speaks of Ben and Jerry as good promoters but not as "real ice cream people." Real ice cream people did it the hard way. It didn't have to be fun. Mattus sees Ben and Jerry as the sort of people who might make money in the ice cream business and then sell out and go into something else. "There's a special kind of people dedicated to their business," he has said. "Certain other people are like bees — first this flower, then the next flower. People like the Krolls and myself, we're horses."

1985

RIGHT-OF-WAY

"THE IRONIC THING is that both of these people came here to find peace," the man said. When he said it, he swept his arm out to indicate a scene of palpable peacefulness — a narrow street with almost no traffic on it, a line of buildings that looked as if they might have originated in the early nineteenth century, some lovely mountains in the distance. He was standing not far from the courthouse in the seat of Rappahannock County, Virginia — a town that is named Washington and is sometimes called Little Washington, to distinguish it from the larger, much less peaceful seat of government in the District of Columbia, an hour and a quarter to the east. The residents of Rappahannock County aren't fond of having their county seat called Little Washington, but the town does have the feeling of a place built on the smaller scale of more settled times. The old brick courthouse is flanked by two diminutive brick buildings that look like toy courthouses themselves. The brochure available to visitors says, "Today the population of Washington, Virginia, barely exceeds that at its 18th Century beginning." In recent years, Washington has acquired a community theater and a restaurant widely known for elegant turns on American cuisine, but there is still not enough bustle to require a public telephone booth.

The theater and the restaurant are, of course, the sorts of institutions brought to rural Virginia by newcomers — along with craft shops and careful restorations and elaborate zoning ordinances. It is only in recent years that Rappahannock County has been thought of as the sort of place that might offer shiitake mushrooms on vermicelli or a remarkable level of peacefulness. In the thirties, when the Shenandoah National Park and the Skyline Drive were established in the Blue Ridge Mountains, along the western border of Rappahannock County, a lot of people were resettled from the mountain hollows into what was then a farm county known mainly for apples and cattle. Some of those who were resettled did not immediately abandon their customary ways of resolving disputes or celebrating good fortune or displaying their resentment at having been forcibly removed from their land. Even before the re-settlement, there were parts of the county where sheriffs' deputies went with trepidation. Rappahannock County, which had always had some large farmland holdings, didn't carry the reputation for random violence that was associated with a couple of the mountain counties nearby, but on a Saturday night in an area like Jenkins Hollow the peace was breached rather regularly.

"There probably aren't more than one or two Jenkinses left in Jenkins Hollow," a Rappahannock lawyer who sounded as if he rather missed the old sort of Saturday night has said. "I suppose it's mostly retired people from D.C. The houses are very well kept." Of the six thousand or so residents of Rappahannock County, a couple of thousand are people who have moved in within the past fifteen or twenty years. As it happened, Rappahannock County represented a haven to a lot of different sorts of people. For a time, there was an influx of hippies, many of whom drifted on and some of whom evolved into respectable shopkeepers or building contractors or schoolteachers. A lot of people who worked for the government in Washington, D.C. — civil servants or military people at their final posting — bought houses in Rappahannock that began as weekend retreats and became retirement homes. Some people who were trying to escape the steady suburbanization of the northern Virginia counties — people who were more comfortable in small towns, people who wanted a place where it was possible to hunt rabbits or raise a few crops — moved from Fairfax County to Prince William County to Rappahannock County. For some rather prominent people in Washington, D.C., Rappahannock County seemed to have the beauty of the Virginia foxhunting country just to the east of it — in fact, it has always had a hunt — but not the social pressure associated with places where the horsy types have collected in great numbers. A lot of people who settled in Rappahannock County found it to be what they sometimes call "a good mix." It's a place where some families have presided over large holdings long enough to hear themselves discussed as feudal and where some families continue to live in the government-built bungalows still known as resettlement houses. It's a place that has tasteful antique shops as well as, on the road to the Shenandoah National Park, a line of stands selling apples and cider and Hong Kong statuary. It's a place where life seems simple but where the guest columnist in the county weekly is Eugene McCarthy.

Although the man standing near the courthouse in Washington, Virginia, might have found it ironic that two of the people who had come to Rappahannock County to find peace had found turmoil instead, he would have seen no irony in the fact that the cause of the turmoil was — at the beginning, at least — an argument over property. The newcomers to Rappahannock County brought with them an urban precision about property — about precisely where the boundary was and precisely who had the right to cross it. They talked a lot about property values. Partly because of their presence, of course, there was more property value to talk about. People in Rappahannock County had always had the occasional title disagreement or boundary dispute, but the new people seemed to bring a new relentlessness to such disagreements. When the disagreement between Patricia Saltonstall and Diane Kidwell began, they were arguing, relentlessly, about a right-of-way.

"I fell in love with it when I saw the hills open up," Patricia Saltonstall says of her first impression of Rappahannock County. That was in 1970, and, like a lot of people who had found the sixties almost too eventful, she was in the market for a peaceful place. She had the sort of credentials that presumably could have been useful in keeping a certain amount of turmoil at bay. Her parents' marriage was a union of two prominent New England families, the Saltonstalls and the Laphams. She had gone to Smith and then married a Yale man whose family owned a factory in Pittsburgh. But by 1970, when she was in her early forties, she had also seen her share of contention. Her first marriage had ended in divorce, and so had her second. Reclaiming her formidable maiden name, she had moved with her three sons to Washington, D.C., and established herself as a society writer for the *Washington Star*. In the mid-sixties, she became caught up in the civil rights struggle; she worked for a while for the federal Community Relations Service and then began to devote just about full time to the District of Columbia school-desegregation case. At the 1968 Democratic Convention, in Chicago, she and a number of companions — most of them convention delegates who had impressive credentials of their own — were arrested for disorderly conduct, and she responded to the experience by threatening to sue the city to stop the practice of strip-searching female prisoners. In 1970, she was working in Washington for Senator Harold Hughes, of Iowa, mostly on matters concerning the problem of alcoholism, and looking for some land to escape to on weekends and summer holidays. She had the sort of taste and accent that might have been expected from a former society writer with a formidable name, but she also seemed like someone who had been affected by her connection with the civil rights movement and the struggles entailed in raising a family on her own — a direct, rather intense woman with a no-nonsense manner and a lot of pride in her own independence.

The land she found in Rappahannock County was a two-hundred-and-seventy-acre farm not far from the village of Flint Hill, in an area along State Route 729 which includes some relatively simple houses on ten or fifteen acres of land and some imposing places displaying signs like "CLIFTON, ESTABLISHED 1675." The farm was what she has sometimes called landlocked — it could be connected to the state road only by a private road slicing through neighboring properties — but that brought the price down and added to the privacy. It was lovely, rolling land, leading back to include an overgrown mountain — Hickerson Mountain — that could be seen from miles away. She bought the place and named it Points of View. There was an abandoned tenant's house, which she began to renovate — rather gradually, since she had not yet come into her inheritance. She wanted a barn — a barn that, like the house, was tucked into the curves of the fields in a way that made it blend with the landscape rather than something that seemed to have been dropped naked on the top of a hill. An architect from Georgetown built her an ingenious, multi-use version of a faded wood barn, which eventually won an architectural award and was pictured in the *Washington Post*. In 1973, a two-hundred-acre farm a few miles down 729 was divided into eight lots that became known as the Lindgren-Whaley tract, and she acquired three lots that joined her land on the other side of Hickerson Mountain. Although her holdings on that side of the mountain were also blocked from 729, they could be reached without hacking up and down Hickerson: the Lindgren-Whaley deed provided that the owners of all lots had the use for all purposes of a fifty-foot right-of-way that ran back from 729 through a ten-acre parcel known as Lot A.

For several years Patricia Saltonstall thought that in Rappahannock County she had found the peace she had sought. Then she started having problems with her neighbors. It may be that the problems started when she changed from a weekender into a permanent resident who was intent on making Points of View an effective agricultural operation — in the late seventies, when, after having come into her inheritance, she decided to make a serious commitment to the farm. In her view, that caused some irritation among the nearby farmers, because it deprived one of them of some grazing land he had been renting cheap and it challenged some of their old Virginia notions about the place of a woman. Whatever notions Pat Saltonstall's neighbors might have had about women, they had different notions from hers about how to approach farming. What they tended to think of as the occasional and inevitable straying of cattle, for instance, she considered "systematic stealing of grazing land" — stealing that was made all the more irritating by the accused neighbor's expressing amiable surprise ("My land! What *am* I going to do with them critters?") and vowing to get at that broken fence just as soon as he could. Some of the neighbors thought that Pat Saltonstall, in her businesslike approach to farming, was inflexible and maybe even self-righteous. "Pat was her own worst enemy," a friend of hers has said. "With her money, she should have just fixed the fence instead of worrying so much about what was right or wrong."

In the view of some people in the area, the real trouble started when Patricia Saltonstall hired Rance Spellman. She had met him during the renovation of her farmhouse; he operated heavy equipment. Spellman came from a family that also had been seeking some space in rural Virginia. His father, who was born and raised and married in Ohio, had gone to Alexandria, Virginia, after the Second World War to work as a heavy-equipment operator, and eventually moved his family out to what the Spellmans had built as a weekend cabin in Culpeper County, only ten or fifteen miles from Points of View. In the meantime, he had managed to create a small heavy-equipment contracting company of his own, despite an inclination to be a lot more comfortable on top of a bulldozer than in front of a ledger book. Rance Spellman worked for that company, and took it over after the sudden death of his father. The first time Pat Saltonstall saw him, he was on top of a bulldozer — a bulldozer whose blade had just hit the root of a treasured old ash tree in her front yard. She remembers his courtesy, and the almost delicate way he handled the huge machine, and his blue eyes.

Spellman was interested in what might be done with the top of Hickerson Mountain. "He said he'd like to do the mountain — clear it, stabilize the soil, fence it," Pat Saltonstall has said. "He was just inspired by it." She hired him to do the mountain. It was soon obvious to her that he was a prodigious worker — a burly young man, six feet two inches tall, who was meticulous about his equipment and precise in his estimates and annoyed whenever darkness finally forced him to quit for the day. It was also obvious, she later said, that with Rance Spellman's help "I could *do* this farm, and it would be fun." In early 1980, she hired him, on a contract basis, to be her farm manager. Eventually, they also had what Pat Saltonstall usually refers to as "a personal relationship." A small solar house had been built for the Points of View farm manager, but Spellman moved into the restored farmhouse with Pat Saltonstall.

It was a relationship they didn't advertise — aware, as Pat Saltonstall says, that in the view of her neighbors "it was not the sort of thing you did with the help." Rance Spellman was in his early thirties, nearly twenty years younger than Pat Saltonstall, and his education was in earth moving and stone masonry and horse training rather than in the sort of subjects taught at Smith. "There was a gap in age and a gap in cultural background," she has said. "But we had a lot in common. He could stand alone, the way I do." She saw him as a sort of blond Marlboro man — an independent outdoorsman in jeans and boots who patrolled the property and, like the cowboys of old, always carried a gun. She admired his competence and his almost religious devotion to hard work. He joked about her being his employer, a relationship he expressed in the diminutive: his private name for her was Bossie. Together, they built up a herd of registered Angus cattle. Spellman cleared more fields and built more fences. On the other side of the mountain, they had some lumber cut and hauled out through the right-of-way road to the mill.

After a time, Pat Saltonstall became aware that where she saw a protector — a handsome and basically rather shy protector — some other people saw a bully. She considered that largely a matter of jealousy caused by Spellman's looks and his "tremendous presence." In her view, "There's a kind of handicap that big men have: sometimes other men feel threatened." In fact, some people in Rappahannock County had found Spellman to be unvaryingly soft-spoken and polite; some knew him for obviously genuine and unselfish acts of kindness toward children or animals. But others saw him as a menacing swaggerer. Nobody had ever seen him actually use his size or his guns to attack anyone, but a number of people seemed afraid that he might. According to his brother, Boyd Spellman, their father, whom Rance had revered, had sometimes seemed too easygoing to be in business, and Rance had been intent on becoming the sort of person nobody took advantage of. Along the way, he had some experiences of the kind that can drain off cheerfulness — two failed marriages, for instance, and the early death of his father, and a stint in Vietnam at a time when most people his age seemed to be going about their business at home. For whatever reasons, Spellman had been in some unpleasant confrontations now and then as a heavy-equipment operator, and as the farm manager of Points of View he seemed to be in more. It got so that the owner of straying cattle had to contend not with a stiff note from Pat Saltonstall but with the possibility that Rance Spellman would impound the cattle and demand board and feed money before giving them back. "They'd done every kind of thing to everybody there," William Buntin, who was the sheriff of Rappahannock County at the time, has said. "They had problems with every neighbor that joins them."

Of course, Patricia Saltonstall might have been right in assuming that some of the ill feeling was brought on by jealousy or prejudice — envy of her money and his appearance and what they had accomplished at Points of View, hatred of the relationship that was suspected between the boss and the farm manager. In the view of a friend of theirs, "They were building a showplace, and I think that people who had always got along with patches resented it." Some of the neighboring farmers said that people who were seriously interested in farming, as opposed to showing off, would not have given priority to putting a pasture on top of a mountain. It did seem, though, that as farm operators Pat Saltonstall and Rance Spellman complemented each other perfectly — his skills and heavy machinery and stunning capacity for work, her resources and organizational ability and encouragement. But to some people in the county their alliance was also what made them particularly threatening. If Rance Spellman was a bully, he was all the more so with Patricia Saltonstall's money and influence behind him. If Patricia Saltonstall was a willful rich lady, she was all the more so with a huge, intimidating cowboy to back her up.

Roger and Diane Kidwell were among those people who kept moving west from the D.C. sprawl to find a little country. They had both been raised in Fairfax County, in the days when it seemed more small-town than suburban; after they were married and began to raise a family, they moved in two or three steps from Alexandria to Amissville, not far from where the Spellman family had gone to find some space. Diane Kidwell was a secretary, and until 1975 she worked at a conference center called the Airlie Foundation, in Warrenton, Virginia, twenty miles to the east. Roger Kidwell also worked there briefly, at the front desk. For the Kidwells, as it turned out, escaping the suburbs did not mean escaping turmoil. In the late seventies, Murdock Head, the executive director of Airlie, was indicted for payment of an illegal gratuity. He was accused of having smoothed the way for the foundation's contract applications by slipping cash payoffs to Representative Daniel Flood, of Pennsylvania, through Flood's aide, Stephen Elko, who had become a witness for the government. The payoffs were alleged to have taken place during the time Diane Kidwell worked in Head's office, first as a secretary and for a time as his administrative assistant. After two trials, Head was convicted and sent to jail. Among those who were or had been connected with the foundation, Mrs. Kidwell, who had been laid off by Airlie before the investigation began, was the only person who appeared as a friendly witness for the prosecution to corroborate Elko's story — an act that caused great rancor among her former colleagues. The payoff scandal was not the only source of turmoil in the Kidwells' lives. Apparently, their marriage had been stormy. In 1970, they were legally separated for a while; Diane Kidwell and the children moved into one of the Airlie buildings. Having sold their house in Amissville while they were separated, the Kidwells moved into a rental house after their reconciliation. Roger Kidwell had started selling insurance, and eventually his wife worked with him, in an office in Warrenton. They had their hearts set on building a house of their own — a house on the top of a hill. In the early seventies, they came across Lot A of the Lindgren-Whaley tract. It seemed perfect, Diane Kidwell said later, except for the right-of-way.

The Kidwells built their house on a hill overlooking Route 729. It's a tidy-looking house that wouldn't have seemed out of place in one of the subdivisions they left as they moved west — two stories, with yellow siding and a carport and a basketball goal and an apartment in the basement for Roger Kidwell's parents. The right-of-way, which existed only in the form of a narrow dirt road coming back toward the mountain from 729, was not a source of disturbance. There was only one house on the lots served by the road — a small weekend cottage that generated little traffic. Eventually, the Kidwells bought a second lot, a twenty-five-acre parcel just across the right-of-way. They had no problems with the Lindgren-Whaley tract's largest landowner, Patricia Saltonstall, even after she hired Rance Spellman as farm manager. Until the dispute about the right-of-way began, in fact, the Kidwells were not even aware of who Rance Spellman was. Roger and Diane Kidwell, both of whom commuted every day to Warrenton, were not among those who spent a lot of time at the lunch counter or filling station in Flint Hill chewing over questions like whether beef prices would ever go up or what the relationship between Patricia Saltonstall and Rance Spellman really was. The Kidwells were not well known in the area except as a family that raised what seemed to be particularly ferocious dogs. (Sheriff Buntin has said that when he canvassed the county for his final election campaign the Kidwell house was the only place where he decided against getting out of the car.) What little contact there had been between the Kidwells and Pat Saltonstall was cordial. Diane Kidwell's brother had been given permission to fish in a pond at Points of View. Like Pat Saltonstall, the Kidwells believed strongly in the importance of maintaining one's property ("We've always been interested in our property, and in keeping our property values") and in the necessity of keeping hunters and other trespassers off the mountain. Although Diane Kidwell and Patricia Saltonstall may not have had the same taste in architecture or the same circle of friends, they had what Pat Saltonstall calls "a fairly normal neighborly acquaintanceship."

The trouble started in the spring of 1982. The subject of the right-of-way came up when Diane Kidwell wrote to Patricia Saltonstall asking if she would contribute to the cost of putting down some new gravel. After that, a lot of issues were raised. Eventually, lawyers for the two parties were exchanging letters, none of them conciliatory. Paragraphs in the county deed book and statutes in the Virginia code were cited. Questions were raised about a gate that had been placed across the right-of-way back near the mountain. Patricia Saltonstall had, in violation of the deed, put it up without the permission of the other lot owners — she said it was to discourage lumber thieves — and the Kidwells had removed it without the permission of Patricia Saltonstall. There was the question of the Kidwells' having installed a cattle guard on the road. There was the question of whether the Points of View lumbering crews had left the Kidwells' gates open. There was the question of whether the Kidwells had been trespassing on the mountain. There was the question of whether Rance Spellman's excavation work on the mountain had interfered with the Kidwells' water supply. At the center of the dispute, though, was Pat Saltonstall's announced intention to exercise her right to make use of a full fifty feet of right-of-way, so that there could be "more frequent and regular use of the road." Since road improvements would begin shortly, she informed the Kidwells, they should remove any shrubbery or trees or posts that they had within the fifty-foot strip stipulated in the deed. The Kidwells didn't want to remove their shrubbery and trees and posts; they didn't want more frequent and regular use of the road. Pat Saltonstall had said that the widening was necessary for keeping a close watch on valuable herds of Angus grazing on the mountain and for putting into effect "other plans I have for one of the lots." The Kidwells thought it was unnecessary except as a matter of spite. Their lawyer said that anyone who attempted to clear the right-of-way without a court order would be held liable for any property damage. Presumably, the lawyer, a young man named David Konick, intended to file for an injunction; but no injunction had been filed by November 8, when Patricia Saltonstall's lawyer, unable to reach Konick, left a message on his answering machine saying that work might begin as early as the next afternoon. It was actually early the next morning when Rance Spellman climbed onto a bulldozer, drove over the mountain he had cleared, and came out on the right-of-way to begin his work.

Sheriff Buntin and a state policeman arrived at the Kidwells' together that morning. Diane Kidwell had phoned Buntin's office to demand that Spellman be stopped, but the sheriff, who had neither the authority nor the inclination to referee a right-of-way dispute, had not hurried out. Diane Kidwell's brother had phoned the state police and warned them that an armed confrontation might take place. When the two lawmen arrived, Rance Spellman was sitting in the driver's seat of the bulldozer, which was parked only twenty yards or so from where the Kidwells' driveway meets the right-of-way. From the appearance of the land around him, he had already done considerable work. He was dressed in his usual outfit of blue jeans and boots and a couple of work shirts and a down vest. He was slumped over. The state trooper climbed up on the bulldozer to have a closer look. Rance Spellman had a small amount of blood coming from his mouth and nose. A volley of shotgun pellets had torn through his down vest. He was dead.

The story that the authorities eventually put together was this: Rance Spellman had begun his work near the Kidwells' driveway — tearing up trees, pushing over gateposts. When Diane Kidwell's brother tried to reason with him, he just smiled — sneered, really — and kept working. After a while, Mrs. Kidwell took a shotgun from the house and, holding it in a way that concealed it from Spellman's view, walked to the family's pickup. She pulled the pickup into the right-of-way, close to the beginning of her driveway, and sat in the front seat with the shotgun next to her. Her brother pleaded with her to come back to the house and wait for the state police, but she said she had decided to take her stand. Her husband watched from the back door; one of her sons watched from a field above the house. For twenty minutes or so, Diane Kidwell watched the bulldozer, which took several swipes perilously close to the pickup. After one of them, she pointed the shotgun out the window and fired one blast at Spellman — shouting, "Get off! Get off!" She said that she thought he was reaching for a gun and she had therefore been in fear for her life. Spellman was armed, as usual. He had a carbine on the bulldozer and a pistol in his shoulder holster. But the carbine was still in its scabbard and the pistol was buttoned up under one of his shirts and the vest.

The only witnesses alive to testify to what had happened were Diane Kidwell and people related to her, and they had been sequestered in the house by their lawyer, David Konick, long enough to have compared stories. The authorities, though, tended to think that the shooting had taken place pretty much the way the Kidwells said it had. The witnesses had reported, after all, that Diane Kidwell had put herself in the path of the bulldozer, which never left the fifty-foot right-of-way. They had reported that Spellman had been shot with a concealed weapon when his own gun was nowhere in sight. They had reported Diane Kidwell's shouting not "Help!" or "Don't shoot!" but "Get off!" If the Kidwells had been trying to concoct a story that would justify the killing of Rance Spellman, it was thought, they would have managed to come up with a better one. The grand jury heard testimony, and four weeks after the shooting Diane Kidwell was indicted for murder.

Rance Spellman's funeral was at Points of View farm. There was an unconventional service, full of symbolism. Spellman's horse stood nearby, with a pair of boots reversed in its stirrups, in the traditional symbol of a fallen cavalryman. Then a cortège of four-wheel-drive vehicles moved slowly up the mountain, where Spellman was buried on the mountaintop he had cleared. Spellman's friends and family were there to mourn him, but it was already apparent that his death had not erased the difference between the view of Rance Spellman held by Patricia Saltonstall and the view of him held by a lot of other people in Rappahannock County. A lot of people were saying, "He had it coming." A lot of other people were saying of Diane Kidwell, "If she hadn't done it, somebody else would have."

In a claim of self-defense, the reputation of the deceased is admissible evidence. Lawyers for the accused can try to demonstrate that their client had been particularly fearful because of having been threatened by someone known for "turbulence, violence, and pugnacity." The trial lawyers Diane Kidwell had hired to defend her — her chief counsel was John Dowd, a former federal prosecutor who had led the investigation of Murdock Head — could be expected to do just that. Protection of home and property is not a ground for a claim of self-defense, but none of the attorneys involved doubted that it was relevant to the way jurors were likely to view the issues. As it happened, an early news story had reported incorrectly that Spellman began his work despite a court hearing's having been scheduled for the very next day, but even jurors who were not under that misapprehension could be expected to have a certain sympathy for a woman watching a huge, sneering man on a twenty-ton bulldozer tear up her property in front of her dream house. Also, Diane Kidwell presented a sympathetic figure — a neatly dressed woman with a careful hairdo and thick glasses and a soft voice. News stories tended to identify her as "43-year-old mother of four."

Still, the prosecution thought it had a case that could overcome sympathy for Diane Kidwell. The commonwealth attorney of Rappahannock County, Douglas Baumgardner, brought in a special prosecutor, because he himself had to testify in a closed hearing concerning a rather bizarre side issue that was not made public until nearly a year later: David Konick, the young lawyer who had been called by the Kidwells on the morning of the shooting and later dismissed, had admitted that, acting on his own, he had wiped the barrel of the Kidwells' shotgun clean of fingerprints, and he was therefore in danger of being indicted himself. (As it turned out, he was not indicted, but his actions were finally made public at a rather awkward moment — the closing days of what turned out to be an unsuccessful race he ran for commonwealth attorney.) The special prosecutor — Steven A. Merril, a former assistant prosecutor in Fairfax County — argued that by Diane Kidwell's own admission she had chosen to confront Spellman, she had hidden a shotgun beside her, she had rejected her brother's plea to return to the house, she had become angrier and angrier as she watched Spellman work, and she had previously seen Spellman reach into his shirt two or three times and come out each time with nothing more dangerous than a cigarette. Whatever the rights and wrongs of the right-of-way argument and whatever the nature of Rance Spellman, Merril said, Diane Kidwell had "absolutely no right to eliminate Rance Spellman from the face of the earth."

The defense lawyers said that Pat Saltonstall's decision to widen the right-of-way to fifty feet was a "spiteful, punitive act," and that Spellman had confirmed that by beginning his work right in front of the Kidwell house, four hundred yards from where the road began. They called as witnesses four or five people who related experiences that led them to consider Spellman violent and turbulent and pugnacious. The owner of some adjoining land, for instance, testified that a front-end loader being used for work on the edge of his property had once been left a few feet onto Points of View land overnight, and that Rance Spellman waited near the machine the next morning with two guns and demanded fifty dollars before he would release it to its operator. There was testimony that just a week or so before the shooting Roger Kidwell and his son-in-law had run across Spellman while they were out cutting wood, and Spellman had challenged Kidwell to step out in the right-of-way path and settle the dispute with bare hands. Dowd said that Diane Kidwell had concealed her shotgun because she didn't want to provoke "this madman on the bulldozer." She testified that Spellman had threatened to turn over the pickup and that, just before he reached toward his vest, his expression had changed to one of rage. Dowd built an impassioned summation on the theme of why Diane Kidwell had walked from the house to sit in a pickup truck right in front of where Spellman was moving earth around. ("Why does a fireman go into a burning house and pull out a child? Why does a man jump into a cold river and pull a young boy out? Why do men do what they do on the battlefield and save lives, with holes in them? Why? Because they are strong, that's why.") He said that Diane Kidwell had indeed been intent on protecting her home ("Nowhere in the laws or Constitution of this country does it say that a citizen on her own property has to submit to the tyranny of a professional bully on a forty-one-thousand-pound bulldozer"), but had fired because she honestly believed that Rance Spellman was about to pull out a pistol and kill her.

The jury couldn't reach a verdict, but only because of a single holdout. Everyone else wanted to acquit Diane Kidwell. Shortly after the trial ended, three prominent landowners from around Flint Hill went to the commonwealth attorney and suggested that, considering the size of the majority for acquittal and the continued feeling against Spellman in the county, it would be a waste of money to try Diane Kidwell again. Merril, who had decided to hold a second trial, thought about trying for a change of venue, but he concluded that Rappahannock County jurors were the appropriate people to hear the case. "I felt people who lived there had a stake in it," he has said. "They have to live there, and they have a right to say what they consider criminal activity and what isn't." Merril thinks that he presented a better case the second time around. He tried to narrow the issues, avoiding as much as possible ensnarlment in the right-of-way dispute; he was more aggressive in his cross-examination of the accused. This time, there was no holdout. Diane Kidwell was found not guilty.

The people who watched the trials with some detachment — reporters, courthouse workers, lawyers who dropped in and out of the courtroom — tend to agree that Merril put forward a strong case. Half a dozen of them took a survey among themselves to predict a verdict before the jury came back in the first trial, and the predictions ranged from guilty of manslaughter to guilty of murder. In retrospect, they tend to agree with Merril that a conviction was nearly impossible. "I feel that a typical jury, in addition to analyzing the facts and applying the law, subconsciously takes out a set of scales," a Rappahannock lawyer with considerable trial experience said after the second trial. "It values the liberty of the accused on one side of the scale, and attaches a certain value or weight to the life of the deceased on the other." The decision of twenty-three jurors in the death of Rance Spellman could be taken as an indication that they placed considerable value on the freedom of Diane Kidwell, a demure wife and mother and grandmother who had no previous criminal record and was hardly a threat to the community. The other way to look at it, the lawyer went on, was that Rance Spellman's life was not given great value — that "the community had decided that someone's life is not worth punishing someone for taking."

That's the way Patricia Saltonstall interpreted the jurors' votes. She also saw the case presented by Diane Kidwell's lawyers in court as an attempt to get someone off the hook by dragging the name of someone else through the mud — someone else who was no longer alive to defend himself. Pat Saltonstall took on that defense herself. She saw her mission as "having his name and his life put in perspective." In August of 1983, nine months after Rance Spellman died and two months before Diane Kidwell's second trial, a number of people in Rappahannock County received an invitation from Pat Saltonstall to "come and celebrate the life of Rance Lee Spellman." The celebration, the invitation said, would include country music, a roast-pig picnic, a dedication of the mountaintop cemetery where he was buried, and the announcement of a living memorial — an agricultural prize to be awarded through a nearby community college. Under Rance Spellman's name, the invitation listed some of the things he had been — including farmer, horseman, mason, welder, artificial-insemination technician, surveyor. The guests — a couple hundred of them — arrived at Points of View to find that a tent had been erected for the celebration. It was decorated with thirty-six nearly life-size photographs of Rance Spellman, one for every year of his life. "We wish to remember Rance not for the cruelty of his senseless death by one act of human violence," the invitation said, "but for the glory of one man who left place upon place more beautiful because of his work."

One piece of Spellman's work that Pat Saltonstall intended to finish was the widening of the right-of-way in the Lindgren-Whaley tract. The legal question of whether she had the right to widen the right-of-way to fifty feet — not what her motives were or whether she really needed to but simply whether she had a right to — was not difficult to settle. In December of 1983, two months after Diane Kidwell's acquittal, a circuit-court judge heard one day of testimony on the Kidwells' motion for a permanent injunction barring the road widening, and in January of 1984 he handed down a ruling denying the motion, on the ground that the deed's grant of the fifty-foot right-of-way showed "unambiguous intent." When the warm weather came, in May, a contractor hired by Points of View farm showed up on the right-of-way to begin the grading at precisely the spot where Spellman had left off. Patricia Saltonstall was also there. In a press release, she said that the work was dedicated to Rance Spellman. "Saltonstall called the new construction 'a clear statement about who was right and who was wrong that tragic morning,' " the press release said. " 'This project had to be completed, not only because we badly need a good farm road up the north side of the mountain . . . but because such a violent act could not be allowed to be the last word on this project.' "

By then, people in Rappahannock County had begun to wonder whether there was ever going to be a last word. Even before the second trial, Patricia Saltonstall had applied for planning permission to build two-family houses on two of her lots in the Lindgren-Whaley tract — she said she would eventually need them for farm workers — and the Kidwells protested to the zoning authorities that she should not be given a special-use permit to build two-family houses in an area zoned for single-family dwellings only. The zoning argument involved not only the same disputants but some of the same supporting characters. Douglas Baumgardner, who as commonwealth attorney had presided over Diane Kidwell's indictment, eventually represented Patricia Saltonstall. The zoning administrator of Rappahannock County at the time was David Konick, who had been accused by Roger Kidwell in a letter to the *Rappahannock News* of using the position to carry on a vendetta against the Kidwell family. As the argument about the new houses was carried through the various levels of appeal, it seemed to blend into the murder trials as part of the endless litigation set in motion by Diane Kidwell's letter concerning gravel on the right-of-way.

After the second murder trial, in fact, contention had burst out on several fronts at once. Responding in the *Rappahannock News* to a letter from a county resident that criticized the verdict, Diane Kidwell managed in the course of defending her own conduct to mention that Rance Spellman's estate had been inherited not by an elderly black man who had long worked for the Spellman family, as had been reported, but by Patricia Saltonstall herself. That one was answered by a letter from Patricia Saltonstall expressing outrage ("How, in the name of any kind of fairness and decency, does Kidwell see this as her business?") and then taking issue with Mrs. Kidwell in detail not only about the will but about the facts of the right-of-way dispute. That one was followed by a letter to the paper from Diane Kidwell pointing out that the burial of Rance Spellman on Hickerson Mountain seemed to be contrary to the burial instructions in his will and contrary to the zoning code, which permitted burial on farmland only in the case of family graveyards.

Perhaps developing her lots in the Lindgren-Whaley tract makes economic sense for Patricia Saltonstall, but the Kidwells see it as a simple act of harassment. ("There's no other reason to build those monstrosities," Diane Kidwell has said.) Perhaps their protest against the houses has been based on the desire to protect their tranquillity and their property values — according to testimony at the zoning hearings, the two houses could generate seventy more automobile trips per day on the right-of-way road — but Patricia Saltonstall sees it as part of a vendetta against her. By now, the disputants can credit each other with only a single motive — the desire to torment. After a couple of letters to the zoning administrator, the Kidwells did not pursue the gravesite complaint ("It was a sensitive issue for some people," Roger Kidwell has said), but that does not keep them from believing that Rance Spellman was buried on Hickerson Mountain so that they would be reminded of him every time they glanced up from their carport. In Roger Kidwell's view, "The house was harassment, the gravesite was harassment. We know there is no end to this thing." Speaking at the same time of the large memorial advertisements that Patricia Saltonstall has placed in the *Rappahannock News* each year on the anniversary of Rance Spellman's death, Diane Kidwell said, "She might be very genuine in her reasoning for doing that, but it's like she wants to remind me. On the ninth, when I pick up my local paper I see his picture. I see that as harassment. I feel like when I'm sixty-five I'll pick up my local paper and there he'll be."

It has been common for some time to hear people in Rappahannock County say that Patricia Saltonstall and Diane Kidwell are, despite the differences in their backgrounds, very much alike. Both of them tend to complain about having been singled out for unfair treatment. Patricia Saltonstall often talks about the difficulty of having been the only girl at her boarding school who was completely cut off from family during the war — her family was in Hawaii — and of having spent her first years in Rappahannock County making neighborly gestures that were never returned or even acknowledged. Diane Kidwell has implied at times that pressure from a variety of enemies was the only reason she was indicted. Each of them sees herself as a woman capable of standing up to the considerable forces allied against her. One way to view what has happened, Diane Kidwell has said, is as "the story of a wealthy Northern woman who came down here to a small Virginia county and wanted to do everything her own way, and the story of the mother and grandmother who stood in front of a forty-thousand-pound bulldozer simply to protect her own property and was forced to shoot somebody to protect her own life." Both women tend to describe their own motives in high moral terms. Asked why she would make an issue over where Spellman was buried, Mrs. Kidwell said that the gravesite was contrary to the burial instructions in his will and "we have a kind of sacred feeling in our family about wills." Patricia Saltonstall has often compared her effort to right what she considers a wrong in Rappahannock County with the efforts of lone black people to right wrongs in the counties of the Deep South. She sometimes says, "I feel like the Rosa Parks of Rappahannock County."

In December of 1985, both the house that Patricia Saltonstall had already built on one of her lots and the house she wanted to build on the adjoining lot were given special-use permits as two-family dwellings by the county Board of Zoning Appeal. The decision did not leave the combatants without a court case. The previous month, just before the statute of limitations for civil litigation was reached, Patricia Saltonstall, in her role as an executor of Rance Spellman's estate, filed a wrongful-death suit against the Kidwells; on her own, she filed a suit claiming three million dollars in damages on the ground that the Kidwells "have engaged in a persistent course of conduct, commencing before the killing of Rance Spellman and continuing up to the present time, to harass plaintiff, to defame her, to invade her privacy, to interfere with the use of the right-of-way . . . and to interfere generally with the use of her property and the operation of her farming business and other farming operations." At around the same time, Diane Kidwell filed a two-hundred-and-twenty-five-thousand-dollar malpractice suit against David Konick, claiming that his suppression of material evidence and subsequent contraventions of the rules of confidentiality had caused doubts to be cast on her innocence. In the reply that Konick filed, he said that Diane Kidwell had "intentionally and maliciously confronted Spellman" in disregard of his advice, and that if he had, in fact, revealed all the confidential information at his disposal she "would likely have been convicted of a felony in connection with the homicide of Spellman." That statement was, of course, of great interest to Patricia Saltonstall. She saw it as an opening to reinvestigate the circumstances of Rance Spellman's death.

No one knows how far the latest law cases will be carried, but the feeling in Rappahannock County is that the Kidwell and Saltonstall forces will manage to find one battlefield or another. It is assumed that by now Diane Kidwell and Patricia Saltonstall hope to drive each other away. It is also assumed that both of them are people not easily driven off. A lot of Rappahannock residents find that a cause for regret; they were tired of hearing about the dispute a long time ago. Sympathy for both of the participants has pretty much evaporated. There are people who say that Patricia Saltonstall is not trying to rehabilitate Rance Spellman's name but working out her own guilt ("Let's face it: if she had just said, 'Rance, wait until tomorrow,' he'd be alive right now"); there are people who think that Diane Kidwell, in her relentless concern with what impinges on her rights or property, somehow seems to have lost track of the fact that she killed someone. (The headline on one letter to a local paper was "SHE COULD HAVE SAID SHE WAS SORRY.") Old-time residents of Rappahannock County are sensitive to the possibility that talk about the murder-trial verdict — particularly in conjunction with another case, in which a man who tracked down his estranged wife's lover and killed him was fined a thousand dollars for manslaughter — will rekindle suspicion among outsiders that Rappahannock might still be one of those counties with backwoods notions about crime and punishment. Some newcomers simply hate the publicity and the turmoil caused by the dispute. Many of them, after all, came to Rappahannock County looking for peace.

1985

GOLDERG CAN GO
HOME AGAIN

SOMETIME IN the middle eighties, my friend Fats Goldberg, the pizza baron, started talking a lot about going home. Many people might have argued that he was home already — he had at the time lived in New York for more than twenty years — but those wouldn't have been people who grew up in the Midwest. For Midwesterners, a home town has no statute of limitations. If a Wall Street trader who grew up in Des Moines says late in the evening, "I better be getting home," he may be talking about a co-op apartment on East Seventy-first Street, but if he says after a day that included an expensive down-tick in automotive issues and a visit by a couple of men from the SEC, "Sometimes I think about going home," he's talking about Des Moines, Iowa. If Fats Goldberg made such a remark, he'd be talking about Kansas City, Missouri. So would I. In fact, after twenty-five years or so in Manhattan I still find myself talking now and then about going back to Kansas City. "We could go back home," I say to my wife, an Easterner, whose home it never was. "I'd buy you a house overlooking the brown waters of Lake Lotawana." I assume my wife has never taken those offers seriously — so far, she hasn't bothered to reply — and at first we didn't take Fats Goldberg's talk seriously, either. I'd known people who talked about going home as a sort of symbolic fallback position ("Why, before I'd do that I'd go on back home"), and I'd known people who had given serious consideration to job offers in their home town. But I'd never known anyone who had actually gone home.

Also, over the years my wife and I and our daughters had spent many hours talking to Fats about what he might do with his future — he often said, "You can't schlep pizzas all your life" — and, considering the fact that the business schemes he mentioned ranged from an edible diet book to something called Goldberg's Pizza Cone, it was natural to assume that we were in the realm of the hypothetical. On a Sunday evening at Goldberg's Pizzeria, we would consume a pizza that the girls had been permitted to make themselves, under Goldberg's unflappable supervision. Then Fats might bring out, say, the prototype of a Plexiglas pizza pusher, designed to keep the eater's hand cool and clean, and present it with one of the Goldbergian expressions of enthusiasm — "This is the ticket" or "This'll straighten you right out." I suppose we treated the proposed move to Kansas City as just another Plexiglas pizza pusher.

I'm not saying that we simply dismissed Fats's schemes. I'll admit to having expressed unqualified enthusiasm for the original title of the edible diet book — *Eat This Book and Lose Weight in Three Days*. Also, when Fats told us that he had put classified ads in a couple of New York papers offering to pay two dollars each for fortunes to put in Goldberg's Funny Fortune Cookies, I submitted at least one fortune: "You would do well to get your elbow out of the mu shu pork." He turned it down. Fats could afford to be choosy; it turned out that there was a buyer's market in funny fortunes. The ads he had placed drew hundreds of responses, which didn't surprise him at all. "In New York, everyone's a writer," he said.

All the business schemes Fats came up with had to do with dieting or eating, the mirrored Goldbergian obsessions. By then, Fats had not actually been fat for many years. At the age of twenty-five and the weight of three hundred and twenty pounds, he had reversed a lifetime as a barrel by taking off some hundred and sixty pounds — an accomplishment I've always liked to think of as losing the equivalent of Rocky Graziano in his prime — and a quarter century later he remained half of the Goldberg I had once known. In fact, it was Goldberg's success in dropping his Graziano that, some years ago, startled me into discussing him in print. One Sunday in the late sixties, at the old Ratner's dairy restaurant on lower Second Avenue, a six-foot wraith approached our table. He was an exceedingly amiable wraith, wearing a bright sweater and white pants. He claimed that he was Larry (Fats) Goldberg, of Kansas City — the same Larry (Fats) Goldberg I had last seen as one of the University of Missouri's rare three-hundred-pound undergraduates. My initial impression was that he was probably an impostor, and before I finally acknowledged him as the real article I gave him a Kansas City quiz that could not have been passed by anyone who didn't have an intimate knowledge of Arthur Bryant's barbecue restaurant, at the old Eighteenth-and-Euclid location. I began chronicling his Manhattan adventures out of an interest in how he had managed to, as he always put it, "stay down." His secret, it turned out, was an inflexible regimen that required a permanent diet except on certain cheating days each week and on semiannual ten-day visits to Kansas City. The fact that Fats went to Kansas City for his eating binges did not, at the time, alert me to what his future might hold. After all, I'd always visited Kansas City regularly, and I had some trouble resisting the food back home myself.

In 1976, I was part of the press corps — or, to be absolutely accurate about it, I *was* the press corps — that accompanied Fats to the Smithsonian Institution for the opening of a bicentennial exhibition that included in its display of American neon a sign that said, "GOLDBERG'S PIZZERIA." In the role of a pool reporter who has the whole pool to himself, I was able to get close enough to record every detail of Goldberg's costume for the occasion: "A faded-blue Western shirt with the collar spread back to display a V of white T-shirt, peach-colored Levi trousers, a Madras sports jacket, and a pair of black-and-white Spalding saddle shoes with authentic red rubber soles — a type of saddle shoe apparently as rare and difficult to replace as a 1947 De Soto."

Not long after my account of Fats's adventures at the Smithsonian was published — it was called "Goldberg as Artifact" — I took a friend who was visiting from Boston to meet Fats for the first time. "I was rather disappointed," my friend said as we walked away from Goldberg's Pizzeria one Sunday evening.

"Disappointed!" I said. "Why, I thought the fat man was at his most charming tonight."

"Not disappointed in him, disappointed in you," my friend said. "I thought you had made Fats up, or at least embellished. You've just been copying down what he says."

At that moment, I realized that I had become Fats Goldberg's Boswell.

In the years after the bicentennial, Fats seemed firmly settled in New York. He was, of course, a pizza baron: the Chicago version he served had won *New York* magazine's prize for the best pizza in the city. He had been mentioned so often in the *Times* — not just in pizza articles but in articles about, say, the comeback of saddle shoes or the Manhattan singles scene — that for a while the editors informally declared him a banned person. He was literally a man about town: because his exercise regimen required taking extraordinarily long walks through the city every day, people were constantly saying to me, "I bumped into your friend Goldberg on Fifth Avenue last week," or "I saw this weird-colored sweater approach me on Fifty-eighth Street the other day, and guess who it was." His circle of acquaintances included just about everyone he passed regularly on his daily walks, since he normally greeted any fellow pedestrians — a Fifth Avenue dowager being helped into a cab by her doorman, a couple of moving men wrestling with a piano — with a cheery "Hi, guys. What's cookin'?" In certain Manhattan fields of special knowledge, he was the man to consult — what Irish policemen as well as Jewish cabdrivers in New York would call the maven. Nobody knew more about accessible public bathrooms on the East Side of Manhattan. Nobody knew more about which museums were best for falling into conversation with female art lovers on Sunday afternoon. Nobody knew more about places appropriate for the classic Goldbergian date — a movie and a cheeseburger, preferably Dutch treat.

So when he talked about going home we naturally didn't take him seriously. "Fats has lived in New York virtually all his adult life," I would say now and then, to reassure myself — although sometimes I made the mistake of saying it in the presence of people who didn't think it made sense to talk about adult life when it came to Goldberg. Some Eastern friends of Fats made no secret of their belief that the life he was living was the teenage life he had been too fat to live as a teenager — from dressing in white Levi's to "checking out the action" at the Museum of Modern Art and continuing to make the basic 1952 distinction between close female pals and what he still referred to as "real girls." I suspect that those people have some analytical theories about why Fats got fat in the first place, and why, after ignoring so many doctor's warnings that the life of a three-hundred-pound man was likely to be not simply uncomfortable but short, he finally mustered the willpower to become permanently thin. But they've tended to spare Fats those theories. When Fats hears Easterners speculate about why people behave the way they do and what it may have to do with their infancy, he's likely to say, "That stuff makes me twitchy."

However long Fats had lived in New York, I finally realized, he seemed serious about going back to Kansas City. He insisted that the decision did not reflect any irritation with New York. As a matter of fact, about the only complaint about life in the city I'd ever heard him make concerned the cost of a movie-and-cheeseburger date. He had priced it at an astonishing forty dollars, including a particularly galling two-fifty for the glass of white wine his date invariably ordered with her cheeseburger. "It tees me off," he always said, "because I know they use jug wine."

In 1985, Fats lost his closest pal. Judy Klemesrud, a *Times* reporter who was from Thompson, Iowa, died in her forties of cancer. She might have been the only person in the world who treated the Fats Goldberg way of life — the inviolable regimen, the monumental cheating days, the sweaters, the Goldbergian notion of a night on the town — as unremarkable, and some of Fats's friends suspected that his talk of going home was another way of saying that Manhattan wasn't much fun for him without her. But

Fats insisted that his reasons for leaving were commercial. In the late seventies, an attractive offer for the pizzeria had come along, and Fats had taken it, thinking he'd live on the payout of the purchase price while he figured out the next step. (He continued to spend a lot of time at Goldberg's Pizzeria as a consultant — under a contract that included one large pizza a day, said pizzas to be cumulative.) In other words, he was technically no longer a pizza baron, and as the day the payouts would end crept closer no commercially viable alternative to the barony emerged.

The Plexiglas pizza pusher hadn't gone beyond the prototype. Goldberg's Pasta & Pizza Sauce had never been manufactured, and his plan for a five-hour, nonstop eating tour of New York had never got past the planning stage. The edible diet book had technical difficulties until Fats changed it into the chewable diet book — it was to be made of sugarless bubble gum — and then it had publishing difficulties. A few of Goldberg's schemes did get off the drawing board. Doubleday published a nonedible diet book of his called *Controlled Cheating*, for instance, and the funny fortune cookies were actually manufactured. But the jackpot Fats had been looking for eluded him. The most memorable result of the fortune-cookie scheme was that Fats had to spend hours in a number of Bloomingdale's stores handing out samples while costumed as a fortune cookie. I don't think that even the real Boswell could have gone very far toward describing the costume except to say that it looked about as much like a fortune cookie as something designed to fit a six-foot man can look. Fats's own description tends to dwell on how many times a person who drinks eight to ten glasses of water a day has to get in and out of a fortune-cookie costume.

At one time, Fats had assumed that he could always open another pizza parlor, but the thought of starting again in New York seemed to make him sigh, particularly when he considered what had happened to commercial rents during the time he was contemplating other lines of work. For years, people had been urging him to open a pizza business in Kansas City. On his semiannual binges, Fats had kept up with some of his old college friends and met a lot of other people. Although editors of the *Kansas City Star* had never felt the need to declare him a banned person, he had a following in the local press. There wouldn't be any trouble obtaining financing in Kansas City, and nobody in Kansas City had ever heard of charging ten or twelve thousand dollars a month rent for the sort of space a pizza parlor required. Everything in Kansas City sounded easy. Then someone came to Fats with a specific Kansas City deal. A businessman of some means wanted to start a Goldberg's Pizzeria in a suburban Kansas City neighborhood called Prairie Village, with Goldberg at the helm under an employment contract, and then branch out into franchises. Fats decided to do it.

The deal sounded sensible, but I found myself arguing, in an indirect way, that it wasn't time for Fats to go home. "My girls don't like the idea of it at all, Fats," I'd say. Our daughters had outgrown the sort of birthday parties that Fats used to enhance by showing up with a heart-shaped pizza that had the birthday girl's initials done in green pepper. I suppose they were also too old to get excited about the opportunity to make their own medium meatball-and-cheese at Goldberg's Pizzeria. In a matter of months, one of them would not be in New York on Sunday nights herself; she was about to go off to college. Still, it was true that they couldn't imagine New York without Fats. Neither could my wife, even after Fats assured her that he would return every year to carve the Christmas turkey. Neither could I. "But I'm your Boswell, Fat Person," I finally said. "I'm supposed to be nearby, in case pearls of wisdom drop from your lips. I'm not *ready* to go back home."

I realize that "unbeknownst to our hero" is not the sort of phrase Boswell would ordinarily use. But early in 1985 some events occurred in Kansas City that would affect Fats Goldberg's homecoming, and they were, I feel certain, not only events unbeknownst to our hero but also events of the sort that might make him a little twitchy. The events revolved around a flamboyant music professor named John Swanay, who operated in Kansas City as a sort of Oscar Wilde character — a sort of character that, I must admit, is not ordinarily thought of in connection with my home town.

Swanay was widely spoken of as a Renaissance man — someone accomplished not only in his own field of musicology but in foreign languages, living and dead, and poetry and philosophy and the theater and gourmet cooking. He affected a waxed mustache and a white beard and a beret. There were people who remained unimpressed by Swanay — some of the students and faculty at the University of Missouri at Kansas City Conservatory of Music would have been happier if he had spent a bit less of his classroom time railing against the philistines and a bit more teaching introductory music theory — but he had attracted what the *Star* called "a devoted band of followers from his students and the upper crust of Kansas City society."

Swanay lived in an apartment that had been carved out of the ground floor of an old carriage house, in a grand old neighborhood that included several of Kansas City's major cultural institutions — the Nelson-Atkins Museum of Art, the Kansas City Art Institute, the University of Missouri at Kansas City. A young man named Mitchell Burroughs lived there with him; Burroughs had shown up a dozen years before, at the age of fifteen, to study yoga with Swanay. The carriage house was decorated with Victorian furniture and cut glass and a profusion of candelabras. On Friday or Saturday evenings, it was often the scene of elaborate dinner parties at which Swanay, working in a tiny kitchen, somehow managed to turn out, say, an authentic Hindu feast or a precise replica of a meal prepared for King Richard II in 1387. The Friday feasts evolved into what amounted to an unlisted, one-seating restaurant — until some city authorities stopped by to mention such bourgeois details as restaurant licensing and the collection of sales tax.

Eventually, Swanay took early retirement at UMKC to fulfill his dream of opening a true gourmet restaurant in Kansas City. Some people who had been brought to one of the carriage-house evenings — Neil Murry III and his wife, Belinda — agreed to become partners in the project. An old house was renovated to become a restaurant called the Painted Lady. John Swanay was the chef. Mitchell Burroughs was his assistant. The administration was handled mainly by Belinda Murry, who continued to work part time as an aerobic-dance instructor at the Mademoiselle Lady's Spa, in the Ward Parkway shopping mall. Relations between her and Swanay were bad. Always a volatile man, Swanay had become even more prone to sudden explosions of temper — perhaps, some of his friends thought, because the pressures of running a restaurant kitchen were way beyond anything experienced by someone accustomed to preparing one carefully arranged banquet a week. A few weeks after the opening of the Painted Lady, Swanay came in one afternoon to find that Mrs. Murry had put a settee in the vestibule without consulting him. He was furious. When Neil Murry dropped his wife off at the restaurant a couple of hours later, Swanay was there to confront her. He had a gun. Before she could say anything, he shot her twice, killing her almost instantly. Then he began chasing Neil Murry, taking shots that missed Murry but wounded a bystander. Finally, Mitchell Burroughs caught up with Swanay in a parking lot. Apparently fulfilling a suicide pact, Burroughs killed his mentor with one shot to the head and then killed himself.

People in Kansas City were, of course, horrified at the tragedy, and there was widespread speculation about what could have turned a Renaissance man, however eccentric, into someone responsible for three violent deaths, including his own. Even someone who had long lived in New York, where violent death is more common, would presumably have reacted the same way to the news — but only after the first, almost instinctive Manhattan response: in that case, the carriage-house apartment must be available. A couple of window dressers got it first. Then, in March of 1986, it became the new home of Larry (Fats) Goldberg, the former New York pizza baron.

"But I don't understand what you do all day, Fat Person," I said.

"I talk on the phone a lot, and I horse around," Fats said.

I was sitting in the carriage-house apartment, in a chair shaped like a baseball mitt — a piece of furniture, it occurred to me, that would have almost certainly driven John Swanay to violence. This was nearly a year after Fats moved back home, and I was trying to catch up, feeling a bit the way Boswell would have felt if he had remained in London while Dr. Johnson traipsed around the Hebrides dropping pithy sayings in the company of people who didn't listen or wouldn't understand or didn't have a quill pen handy or couldn't read and write. I don't mean that Fats and I had completely lost contact. I had been to Kansas City half a dozen times to see my mother — she happens to live only two floors away from Fats's mother — and each time Fats and I had spent an afternoon or an evening in activities that I suppose fall within the category of horsing around. One afternoon, for instance, we sniffed out a new barbecue joint not ten blocks from where my own grandfather once ran a grocery store, checked out the steers at the cattle barn of the American Royal Livestock Show, and, thus inspired, drove to the national headquarters of the American Polled Hereford Association to buy some of the APHA mechanical pencils that have a tiny cow floating in a plastic bubble at the tip, where most pencils have erasers. (Arthur Bryant used to hand out the same sort of mechanical pencils, except that the motto inscribed on his was not "THE TREND IS TO POLLED HEREFORDS" but "THE HOUSE OF GOOD EATS.") Also, Fats had returned to New York for both Halloween and Christmas, the two holidays we celebrate with considerable vigor at our house. We all thought that he seemed cheerful enough, except for the moment on Halloween when a pained look flashed across his face as I informed him that his fortune-cookie costume was in our basement, just in case he wanted to zip himself up into it for the Village Halloween parade. But Fats has always seemed cheerful. He had seemed cheerful even when he was walking around Bloomingdale's in his fortune-cookie costume — a foray into merchandising that he later summed up simply as "the worst experience of my life." But as the end of Fats's first year in Kansas City approached I had decided that I'd better make a special trip home to bring myself up to date on how he was faring. What are Boswells for?

I had asked Fats what he did all day because I knew that one thing he was not doing was running a pizza operation in Prairie Village. Fats had backed out of the deal just a few weeks after he ar-

rived in town. After that, he hadn't done much in a business way
beyond running a Controlled Cheating diet group, which met
weekly in a cafeteria at the Ward Parkway shopping mall. The news
that Goldberg was out of the Prairie Village operation had caused
concern among some of his fans in New York — after all, that deal
was supposedly the reason Fats had moved to Kansas City — but
Fats himself seemed unfazed. He said he'd open a spot in Kansas
City sooner or later. He said four separate groups of investors had
expressed interest in backing him. He said he could always find another location. "Everything's easy here," he said to me. "In this
town, lawyers call you back."

On one trip to Kansas City, I had actually gone with Fats to take
a look at some space on the Country Club Plaza — or, as we ordinarily say when out-of-town visitors are within earshot, the world-
famous Country Club Plaza. Built in the thirties with a Spanish
motif that suggests an exceptionally tidy Granada, the Plaza is still
probably the most desirable place in town for a retail business.
Goldberg's Pizzeria would have been the only pizza parlor on the
Plaza, but Fats expressed some reservations about the precise site
of the space and the price being asked for the lease and fixtures of a
bar that was operating there. On my next trip home, I asked him
how the Plaza deal had turned out, and he said he had cooled on
that one, partly because his mind had begun to turn away from
pizza and in the direction of bagels. "I think bagels are the ticket,"
he said. "What do you think?"

"I'm not sure I feel qualified to comment, Fat Man," I said. As it
happens, one of the most treasured childhood remarks of my older
daughter was that in Kansas City bagels tasted like just round
bread, but I had no way of knowing whether quality in bagels was
the sort of thing that preoccupied a significant number of the full-
time residents.

When I arrived for what I had begun to think of as the twelve-
month inspection and lubrication, Fats was still extolling bagels, although he assured me that a pizza operation was still a possibility.
He didn't seem to be in any hurry to make up his mind, even
though he talked a lot about the necessity of finding something

to do before the New York pizza payouts came to an end.

"If I'm not working this time next year, it's going to be Aid to Dependent Children time," he said.

"You don't have any children, Fats," I reminded him.

He ignored that. Apparently, he had been speaking Goldbergian metaphor, and I, being out of practice, had missed it.

I didn't have to ask Fats about who was available to horse around with when I wasn't in town. The first report I had brought back to New York about Fats's new life in Kansas City was that he had fallen in with a good crowd. The crowd's headquarters was, to my surprise, an elegant shop called Asiatica. Fats had met the proprietors through a pal of many years, a restaurant consultant named Bonnie Winston — although it turned out that he had known one of them, Fifi White, many years before. When Fifi was in high school, Fats, just then turned loose by the University of Missouri as the heaviest graduate of the School of Journalism, had worked for her father's company in a job he describes this way: "I was hired to write a catalogue, but I mainly counted Japanese thong sandals and threw them in a bin." Now that Fats and Fifi are both grownups, he has confessed that he used to fantasize about her as he counted sandals, but he has also admitted that he might have had a somewhat stronger fantasy concerning the spaghetti and meatballs at an Italian place just down the street. Since the sandal-counting days, Fifi has been a graduate student in the history of art at Columbia — her special interest was always in textiles — and a weaver and a collector of rare and antique textiles and, eventually, a designer. She now turns out chic, understated, expensive women's clothing made of kimono cloth and other old fabrics brought from Japan. She is also, on occasion, an informal consultant to Fats Goldberg on matters of dress. I doubt if her sense of style or her knowledge of fabrics makes that task any easier, but she must draw strength from having had up-to-date experience as the mother of two teenagers. Fifi can reproduce practically verbatim a conversation she had with Fats about what he should wear to the funeral of a friend's mother-in-law.

"How about my plum number?" Fats asked, referring to his plum-colored corduroy sports jacket. "I'm thinking of wearing it with either my white 501s or my banana-yellow 501s."

"I have to admit that plum and banana yellow has never been my favorite combination, Goldberg, but the important thing is that you're there."

"I was thinking of my checkerboard sweater," Fats said, mentioning a garment that bursts through the restraints of the conventional two-color checkerboard.

"Well, of course, the checkerboard sweater will provide a link for just about any color combination . . ."

Fifi White's partner at Asiatica, Elizabeth Wilson, was also a graduate student in art history, specializing, at Berkeley, in Chinese paintings of the thirteenth century. During a year spent in Taiwan on a grant, she met Marc Wilson, a Yale graduate student with precisely the same specialty. They were married, and Marc Wilson eventually became the director of the Nelson-Atkins Museum — whose Chinese collection, not to boast, is even more famous than the Country Club Plaza. After a time, Elizabeth Wilson opened a shop to sell antiques and other objects that had caught her eye on trips to the Far East — a shop that would not be out of place at Sixty-fifth and Madison, except that one of the exquisite Chinese chairs is often occupied by a thin man wearing running shoes, white Levi's, and an orange sweatshirt over a red turtleneck.

From that perch, Fats can continue his opinion survey on the question of pizza versus bagels. He can arrange for company if he wants to go to the movies or — on cheating days — wants to repair to a fried-chicken joint and do what he calls "some heavy-duty business." He can regale his pals with stories of the real girls he has met at events like singles night at Bob's IGA supermarket in Overland Park — a gathering at which the ice-breaking activities include dancing to a live country band and competing in Oreo-stacking contests. I once asked Elizabeth Wilson what Fats did when the conversation turned from Oreo stacking to, say, medieval Chinese painting. We're talking here, after all, about a man who at the height of his Manhattan museum-crawling days made a policy decision to "work the lobby" of the Whitney rather than go in, since it resulted in as many dates and saved the dollar-fifty admission.

Elizabeth said that she had engaged in only one extended debate with Goldberg on the subject of aesthetics — a debate prompted by some negative comments one of the guest speakers at the Nelson had made on the paintings of Andrew Wyeth. Elizabeth's position was that some painters are demonstrably superior to other painters — that, for example, Picasso was a better artist than Walter Keane, who used to turn out those big-eyed-children paintings that made so many people want to close their own eyes. Goldberg's position was that it was all a matter of what a person liked. I could see the problem. Fats is completely nonjudgmental. His friends acknowledge, for instance, that when it comes to truly cutting gossip he is absolutely worthless.

"How did the rest of the argument go?" I asked.

"Well, I turned it right away to barbecue," Elizabeth told me. "I said, 'You can't tell me that there is no difference between a barbecue-beef sandwich at some place like Bryant's in its heyday and the barbecue-beef sandwich you find at the Kmart snack bar sitting under the hot light. There are standards that can be measured — the sauce, the quality of the meat.' "

"Brilliant!" I said, thinking that all those years of graduate school had not been wasted on Elizabeth Wilson. "What did he say to that?"

"He said that some people like Kmart barbecue-beef sandwiches, and it all depends on what you like."

It was Elizabeth Wilson who told Fats about the Swanay apartment. The Wilsons live in one of half a dozen apartments that have been carved out of the main house — a large stone pile on the other side of the driveway. Fats says it's all sort of like a fraternity-sorority house, although I suspect his apartment is the only one that actually includes among its design elements a fraternity paddle and a group picture of the brothers. Fats is strong on memorabilia. His apartment also has a life-size cardboard cutout of Fats at three hundred and twenty pounds, a seat taken from Yankee Stadium during the renovation, a picture of the grocery store his parents ran just underneath the family living quarters ("seventeen steps down to my food heaven"), a *Chicago Tribune* newsdealer's apron that Fats got when he sold ads for the *Tribune* as a fat man, a copy of *Controlled Cheating* in German (*Schwindel-Diät*), a color picture of Fats and his very own Boswell at the Smithsonian opening, a 45-r.p.m. record of "Caravan" that dates from a time just after college when Fats was a disk jockey known as the Sheik of Columbia, a shirt he was given for having modeled it in an Asiatica brochure, and the leather medicine pouch he made when he was inducted into the Great Tribe of Mic-O-Say at Camp Osceola Boy Scout camp and thus became for a time Brave Smoke of Many Fires.

I was astonished that Fats still had his Mic-O-Say pouch — it made me wonder, just for a moment, what ever happened to mine — and I was puzzled about why the Asiatica shirt was hanging in the living room. Fats said he had decided that he couldn't possibly get full value out of a three-hundred-dollar shirt — even a three-hundred-dollar shirt he got free — by wearing it, so he put it on display. "My whole wardrobe isn't worth three hundred dollars," he said. He quickly added, though, that his Spalding saddle shoes were probably priceless. "I only break my Spaldings out for special occasions, when I really want to get tootsied up," he said as he unwrapped them to give me a look. I hadn't seen them since the Smithsonian opening — if Fats had found an occasion worthy of his Spaldings in the ten years after that, I hadn't been there to record it — and I told him they were looking good, the plaid laces having been a splendid addition. Fats flicked what may have been a speck of dust off one of them and said, "I expect to get straightened out in the Louis Funeral Home in these some day."

We were walking to lunch before it struck me for the first time that Fats was now living permanently in what for him had always been a dietary DMZ — a place where he had always concentrated so hard on "heavy-duty eating" that it was common for him to gain fifteen pounds in a ten-day visit. Fats said he made the adjustment with no problem. He simply transferred his New York eating regimen to Kansas City: he eats on Wednesdays and Saturdays, and allows himself eighteen additional cheating days a year. He doesn't binge in New York. There are eating experiences in New York that he misses — pastrami, corned beef, the Palm steakhouse, bagels that taste nothing at all like round bread — but he is more certain than ever that, all in all, he would rather eat back home. "New York undoubtedly has the best restaurants in the world, but they're not for me," Fats said. "I like barbecue, fried chicken, cheeseburgers — straight-ahead stuff."

"What did you have on your last cheating day, Fats?" I asked.

"Let me see," Fats said. "I started with a twist from Lamar's Donuts and an apple fritter from the Price Chopper and some coffee. Then I had three breakfast pizzas at David's Cookies. I was trying them out for a little number I do on KMBZ once a week called the Lone Eater. They were pretty good. I rated them at two and a half burps. Then I had a triple cheeseburger with everything at Winstead's, plus French-fried onion rings and a frosty. A dip of chocolate almond ice cream at Famous Amos, in Prairie Village. A forty-six-ounce Pepsi. A slab of ribs at Wyandot Barbecue and French fries and half a quart of Coke. Then a pint of chocolate chip ice cream. I can't eat as much as I used to. I used to be nonstop. I used to move right along."

By then, we had arrived at the restaurant, the Prospect of Westport — a place whose menu turned out to include mascarpone torte and black bean pâté and ratatouille pie and tomato-jalapeño pasta and a number of other items that didn't seem to fall into the category of straight-ahead stuff. Bonnie Winston, who advises the Prospect, had joined us for lunch, and the presence of someone in the trade naturally turned the conversation toward Fats's commercial future. I asked Bonnie if Fats should go into the bagel business or the pizza business.

"I don't think it matters," she said. "The product is incidental. Larry is a terrific standup comic waiting for a place to land. He'd do well in any kind of place." Then she looked at Fats and added, "But it's time already."

Fats agreed that it was time, but when the subject came up again after lunch he still sounded reluctant to make a move. Fats and I were driving out to visit our mothers, after a detour at McLain's Bakery so that he could pick up a few bear claws for his mom. ("The old lady's a sugar junkie, kid.") He said he'd be happier about going into business again if he had a partner — preferably a female partner — to work alongside him and talk over problems with him.

"I think what they call one of those is a wife, Fat Person," I said.

"I can't just jump into a deal," Fats said, ignoring, as usual, the reference to marriage. "It's got to feel right."

Then the conversation turned to the chewable diet book. That and the pizza cone had been Goldberg's most persistent schemes in New York. He had finally decided that the pizza cone would always be crippled by its appearance. "The visuals are no good," Fats said. "People want to see the stuff, and in the pizza cone it's all wrapped up." The chewable diet book was another matter. "It's the greatest idea that ever happened," Fats said. "I'm going to get the job done one of these days, and then I'll be on easy street."

That evening, Fats called to say that after months of silence he had heard from the bar proprietor who owned the lease on the space we'd inspected on the Plaza. The bar proprietor was apparently ready to come down considerably on his price. "Things are moving right along," Fats said. "This might be the ticket."

The next day, we didn't talk about the Plaza pizza opportunity right away — Fats and I were driving out to the Ward Parkway shopping mall early, so that I could join him on his morning walk — because I'd been wondering whether life in Kansas City had turned out to be what he'd envisioned during all those years he lived in New York. People in New York who talk about going back home, after all, have fears that their home town has changed a lot while they were gone, and fears that it hasn't. The vision of home town that most of us cling to has nothing to do with authentic Hindu banquets or elegant clothes made of kimono cloth. How would we respond if we went home expecting apple pie and found ratatouille pie instead? On the other hand, a Midwesterner in New York may know of ghosts of adolescence that lurk, unchanged, in his home town; he may be unsettled by the thought of finding himself in the supermarket line with both of the people who remember precisely how he behaved on graduation night. Moving back would mean facing the closeup perils of what I have always thought of as the Midwestern Adjustment to the Psychoanalytic Theory: Everybody's who he was in high school.

Fats said none of that had proved to be a problem. He is not the sort of person who would let something like the transformation of American society over the past thirty years affect old habits. A few months before my visit, he had led a visiting reporter from the *New York Times* on a tour of the sort of restaurants he calls grease pits — the telling quote from Goldberg was "Let's face it: grease makes things taste good" — and seemed genuinely puzzled when some boosters didn't think the resultant article on the way Kansas Citians eat reflected the sort of image the city is trying to project. The ghosts Fats finds in Kansas City are ghosts of another person — the Fats Goldberg who still had his Graziano. "It's like coming into a new city," he told me. "It's a whole new life. Before, I spent my time finding something to eat. I left here a fat guy everybody wrote off. I didn't have any dates. I didn't go to any parties. No one spoke to me except to ask me to move my 1937 Oldsmobile because it was leaking oil on the driveway." Fats drives a snappy red Honda now, and there is often someone on the passenger side. In fact, he took out the salesperson from the Honda agency for a while, until he finally decided that he would never be able to replace her softball team as an object of her affection.

"What do you miss most about New York?" I asked.

"I miss the spritzing on the streets — the yelling, the screaming," he said. "Here, people don't even honk their horns." Fats is enough of a New Yorker to find it off-putting to walk down the street for miles without hearing anybody call anybody else any names at all — which is why we were heading for the Ward Parkway shopping mall. Fats, who walks half an hour a day and two hours on Sunday, sometimes uses Loose Park, a pleasant park just south of the world-famous Country Club Plaza, but he usually does his walking on the second level of the Ward Parkway shopping mall. At Ward Parkway, he gets climate control, convenient rest rooms, and, most of all, company. Ward Parkway has been a center for mall walkers for years. Before ten, while most of the stores are still closed, several dozen people can usually be found making the circuit of what becomes a third-of-a-mile track on the mall's second level. Most of the walkers are in their middle years or older. Some of them are outfitted in matching sweatclothes and running shoes; some of them stroll along in street clothes, as if they were window-shopping. Fats seemed to know most of them. He waved at some of the strolling couples and said hello to a couple of the serious walkers who were, as Fats would put it, "really going to town." Before he started making the circuit himself, he checked in with the crowd of retirees who, after their early-morning walks, gather at the tables in front of Swensen's Ice Cream — tables that have umbrellas protecting them from whatever sun and rain can find their way into an indoor shopping mall — and drink thirty-seven-cent cups of coffee (unlimited refills) from the Woolworth snack bar next door. Then, after a cheerful "Hiya, guys, how you doin'?" to two white-haired women who were moving along at a moderate pace, he began his morning walk.

I had thought Fats and I might talk about the Plaza space while we walked, but I found that I couldn't keep up with him unless I broke into a run every so often. Apparently, only three or four walkers at the Ward Parkway shopping mall can keep up with him. Fats walks with his arms held high in front of his chest — an elderly woman he met in Loose Park told him he'd get more oxygen that way — so he looks like someone who has something on his hands that he doesn't intend to get anywhere near his body. He seems to be completely flat-footed, maybe from dragging around a Graziano all those years. As he races along past J. C. Penney and Benetton and Function Junction and B. Dalton and Baker's Qualicraft Shoes, he looks as if he might be competing in a race that the American Podiatry Association holds for people with sore feet — and winning.

Shortly after Fats started, Fifi White showed up, and I made the circuit with her for a while. I told her that she seemed to walk almost fast enough to walk with Goldberg.

"Maybe you can put in a good word for me," she said. She explained that as of now she was permitted to walk with Goldberg only during the last thirty minutes of his Sunday outing and on an occasional afternoon "stretch." The Sunday arrangement was the result of Fats's having figured out, with the aid of a calculator, that slowing down to Fifi's pace for half an hour would mean losing the equivalent of only twenty or thirty fewer calories than would be lost at full speed. Fifi was not surprised that Goldberg altered his schedule for her at the sacrifice of thirty calories — she and Fats are quite close — but I don't think she'd take any bets on what would have happened if the calculations had shown a difference of seventy-five or a hundred. Goldberg, Fifi reminded me, is amiable but set in his ways.

Fats finally finished, and joined me at one of the Swensen's tables. He didn't even seem winded. Suddenly, apropos of nothing, he said, "Do you know what I miss in New York? The Carlyle Hotel."

"You mean the sense of elegance?" I asked.

"No, no," Fats said. "The bathroom. It's all white marble in there. I love the Carlyle. When I win the lottery, I'm going to live at the Carlyle."

"You ought to move back," Fats said the evening before I was due to leave Kansas City. "At least you ought to get a pied-à-terre." As if he couldn't quite bring himself to use a term of French origin, Fats pronounced it "peed-a-tare."

"I don't think people keep pied-à-terres in Kansas City, Fat Man," I said. "Except maybe people from Fort Scott or Sedalia."

"Don't you ever miss Kansas City?" Fats asked.

I had to admit that I was enjoying the horsing around. Fats and I were on our way to Stroud's fried-chicken restaurant to lay in a supply of the sweatshirts that carry Stroud's spectacular motto: "WE CHOKE OUR OWN CHICKENS." From there we planned to hit the Corinth Square shopping center. I'd admired some bright-orange-and-red work gloves Fats had just bought — orange and red are practically Fats Goldberg's national colors — and he thought I owed it to myself to visit the hardware store where they were selling for a dollar seventy-nine a pair. There had been some talk of going from Corinth Square to the Swope Park zoo — not far from Shelter House No. 4, which my family had always favored for Fourth of July picnics.

I also had to admit that Fats seemed fine in Kansas City, although I wouldn't say that means the Wall Street trader from Des Moines can put aside any fears he may have about going home. Fats is, to say the very least, a special case. He travels light. He carries his routine with him. He says hello to everyone he sees, wherever he is. He is someone who was cheerful even while costumed as a fortune cookie. "Listen, I'm just happy to be here," he told me. "I was supposed to check out thirty years ago. I'm glad to be alive. They'd have put me in a piano crate and lowered me into the ground."

His pals Fifi and Elizabeth agreed that Fats was fine, but they figured the sooner he went into business the better. ("He needs a stage.") Fats had, in fact, made a few more phone calls about the pizza parlor on the Plaza, and he said the deal continued to look promising. If he didn't do that, he said, he'd simply do something else — in Kansas City. He lived there. Just to confirm that, I got out the telephone directory that night and looked at the column headed "GOLDBERG." Sure enough, about halfway down was a listing for "Larry Fats."

"It's too bad you can't stay tomorrow," Fats said when I left him the next morning at the Ward Parkway shopping mall. "It's a cheating day."

"We'll do it next time, Fat Man," I said. "I've got to get home."

A week after I got back, Fats reported by telephone that the Plaza deal was moving right along, but a couple of weeks after that he said it had fallen through.

"Are you going to look for another spot?" I asked.

"Oh, sure," Fats said. "But do you remember my idea of a food tour of New York?"

"Vaguely."

"Some travel lady wants to do it here."

"Do you mean you'd take them for a tour of the grease pits?"

"Oh, I think I might stop for a piece of lettuce somewhere," Fats said. "Then maybe we'd have a special tour for just barbecue. What do you think?"

"It's better than the Plexiglas pizza pusher."

"This might be the ticket," Fats said. "She thinks it's the best idea in the whole world. She's ready to move right along."

1987

YOU DON'T ASK,
YOU DON'T GET

THEY STARTED OUT as the Ermines. It sounded fancy. There were four of them in the group, all students at Stitt Junior High School in the Washington Heights section of upper Manhattan. The group, like the neighborhood, was mixed — part black, part Puerto Rican. It came into existence when Herman Santiago and Joe Negroni, who had been singing together, merged with Sherman Garnes and Jimmy Merchant. This was in 1955. The Ermines sang on the street, the way kids from such neighborhoods later did break dancing on the street — but not for money. "It was a fad at the time to be a vocal group," Jimmy Merchant said many years afterward. "It wasn't just like roller-skating. It was a higher-class fad — a quality fad. It tied in to being known, and getting girls." Apparently, Merchant and Sherman Garnes didn't consider the Ermines a quality name, so the Ermines became the Coupe de Villes. Car names were popular then. There were at least two other groups named after Cadillacs. For a while, the Coupe de Villes had a fifth member — five was the standard number for street-corner-harmony groups — but apparently he was never able to overcome the bedrock disadvantage of having no talent for singing. Or maybe he found some other way to get girls. Such details in the early history of the group tend to be hazy. Why would junior high school kids who sing together think that their after-school activities were worth remembering with great precision?

Everyone agrees, though, that the geographical center of the group was West 165th Street, between Edgecombe Avenue and Amsterdam Avenue. Stitt Junior High School was there. Sherman Garnes and Herman Santiago lived on the block. So did another Stitt student, named Frankie Lymon. He was a couple of years younger and a lot smaller than the four Coupe de Villes, but in some ways he seemed more mature — someone Jimmy Merchant thought of as "this midget who was a man." Although Frankie was not yet thirteen, he sometimes worked as a clerk in a convenience store called the Excel-O Mart, on the corner of 165th and Amsterdam. He had sung publicly, not just in Stitt talent shows but with his father's gospel group, the Harlemaires. He was, in the words of Herman Santiago, "extremely talented and bright and very cocky." According to one version of how Frankie joined the group, he happened to be hanging around a 165th Street stoop one day when Herman Santiago was having trouble hitting the high notes as the lead singer in one of the first original songs the group had come up with — "I Want You to Be My Girl." There are other versions of the story, all having to do with a voice that had no trouble with the high notes. Frankie had a sort of gospel tenor — a high, strong voice of remarkable clarity. Particularly in conjunction with Sherman Garnes's bass, an unusually low bass for a fifteen-year-old, it helped give the Coupe de Villes a sound of their own. Except that sooner or later the Coupe de Villes were no longer the Coupe de Villes. They had become the Premiers.

One of the tenants of the building that held the Excel-O Mart was a young man from Philadelphia named Richard Barrett, who sang with a group called the Valentines. Barrett had some prestige on West 165th Street: the Valentines sang indoors. They were singing then at the Apollo Theatre, on 125th Street, in fact, and they had done pretty well with a record called "Lily Maebelle." According to Barrett, he met the Coupe de Villes because they used to sing "Lily Maebelle" outside his window — they presumably knew that he was beginning to work part time as an A. & R. man for a record company downtown — and he finally told them that if they'd quit bothering him when he was trying to sleep he'd come over to their rehearsal at Stitt to hear what they could do. There are other versions of that one, too. None of them contest the basic fact that Richard Barrett, impressed by what he heard, took the group downtown and presented it to George Goldner, the record-company proprietor who had put out "Lily Maebelle."

Downtown meant white. It didn't mean RCA Victor. In the mid-fifties, respectable, mainstream pop music — the kind heard on records put out by Victor and Capitol and Decca — was dominated by crooners. There were a few black recording artists, of course, but the customary response of pop-music producers to an appealing song they heard sung on a black rhythm-and-blues label was to "cover" it — re-record it with a white star. The attitude of the pop-music industry toward rock ranged from such quiet absorption to outright hostility. In their book *Rock 'n' Roll Is Here to Pay*, Steve Chapple and Reebee Garofalo quote from some testimony before a congressional committee in 1958 saying that rock was "the most brutal, ugly, desperate, vicious form of expression it has been my misfortune to hear," that it was written and sung "for the most part by cretinous goons," and that "by means of its almost imbecilic reiterations and sly — lewd — in plain fact dirty — lyrics . . . [it] manages to be the martial music of every sideburned delinquent on the face of the earth." The concerned citizen who so testified was Frank Sinatra.

The producers who actually put out rhythm-and-blues records were on the fringes of the industry — hustling independents who were sometimes imaginative in their judgments and almost always creative in their bookkeeping. George Goldner had moved into rhythm and blues from Latin, another fringe. He was known in the business as a good promoter and a bad horseplayer. "I think in my heart if he hadn't gambled he wouldn't have shorted anybody," Richard Barrett has said. "But everybody shorts somebody." When it came to handling money that somehow didn't find its way to the black teenagers who were often both the performers and the writers of rhythm-and-blues songs, the difference between George Goldner and the other entrepreneurs of early rock might have been that the others didn't have horseplaying as an excuse. The Premiers, on their first business trip downtown, were wowed by George Goldner. Thirty-five years later, Jimmy Merchant still had a picture in his mind of what Goldner was wearing: "He had an embroidered shirt, long pointed shoes, and black silk socks. You could see through the socks, they were so silky. He had on a mohair suit."

Goldner agreed to record a 45 by the Premiers, apparently squeezing the session into the dinner break of a recording session with a group called the Millionaires. Herman Santiago was still doing most of the lead singing then; the novelty of singing R&B songs in a Hispanic accent had been part of the group's appeal to Barrett. But, for one reason or another — maybe because Santiago had a cold that day, maybe because of Goldner's preference — it was Frankie Lymon who was the lead singer of the Premiers at the recording session. Except that they were no longer the Premiers. When the record came out, in late 1955, the group was called the Teenagers, the lead singer was Frankie Lymon, and the song was one of their own, developed on West 165th Street — "Why Do Fools Fall in Love?" It was an instant, stupendous hit.

"Why Do Fools Fall in Love?" went to No. 6 on the charts — not the rhythm-and-blues charts, the pop charts. Under their final name — Frankie Lymon and the Teenagers — the group broke through to become a phenomenally successful crossover act. They didn't play the Apollo; they played "The Ed Sullivan Show." (In Sullivan's teaser announcements through the program about what was still to come, he continually referred to Frankie as Frankie Robinson.) The Teenagers were not considered threatening to whites, probably because of Frankie, who came across as the sassy, pint-size kid brother who would never grow up. Bouncing around in front of the group, Frankie managed to ask all the questions — Why do fools fall in love? Why do birds sing so gay? — and never quit smiling. The Teenagers came in a squeaky-clean package — processed hair and the sort of clothes familiar from Hollywood campus movies of the forties, including letter sweaters. At one point, Frankie led them in a syrupy appeal to parents called "I'm Not a Juvenile Delinquent." Although they never came up with a song to equal the blockbuster "Why Do Fools Fall in Love?" they had three or four more hits. And they were stars. For thousands of other kids singing what some people called streetcorner harmony and other people were beginning to call doo-wop, the Teenagers were the model, the proof that a miracle could happen. In a way, the Teenagers were rock stars before the era of the rock star — before it was even clear how rock stars were expected to behave. Jimmy Merchant has said, "We were the first people to get out of long limousines with sneakers and jeans on."

Stardom lasted almost exactly eighteen months. After a tour of Great Britain, Frankie split off to do a single act, and the four remaining Teenagers got themselves another lead singer. Frankie couldn't repeat his hits, and neither could the Teenagers. Frankie had some other problems. His voice was changing — a change that would leave him sounding like a perfectly adequate but unremarkable crooner. Even worse than that, he was a junkie. He did club appearances as a solo for a while, but as his drug problem worsened he had more and more trouble booking jobs. Jerry Blavat, a disk jockey who has always specialized in the songs of the fifties and sixties, gave him an occasional hundred and fifty dollars or so to appear at one of the record hops Blavat held in Philadelphia — events at which the guest star had only to lip-synch to his record. Before Blavat became a d.j., he had been the road manager for Danny and the Juniors, and he remembered Lymon from those days as a mischievous kid whose idea of backstage entertainment was to hide Paul Anka's shoes just before Anka had to be onstage. It was a different Frankie Lymon who lip-synched in the middle sixties. He was beginning to look puffy. He was missing a couple of teeth. He had started borrowing from people in the business. Sooner or later, he was panhandling or stealing. He was arrested at least once for possession, and once for stealing a set of drums. Occasionally, he'd be hospitalized for a cure. More than once, he announced his reformation with some fanfare. On one of those occasions, in January of 1967, a piece in *Ebony* quoted him as confessing, among other things, that he had been a juvenile delinquent after all — someone who smoked a lot of marijuana in grade school, and was pimping for local girls before he was twelve, and had what amounted to a stable of older women during those eighteen months when he was cast as a cute little cutup.

Around the time of the *Ebony* piece, Lymon went into the Army, apparently as an alternative to going to jail. At Fort Gordon, outside Augusta, Georgia, he seemed to be in better shape than he had been in for some years. He was hardly a model soldier. He was never finicky about staying on the base when he was supposed to be on duty, for instance, and he eventually ended up with a less than honorable discharge. In August, though, the scrapes he got into seemed less serious — drinking bouts instead of heroin addiction, for instance, and arrests for driving without a license rather than for theft. His lawyer, Maxwell T. Cohen, was moved to write Lymon that those who cared about him "rejoice in the fact that the sun is beginning to shine for you." In Augusta, Frankie married a respectable woman, an elementary school teacher named Emira Eagle. After his discharge, they lived with her mother, but they discussed building a house of their own. For a while, Frankie appeared on weekends at the Capri Lounge in the local Howard Johnson Motor Lodge. His wife, having caught on to how Frankie dealt with ready cash, went to the Capri Lounge herself to pick up his paychecks. Emira Lymon was hoping that Frankie would be able to use Augusta as a base — another bar, called Trudy & Bill's, had expressed some interest in booking him — and take short road trips while she remained at her teaching job. Then, in February of 1968, he apparently got an encouraging call from his new manager about a weekend job in New York. He left in the middle of the week, planning to stay at his grandmother's — the apartment he had grown up in on 165th Street. A couple of days later, Emira Lymon got a call from New York. Frankie had been found dead in the bathroom of his grandmother's apartment. He had died from an overdose of heroin.

Frankie Lymon was twenty-five years old when he died, and he had been a has-been for more than ten years. The other Teenagers didn't fare a lot better than Frankie. Some of them had problems with drugs or alcohol. In another ten years, Joe Negroni and Sherman Garnes were also dead. Jimmy Merchant was driving a cab. Ordinarily, that might have been that. Among rock-history buffs, the Teenagers would have been remembered mainly as an early example of a successful crossover group, and Frankie Lymon would have been remembered mainly as an early example of a rock singer destroying himself with drugs. What kept Frankie Lymon and the Teenagers from being confined to those footnotes of rock history was one monumental hit song — "Why Do Fools Fall in Love?"

A pop song was once thought of as the paradigm of a creation that is on everyone's lips for a few moments and is then forgotten forever. As it turned out, though, nostalgia for the early days of rock became almost a spinoff industry in itself. "Why Do Fools Fall in Love?" became what is sometimes referred to as a rock classic, a staple of oldies albums and rock-trivia quizzes. In 1973, it was featured on the soundtrack of the film *American Graffiti*, a film that had a lot to do with the demand for oldies. In 1981, Diana Ross did a recording of "Why Do Fools Fall in Love?" that went nearly to the top of the charts. It was clear by then that the songwriter royalties for "Why Do Fools Fall in Love?" would represent a serious income for the foreseeable future. As it happened, though, precisely who wrote "Why Do Fools Fall in Love?" was one detail in the early history of the Teenagers that was particularly hazy.

There was a time in American popular music when a song reached the public almost entirely through sheet music. The song's publisher produced and distributed and promoted the sheet music — more or less the way a book publisher produces and distributes and promotes a book — and for that received fifty percent of the royalties. Now that a song reaches the public mainly through records or tapes or videos, the publisher's role has been reduced to registering the copyright for the song with the Library of Congress and dealing with the royalties from soundtracks and re-recordings. (Royalties from radio stations and nightclubs and jukebox operators are collected by one of the monitoring organizations, ASCAP or BMI, and sent in separate checks to the writer and the publisher.) One thing that hasn't changed is the percentage of the take: the publisher still normally gets fifty percent of the royalties. "Why Do Fools Fall in Love?" was published by one of George Goldner's companies — another one of his companies, Gee, put out the record — and the writers of the song listed on the copyright that Goldner registered with the Library of Congress were Frank Lymon and George Goldner.

Like many of the early rock entrepreneurs, George Goldner may have grown up on the street himself, but not West 165th Street. How could he have been one of the writers of "Why Do Fools Fall in Love?" Richard Barrett says, "He might have tried to change a word or two here and there." Then again, he might not have. Although listing someone's name as a writer of a song legally means that he literally participated in writing the song, it was common practice in the fifties for an R&B record producer to tell a group that he'd have to have a writing credit if it wanted its song recorded — or to put his name on the copyright application without telling the group anything. "We had no idea of the value of a song then," Barrett has said. "We had no idea what the value of a copyright was. And they weren't going to tell any black people about that anyway." So George Goldner had half of the royalties as the publisher and half of the remaining half as a co-writer. In the late fifties — after "Why Do Fools Fall in Love?" finished its first run on the charts but before the onset of the oldies craze — Goldner may not have had much of an idea of the future value of the song himself. As it turned out, though, the future value would not be his. Because of his gambling habit, Goldner was losing control of his business. First, he had a partner in the group of companies that included the companies that had published and recorded "Why Do Fools Fall in Love?" Then the partner took over, and Goldner was completely out of the picture. The partner was a man named Morris Levy.

Morris Levy was a seventh-grade dropout from the Bronx who eventually became one of the most powerful figures in the record industry. He started his career in the entertainment business as a nightclub checkroom boy, and went from there to a job developing nightclub pictures and from there to operating hat-check and darkroom concessions. Then he ran some nightclubs, including Birdland, in New York, and promoted concerts — all of which led to the record business. Through it all, he was a friend, and occasionally a business partner, of mobsters; he was also the Man of the Year at United Jewish Appeal dinners, and a planter of forests of trees in Israel, and a man deferred to by ostensibly more respectable record executives, and a financial supporter of the congressional black caucus. The walls of his office, on Broadway, were adorned not only with gold records but also with an array of plaques from institutions he had supported and with a photograph of him with Cardinal Spellman, of New York, and, as it later turned out, with a listening device planted by the Federal Bureau of Investigation. He spoke in a raspy voice, often using the sort of grammar and the sort of language that would not have inspired that final educator in the seventh grade to promote him to the eighth grade. A lot of people in the business were afraid of Morris Levy. There were people who said that he was, whatever his faults, a standup guy — an implacable opponent who demanded three eyes for an eye, but a loyal friend who would look after the financial needs of a pal's widow even if she was in fact pretty well off. There were other people who said that he was a vicious, conniving, thoroughly dishonest thug. Nobody claimed that he was easy to do business with.

Levy was one of the people Lymon pestered for money in the sixties. In 1965, when Lymon was arrested in California and was desperate for cash, Levy bought his rights to "Why Do Fools Fall in Love?" for a sum that was probably something like fifteen hundred dollars. Apparently, Levy simply told BMI to start sending Lymon's share to him, and BMI complied. A year before Lymon signed over his rights, Goldner had written a remarkable letter to the Register of Copyright at the Library of Congress, saying, "This is to acknowledge that the attached schedule of compositions which contain my name as writer should properly have the name of Morris Levy in my place." The schedule listed "Why Do Fools Fall in Love?" and forty-nine other songs, including even a couple of

Latin tunes, like "Algún Día" and "Big City Merengue." When
Diana Ross did her hit recording, the record label said, "Words and
music by Frankie Lymon and Morris Levy." Levy, as the publisher
and the co-writer and the owner of Lymon's rights, got a hundred
percent of the royalties. He got a hundred percent of the *American
Graffiti* royalties. When the American Greetings Corporation
made a commercial featuring "Why Do Fools Fall in Love?" a
hundred percent of the royalties went to Morris Levy.

The copyright law of the United States was thoroughly revised in
1978. The old law, which remains in force for anything written before 1978, has in it a provision that lawyers sometimes refer to as
"a second bite of the apple." It's a provision that seems to have
been included on the theory that writers are a feckless lot whose
families need an extra measure of protection. Under the old law, a
copyright offers protection for twenty-eight years, renewable for a
second term. A copyright holder can sign away his rights for both
terms. But if the copyright holder signs away his rights forever and
dies before the first term is up, the rights revert to his heirs for the
renewal term. Twenty-eight years after the original copyright, they
can take out a renewal copyright as if he had not signed anything.
They get a second bite of the apple. In other words, Frankie
Lymon, whose personal life had been in disarray since grade
school, had done at least one thing for his family: he had died before the first copyright term was up.

In 1984, twenty-eight years after Goldner applied for the original copyright, a young New York copyright lawyer named Richard
Bennett filed for the renewal of the copyright in the name of Emira
Lymon, who had never received any money from Frankie Lymon's
songs. "What Goldner did was a common practice," Bennett said
later. "The record business in those days had a system of morality
that was slightly below the Mafia. Goldner's fatal mistake was that
he was a fifty percent thief, and not a hundred percent thief.
Lymon's name was there, so the widow could take out a copyright
and demand her money." Bennett did more than make a claim for
Emira Lymon for the renewal term: he filed a suit in federal court

in New York against Morris Levy, two of Levy's companies, BMI, and Maxwell T. Cohen, Frankie Lymon's lawyer. In a fifty-five-page complaint, Bennett alleged that the defendants had committed fraudulent acts against Frankie Lymon and his widow — not to speak of breaches of fiduciary obligation and copyright infringement and violations of the Sherman Act, the Lanham Act, and the RICO statutes. He said that both Morris Levy and George Goldner had fraudulently represented themselves as co-authors of a song written entirely by Frankie Lymon, that BMI had redirected royalties to Levy without so much as a casual inquiry, that Maxwell T. Cohen had basically been acting for Levy rather than for Lymon, and that what was meant as a release of only performer's rights to Levy had been altered to include all future copyright royalties.

Bennett was working with Chuck Rubin, of the Artists Rights Enforcement Corporation. Rubin, a former agent, is in the business of helping singers and writers from the early days of rock and roll collect money owed to them — a task that sometimes requires research coupled with persistent letter writing, and sometimes requires a lawsuit. When Rubin began his business, in 1981, many of the figures of early rock had pretty much given up on the idea of collecting any money. "It's so tough getting paid when you're on *top*," Rubin has said. "They couldn't believe they could get any money years later." His first successful case involved prying some performers' royalties for the Teenagers out of a television series called "The Roots of Rock and Roll." While working on a followup case for the Teenagers, he learned from one of Frankie Lymon's brothers that the author of "Why Do Fools Fall in Love?" had left a widow.

Although Rubin has been called "a white knight of rock" by the *New York Times*, he has also grown accustomed to hearing himself referred to as a hired gun or even a scavenger: he ordinarily takes fifty percent of whatever is recovered. Emira Lymon's family lawyer, a sole practitioner in Augusta named William McCracken, was not alarmed by the fifty-fifty split, as long as the lawyers' share didn't come out of his client's half. McCracken figured that Rubin's cut was no more than what is taken by people who trace lost heirs, and, having himself once made an inconclusive pass at finding out about Frankie Lymon's royalties, he believed that orchestrating a recovery effort would require a specialist. Rubin, who eventually estimated the past and future royalties of a classic like "Why Do Fools Fall in Love?" at "a conservative million," had begun to investigate how much of that money might rightfully belong to Emira Eagle Lymon. "That," he later recalled, "was when we ran head on into the face of Morris Levy."

Although Morris Levy's name appeared as Frankie Lymon's co-writer, there was a widespread assumption in the music business that Levy's writing was confined to checks, and that he wrote those only if he saw absolutely no alternative. According to Richard Barrett, one of Levy's mottoes was "You don't ask, you don't get." Barrett, the acknowledged discoverer of the Teenagers, has said that Levy was not even in the record business when "Why Do Fools Fall in Love?" was written. The two surviving Teenagers were available to testify that they hadn't met Levy until a year after they recorded "Why Do Fools Fall in Love?" None of that meant that Levy would not contest Emira Eagle Lymon's claim to previous royalties, or even her attempt to collect Frankie Lymon's royalties for the renewal term. In the record business, a common response to a reminder that money was owed someone was "So sue"; Levy's companies were customarily involved in half a dozen lawsuits. Levy's response to being confronted with claims that he had, in effect, stolen "Why Do Fools Fall in Love?" came down to "So prove it."

Even Levy's friends said that he gave no quarter to his enemies, and Chuck Rubin, a man whose business could exist only on the premise that people like Levy were crooks and exploiters, was becoming more his enemy every day. Levy, asked about Rubin during a deposition, said, "Chuck Rubin is a guy who didn't happen in the business, and then he created a new business of harassing people and suing people and starting lawsuits and threatening people, and my personal opinion would be he'd sell his mother for a nickel." Also, Levy was not accustomed to backing down or apologizing. He was not simply the sort of man who hung out with gangsters but the sort of man who bragged about hanging out with gangsters, and challenged the authorities to prove that he and his friends had done anything illegal. Norman Sheresky, who acted as Levy's divorce lawyer two or three times, says he once set up a meeting between Levy and another friend of his, a television producer who was investigating the commercial possibilities of a soap-opera theme song. The two men seemed to hit it off. Levy offered the producer not only a substantial advance but a royalty percentage that was way beyond what other publishers had proposed. When the producer asked him how he was able to make such an offer, Levy replied cheerfully, "Because I'm going to fuck you on the royalties. You'll never see a dime."

In a deposition taken by Richard Bennett, Levy said flatly that he had been one of the writers of "Why Do Fools Fall in Love?" ("I made some changes in the lyric") and that he had written many other songs ("Maybe thirty, forty. I don't know exactly"). All this writing, Levy explained, was collaborative. "It's not like you see a composer sitting at a piano and writing a whole bunch of music," he testified during that deposition. "I think I would be misleading you if I said I wrote songs, per se, like Chopin."

Maintaining the rights for the renewal term seemed like a much more formidable challenge for Levy than resisting Emira Lymon's claims for royalties during the first twenty-eight years. The law was absolutely clear that Frankie Lymon's share of the copyright would revert to his widow. Emira Eagle Lymon would not accept a rather modest settlement Levy offered for those rights and for what she claimed was owed her during the original copyright term. But Levy was not left without a defense. He said that it was not at all clear that Emira Eagle Lymon was in fact Frankie Lymon's widow.

Levy may well have remembered that in New York in the sixties Lymon seemed to have had a wife called Mickey — not from Georgia, not a schoolteacher, and, alas, not terribly respectable. There had been a reminder of Mickey just a couple of years before Bennett's suit. After Diana Ross's version of "Why Do Fools Fall in Love?" became a hit, a woman then in the Delaware County Prison for shoplifting — a woman who was using the name of Jacqueline

Green but had also been Mickey Phillips and Elizabeth Waters — told a young Philadelphia lawyer named Dwight Peterson that she was the widow of Frankie Lymon and should be due some royalties. Peterson wrote a few letters — he wrote to Levy's company Roulette Records, among others — and was simply ignored. Finally, he managed to get a reply from BMI, informing him that all royalties had been transferred to Morris Levy years before. To Peterson, who was unaware of the second-bite-of-the-apple provision and not overconfident of the reliability of his client's information, that had seemed to be about as far as he could go.

Six weeks after Bennett's complaint was filed in federal district court, Peterson got a call from an excited Elizabeth Waters. She told him to look in the *Philadelphia Daily News*. An entertainment column written by Masco Young was headlined "ROYALTY WINDFALL FOR SINGER'S WIDOW?" The item said, "The mushrooming interest in the golden oldies tunes of the '50s and '60s has created a windfall of royalties. According to what Our Town's Jerry Blavat tells me, 'There's a nice chunk of dough that has been accumulating at Roulette Records all these years for Frankie Lymon's estate, and the only known legitimate heir is a Philadelphia girl he married in January 1964 in Virginia. Her name at the time was Elizabeth Waters.'" Peterson phoned Blavat, the oldies disk jockey, who was a longtime acquaintance of Levy's, and this time he had no trouble at all getting through to Roulette Records. In fact, Blavat escorted him to New York in a limousine. Elizabeth Waters wasn't along herself; she was back in prison for retail theft. At Roulette Records, there was, of course, no chunk of dough that had been accumulating for Frankie Lymon's widow — it had all gone to Levy — but there was a deal to be made. As it worked out, Elizabeth Waters agreed that Levy could remain the publisher of "Why Do Fools Fall in Love?" for the renewal term; she was given a ten-thousand-dollar advance against the royalties that would be due to Frankie Lymon; money was promised for her legal fees involved in contesting Emira Eagle Lymon's claims to widowhood; and, concerning whatever might have happened to the royalties from "Why Do Fools Fall in Love?" during the first twenty-eight-year term, she agreed to let bygones be bygones.

Levy had also found a third widow — Zola Taylor, at one time the female singer for the Platters, who had once shown up in the columns as having tied the knot with Frankie in Las Vegas. Richard Bennett took to referring to Zola Taylor as "Levy's bullpen widow." Levy made the same deal with her that he had made with Elizabeth Waters. All this stopped Emira Eagle Lymon's suit against Levy before his lawyers had even answered the complaint: if she was not in fact the authentic widow, she could neither claim the second bite of the apple nor claim standing in court to argue about what had happened to her share of the first bite.

One supermarket tabloid, the *Star,* headlined its story "THREE 'WIDOWS' FIGHT FOR MILLIONS FROM WOMAN-CRAZY TEEN SINGER." The presence of the three widows resulted in the most television coverage Frankie Lymon had received since the days of "The Ed Sullivan Show." They were on "Entertainment Tonight" and CBS's "West 57th." (Morris Levy also appeared in the "West 57th" segment, and uttered what became an industry classic on the joys of collecting copyrights: "It's always pennies — nickels, pennies. But it accumulates into nice money. It works for itself. It never talks back to you.") There was some jockeying about which court was going to decide who the legal widow was. At some point in the blizzard of motions and countermotions, Richard Bennett and Chuck Rubin had a falling-out. William McCracken flew up to New York and replaced Bennett with Ira Greenberg, a commercial litigator who had gone to Harvard Law School with an Augusta lawyer McCracken knew. Finally, in late 1987, three years after Bennett filed his complaint, a trial began in the Manhattan Surrogate Court, with Surrogate Marie Lambert presiding.

Judge Lambert, a dramatic, contentious activist on the bench, was summed up by Barbara Goldsmith, in her book on the epic dispute over the estate of J. Seward Johnson, as "part Portia, part Tugboat Annie." In the Lymon case, a settlement that Judge Lambert had been pressing was rejected by Emira's side, and there were some who thought that the judge sounded particularly irritated with Ira Greenberg. On the other hand, she sometimes sounded irritated with Frankie Lymon. ("This man lied all over the place. If I am to believe all the testimony here, the man never told the truth.") In the words of one of the attorneys who participated, "It was a four-day trial that lasted ten days." Emira Eagle Lymon came to court with some advantages. Although she had been married to Frankie Lymon for only eight months, she was his wife when he died — the one whose name was on the death certificate, the one who was the bereaved widow at the funeral — and New York law carries a strong presumption that someone's final wife is his widow. A churchgoing Baptist who was still teaching school in Augusta, she had married Frankie in the Beulah Grove Baptist Church, in the presence of her family. (Frankie, it almost goes without saying, was late.) In background and demeanor, she had little in common with her two rivals. Elizabeth Waters Lymon was obviously not going to be able to get through her testimony without some exposure of her police record in the areas of shoplifting and prostitution. Zola Taylor Lymon — who in the twenty-five years since she was known as the dish among the Platters seemed to have added some weight and a lot of brass — had led a colorful life even by the standards of the Manhattan Surrogate Court.

But it wasn't a contest for respectability. There was no jury. The only question was who was legally Frankie Lymon's widow. Whether Elizabeth Waters had been sought out by Morris Levy for his own ends or not, her case was hardly frivolous. She had met Frankie around 1961, when she went backstage at the Audubon Ballroom, where he was appearing during his gradual slide toward panhandling. ("I seen Frankie at the time he was a very sad, lonely person," she said in a deposition. "His career didn't look promising at all. But his personality came over very strongly with me, and that was enough for me. We fell in love; that was it.") The two of them undoubtedly lived for a time as man and wife. She had borne his child — a daughter, who died almost immediately after birth. Elizabeth had been through a lot with Frankie — the promises, the bursts of charm, the inevitable disappointments. The moment in her testimony that seemed to stick with everyone was when she said to the surrogate, "Frankie could fool you, he could fool me, Frankie could fool God. That's why we're here today."

Elizabeth Waters Lymon had gone through what appeared to be a conventional wedding ceremony with Frankie Lymon; she had a license issued by a justice of the peace in Alexandria, Virginia. The problem was that she had been legally married to someone else at the time. Still, there might have been enough evidence to show that she was Frankie's common-law wife after a divorce decree from her previous marriage came through, in 1965 — except that New York is not a state that recognizes common-law marriages. Her case had to be built on testimony that she and Frankie were living in Philadelphia. It was testimony that the other side tried to counter by presenting evidence that while she claimed to be living in Philadelphia she was being picked up for prostitution all the time in New York.

Zola Taylor Lymon, the bullpen widow, had a case that was not nearly so strong. Her problems started with her claim that the marriage reported in the columns as having taken place in Las Vegas actually took place in Tijuana — her description of the events sounded less like a wedding day than shore leave — and with her inability to produce a marriage license for a ceremony in either place. And there was also testimony that the wedding had been not an actual wedding but a publicity stunt to put some life into two deflated careers. (Zola would have objected to that description of her career. She said in court that at the time she was doing pretty well with Zola Taylor's All-Male Revue: "I had a singing group called the Fabulous Fi-Dells, and I had a ventriloquist called Aaron and Freddy, which, as a matter of fact, these are now stars.") Zola testified persuasively, and rather graphically, that her romance with Frankie dated all the way back to a night in 1956, when the Platters and the Teenagers were appearing in Bangor, Maine, with a touring company that also included Chuck Berry, the Coasters, the Penguins, Bo Diddley, the Teen Queens, LaVern Baker, Big Joe Turner, Fabian, Frankie Avalon, and the Drifters. There seemed to be no doubt that Frankie Lymon had lived in Zola's house in California for a while around 1965 — he had apparently explained to Elizabeth Waters that Zola's feelings for him were more or less maternal — and that there had been an edgy confrontation when Elizabeth arrived in California herself. During the trial in the Manhattan Surrogate Court, though, Elizabeth Waters and Zola Taylor found themselves chatting amiably about the old days. Before the trial was over, they had reached a settlement of their own, without benefit of counsel. In what someone referred to as "an accord reached in the ladies' room," they decided that if either of them won the case they would split the take fifty-fifty.

Judge Lambert decided for Elizabeth Waters. Before the ceremony in Alexandria, Elizabeth had testified, her lawyer advised her that she was free to marry. The surrogate ruled that under Pennsylvania law someone who marries in the belief that no impediment exists and then cohabits with her partner after the impediment is removed is legally married. If Frankie was legally married to Elizabeth in 1964, of course, he was not free to marry Zola Taylor in 1965 or to marry Emira Eagle in 1967. The decision brought glee in Philadelphia. "She was speechless, actually unable to talk," Dwight Peterson told a reporter who had asked about Elizabeth Waters's response. The decision was also a victory for Morris Levy, but Levy's celebration must have been restrained: at a court appearance the preceding week, he had been sentenced by a federal judge in Camden, New Jersey, to ten years in prison.

Levy was appealing his conviction, but, after twenty-five years or so of what he referred to as harassment by the FBI, it appeared that the federals had finally nailed him. Levy was convicted of involvement in a plan to extort money from a Philadelphia-area record distributor who, in a complicated deal, was refusing payment on the ground that he had not received the records he had been promised. Levy's co-defendants — also convicted — were Dominick (Baldy Dom) Canterino and Levy's longtime associate Gaetano (Corky) Vastola, who had broken the record distributor's jaw. The record business being what it is, Corky Vastola is registered at the Library of Congress as the writer of a few songs himself. The news accounts, though, did not describe him as a songwriter; they tended to identify him as something like "a chieftain in the De-Cavalcante crime family of New Jersey."

Emira Eagle Lymon appealed the surrogate-court decision by Marie Lambert. In writing the appeal, Ira Greenberg sounded like a man much put upon who was finally having his say: "The surrogate was able to reach this conclusion only by riding roughshod over the very strong presumption of the validity of a last marriage. She also strong-armed the facts, perverted the Pennsylvania law applicable to Elizabeth's claim, excluded probative evidence offered by Emira, and ultimately adopted a story (Elizabeth's) which the surrogate herself called 'wacky' at trial." A year later, the Appellate Division did in fact reverse the surrogate's decision, in favor of Emira Eagle Lymon, and eventually the New York State Court of Appeals upheld that ruling. There was no further appeal: Emira Eagle Lymon was the legal widow of Frankie Lymon. Elizabeth Waters may have been speechless at that decision, too, but there was nobody there to record the moment. She was back in jail — in the State Correctional Institution at Muncy, in central Pennsylvania, for retail theft. Dwight Peterson — who, like a lot of the people involved, had grown fond of his client during the years of the widows' case — said later that it was a shame the efforts Elizabeth had made to straighten herself out hadn't proved successful. "She just has a nasty habit of walking into a retail store and taking things that don't belong to her and forgetting to pay for them," he said.

Presumably, the final decision that Emira Lymon was Frankie Lymon's widow would enable Greenberg to take up the federal suit against Morris Levy, BMI, and others which Richard Bennett had filed five years before. But there were complications. The falling-out between Chuck Rubin and Bennett had been largely over the role of Jimmy Merchant and Herman Santiago, the surviving Teenagers. The oldies craze had not enriched Merchant and Santiago, although they appeared at oldies evenings from time to time and had once put together their own Off Broadway musical celebration of the Teenagers, filling out the group with Sherman Garnes's brother, one of Frankie Lymon's brothers, and a female vocalist to do Frankie's tenor. According to a lawsuit Bennett had filed even before the surrogate-court trial began, Emira Lymon and the surviving Teenagers had agreed from the start that each of them would receive a third of the royalties — she needed their eyewitness testimony about the origin of the song, but her participation

alone would guarantee a renewal of copyright under the old law —
and then she was "induced to repudiate her promise by her agent,
Charles Rubin, and possibly others." According to Rubin, Bennett
had been fired and was simply trying to shoehorn himself back into
the case. Bennett's suit, filed in federal court against both Emira
Lymon and Morris Levy, contended that Merchant and Santiago as
well as Frankie Lymon had written "Why Do Fools Fall in Love?"
Greenberg managed to have Bennett dismissed by the court as lawyer of record for Merchant and Santiago, on the ground that it
would conflict with his role in the original case. But Bennett's dis-
missal did not get rid of the Teenagers, and neither did a suggestion
by Greenberg to Bennett that Emira Lymon's side might find it
worthwhile to provide Merchant and Santiago with a small
settlement — exceedingly small, in Bennett's view — to avoid
trouble.

By this time, Levy was presumed to have far more serious problems to deal with than the copyright of one song. His appeal on the
felony conviction had failed, and the only reason he was not in federal prison was that his doctors had presented evidence to the
court that he was gravely ill with cancer. Also, he had sold his holdings in the companies involved — the publisher of "Why Do Fools
Fall in Love?" was now a company called Windswept Pacific —
and it was assumed that the new owner, with no personal stake in a
grudge match with Chuck Rubin, would just as soon get the matter
over with. But no real progress was made toward a settlement.
Then, in May of 1990, Morris Levy died of liver cancer, at sixty-
two. Richard Barrett said that he talked to a dozen or more people
in the industry the day after Levy's death and nobody had one decent thing to say about him. There were in fact a few decent things
said at his funeral. The principal eulogy was by Norman Sheresky.
Noting that his client "took people the way they were — warts
and all," Sheresky said, "Morris had plenty of warts, but he was
beautiful."

Not long after Levy's death, serious negotiations began among
lawyers for Emira Eagle Lymon, the Levy estate, BMI, and Windswept Pacific. A year or so after the Court of Appeals' ruling de-

cided who was Frankie Lymon's widow, the deal was about done. Under its provisions, Emira Eagle Lymon will receive a lump sum — her fifty percent net share would be somewhere around half a million dollars — plus a percentage of the royalties that "Why Do Fools Fall in Love?" generates in the future. She doesn't think receiving all that money will drastically change her life. Unlike her late husband, she has not led a life with many twists and turns. She is now a rather handsome, sturdy-looking woman, with the no-nonsense manner of someone who has dealt with hundreds of schoolchildren. She has never remarried. When she met Frankie Lymon, she was in her third year of teaching. Now, a quarter of a century later, she has taught some children of her former students. Except for a few months in the early seventies, when desegregation of the Augusta schools required some shifting around of teachers, she has spent her entire career at W. S. Hornsby, a sunny primary school across a double-lane from a black subdivision. She is still active in the Beulah Grove Baptist Church. She still lives with her mother, in a neat brick house in a subdivision built on some pleasant, rolling land. She tends to speak of the effort to win Frankie Lymon's royalties as an ordeal that had to be endured. She dreaded having to testify in court. She was pressed by both parties during the dispute between Rubin and Bennett, each of whom presented himself as her true protector. Herman Santiago and Jimmy Merchant phoned a lot to plead their cause. For a time, she had, in a sense, lost her good name: in the year between the surrogate-court decision and the reversal on appeal, she was, at least in the view of one court, someone who had never been legally married to the man she lived with. By chance, some of the most stressful periods of the royalties struggle coincided with some serious illnesses in her family. Talking about all of this around the time a settlement finally appeared certain, she seemed to reach for the language of Beulah Grove to sum it up: "I've really been up the rough side of the mountain. The smoke was so heavy in my eyes, I didn't know where to grasp." The first thing that comes to her mind when she is asked how she might spend the money coming to her is some minor remodeling in her house — particularly the installation of a kitchen vent that she thinks will help protect the living room upholstery. She has no plans to quit teaching. In four years, she will be eligible for a pension.

Some of the money Emira Lymon receives will presumably have to be set aside on the chance that the surviving Teenagers succeed in their effort to share in whatever she gets. The claim by Herman Santiago and Jimmy Merchant to have co-authored "Why Do Fools Fall in Love?" may be weakened by the fact that they waited so many years to exert it. On the other hand, they are the only people left alive who can testify as eyewitnesses of the moment of creation, and they have at least one interesting piece of evidence: the first 45-r.p.m. single of "Why Do Fools Fall in Love?" listed as the song's writers not just Frankie Lymon and George Goldner but also Herman Santiago. According to the surviving Teenagers, Goldner had told them that Merchant's name would have been present as well except that a 45-r.p.m. record had so little room on the label.

In all the legal maneuvering, the question of who actually wrote "Why Do Fools Fall in Love?" has never made it into court, but it's unlikely that even days of testimony would provide any dependable answers. The people who were there have had their say, and there isn't a lot of overlap. The story most often repeated by people writing about the early days of doo-wop is one version or another of a tale having to do with a young man named Richard — not Richard Barrett but another Richard, who lived in the same building on 165th Street that Sherman Garnes lived in. "A lot of times, we used to rehearse in Sherman's building," Herman Santiago once said. "And in Sherman's building there was this person who knew us, and he used to listen to us pretty regular, and one time he said, 'Look, here are some letters that my girlfriend has written me. Why don't you look through them and see if you guys can come up with anything?' "

"He was at that time a Coupe de Villes groupie," Jimmy Merchant added. "We hadn't changed our name to the Premiers yet."

"When Richard gave us those letters, myself and Jimmy Merchant, we looked through them," Santiago said. "We read them and we looked through them. We tried to get ideas, just to see what we could come up with. I remember that part of the letter the girl was saying that she was angry at this person because she loved him so much and he didn't feel the same way she felt. And as I kept reading she was in pain, and she was waking up early in the morning and she used to hear the birds outside her window. That's basically what we had the idea from."

In another version, a poem in the letters used the very words that inspired the song and became one of its main lines: "Why do birds sing so gay?" What Santiago and Merchant say is that they worked the sentiments of the letters into a song lyric and then Frankie Lymon helped with the tune, so an accurate credit line would have read "Words by Herman Santiago and Jimmy Merchant, music by Herman Santiago, Jimmy Merchant, and Frankie Lymon." Richard Barrett seems to accept some version of the way the love letters became a lyric, but in his telling the tune evolved through his effort to help the kids put the song to music and the fact that he knew only four chords on the piano, so maybe the credit should read "Music by the Teenagers and Richard Barrett."

The story Frankie Lymon told his new wife in Georgia apparently didn't include any of this. Asked in one deposition what Frankie had told her about the origin of the song, Emira Lymon said, "He had written the song at twelve because he had fallen in love with a teacher and she told him that he was nothing but a kid, he was too young for her. And that is why he wrote 'Why Do Fools Fall in Love?'" The part about falling in love with his teacher at twelve has a nice ring of Frankie in it, but so, in another way, does the version reported in the 1967 *Ebony* piece: "The original song the group had chosen for their audition had been inspired by an essay which Frankie had written a few weeks earlier for his seventh grade English class at Stitt Junior High School. Appalled by sordidness all around him, the common-law relationships of many grownups in his neighborhood and the unhappy married lives of others, the precocious 13-year-old had chosen 'Why Do Fools Fall in Love?' as the cynical theme for his essay."

Elizabeth Waters was also asked during a deposition what she knew about how "Why Do Fools Fall in Love?" was written. She gave a sort of circular answer, which was her general style of testimony. She said something about how Frankie sometimes didn't feel like doing what the teacher told him to do, and something about how the later songs were done with more professionalism. Then she turned back to "Why Do Fools Fall in Love?" She said, "That first one was off the top of his head."

1991

I'VE GOT
PROBLEMS

THE FIRST PHONE CALL made to Arthur Kirk once a Nebraska State Patrol SWAT team was in place around the Kirk farmhouse was from Jim Titsworth, a reporter for the *Grand Island Independent*. Titsworth had interviewed Kirk that afternoon in the driveway of Kirk's farm, near Cairo — a fading little farm town in flat corn-and-wheat country fifteen miles northwest of Grand Island. At the time, Kirk seemed calm — he had just driven into the farmstead with a truckload of newly cut beans — but he was still angry about his confrontation earlier in the afternoon with some Hall County deputy sheriffs who had come out to serve legal papers for a Grand Island bank. The deputies had no right to come on his land, Kirk told Titsworth — he had what he called "a federal post" on it, excluding government officials as well as ordinary trespassers — and they had no business carrying out "the bankers' dirty duties." He didn't deny that he had pointed a pistol at the head of one deputy; in fact, he pulled a long-barreled .41 magnum out of his coveralls to show it to Titsworth. About an hour after the interview, Art Kirk called the offices of the *Independent*, but Titsworth was out. Kirk left his name and a short message: "I've got problems."

He had serious problems. Jim Titsworth was returning the call that evening from a command post at the headquarters of Troop C, the Nebraska State Patrol's Grand Island detachment. The Hall

County Sheriff's Department had obtained a warrant for Art Kirk's arrest and had asked Troop C's SWAT team for help in bringing him in. Titsworth was using the call from Troop C headquarters partly to nail down some facts for his story — he wanted to know how many acres Kirk had been farming before his operation began to shrink; he wanted to make certain that he had the correct first name of Kirk's wife — but he had also been asked by the state police to do whatever he could to feel out Art Kirk's state of mind. Kirk answered Titsworth's questions — he had once farmed about two thousand acres; his wife's correct first name was Deloris — but he seemed more interested in talking about the problems brought on by his confrontation with the deputies. He said that the deputies had brandished guns themselves. He said that a Sheriff's Department car had followed him when he went out afterward to cut beans on some rental land several miles away. He said that an unmarked Cessna had been making passes over his house. He had seen roadblocks being put in place on country roads near his farmhouse. His wife had apparently been detained on her way to the farm from Grand Island. Kirk said that his phone had an odd sound in it; he was convinced that it had been tapped for some time. In answer to Titsworth's questions about financial problems — the setbacks that had eventually brought the court papers from the bank — Kirk talked mainly in general terms. "You always thought, you know, that things would improve," he said. "But they have gotten worse." He was quite specific, though, on who was leading the forces against him.

"Mossad," he said to Titsworth. "You ever heard of that?"

"What's that?" Titsworth asked.

"Mossad."

"No, sir, I'm not familiar —"

"M-o-s-s-a-d. Look that up. That's what I'm fighting. That's who I'm dealing with. There isn't much hope. They are the most ruthless people. You think the NKVD and the Gestapo were ruthless — you look up the Mossad and see what they've been involved in."

"I've never heard of that name," Titsworth said.

"I know who I'm fighting."

Titsworth tried a couple of times to suggest that Kirk's problems with the sheriff could be settled without violence. "You know, what you ought to do is you ought to try and call somebody and get this thing over before — just to be sure no one gets hurt," he said shortly after the phone conversation began.

Art Kirk laughed. "They'll be somebody get hurt," he said. "About all I got hopes of doing is taking as many of them with me as I can."

"Another one sneaking down to the north, just like the last one," Kirk said.

He was on the phone with Jan Steeple, a deputy sheriff he happened to be acquainted with, and as he spoke he peered out the window toward movements in the farmyard. It was their second conversation of the day. After the confrontation with the deputies, Steeple had phoned from the sheriff's office and discussed the possibility of coming out to talk to Kirk about his problems. But Kirk, a man who was known to have a lot of guns, had insisted that Steeple leave his gun in the mailbox at the side of the road, and the visit had been ruled out as too dangerous. Talking to Steeple again, Kirk berated him for not showing up. He complained that his wife was being prevented from returning home. He complained that his telephone had been tapped. He complained about having had a motorcycle stolen from his barn some weeks before. Steeple tried again to persuade Kirk to come out of the house unarmed.

"I'm coming to no goddam place," Kirk said. "If you want to talk to me, you know where I'm at, and I'll be here."

A State Patrol sergeant who had some training in negotiating armed stand-offs took over from Steeple. He spoke calmly, in a tone of generalized sympathy. ("I understand what you're saying, Art, and you have some reasons to be upset.") He avoided comment on the specifics of Kirk's complaints. But Kirk seemed to grow angrier as the conversation went on. His voice became high-pitched. Some of his grievances were expressed in a sustained, obscene shout. Eventually, he talked about how the attack on his house might begin — tear gas, or a flamethrower that could burn him to a crisp, or a volley of gunfire.

"Art, nobody wants to shoot you," the sergeant said.

"Well, then, damn it, come up here and talk to me," Kirk said. "I don't want to shoot you, either, but, damn you, you respect my rights."

Kirk said that the deputies he had driven from his property were cowards. He railed against "filthy, lying members of the bar — outlaw bastards." Speaking of a lawsuit he had filed without assistance from members of the bar, Kirk said, "I filed a suit against the goddam bank that's been misusing me for years and years and years, unbeknowned to me, until I started reading the laws myself . . . I found out them dirty rotten son of a bitches have done everything despicable that they can think of to me. Everything you can think. It's unimaginable. It's covered by the U.S. Constitution and U.S. titles passed by Congress, the highest lawmaking body in the land, and they tell me that my suit is meritless. I'm going to tell you something: if the Constitution and the laws Congress passes are meritless, them son of a bitches are completely discredited."

Sometimes Kirk seemed to ramble. He said that he was a son of Abraham whose birthright had been claimed by Lucifer, and that the bankers had been Luciferized. He made an extended play on words comparing the service of court papers to a bull's servicing a cow. Most of the time, though, he focused on the shoot-out that he seemed certain was about to take place. He said he was unafraid — a man who had never let anyone walk over him and wasn't going to start now. "You ain't going to walk over me until I'm cold," he said. "And if you want to make me cold I'm not afraid of it. I've led a damn good life, and I'm not ashamed of nothing I ever done." He said he had fired guns all his life ("Nobody's going to take my guns. Is that kinda clear?") and could even have brought down the Cessna. "I don't intend to kill anybody," he said. "But if you force me, if you shoot at me, damn you, there will be hell to pay. I intend to make the toll as great as I can. That's the only thing you leave me now, and that's what I'll do."

At other times, Art Kirk seemed to be asking why he could not simply be left alone. "Why all this goddam monkey business?" he asked. "Why don't you let me try and make a living?"

"Art," the sergeant said, "I didn't have anything to do with what's —"

"Goddam fuckin' Jews!" Kirk shouted. "They destroyed everything I ever worked for! I've worked my ass off for forty-nine goddam years, and I've got nothing to show for it! By God, I ain't putting up with their bullshit now. I'm tired, and I've had it, and I'm not the only goddam one — I'll tell you that."

"Yeah, but, Art —"

"Farmers fought the Revolutionary War and we'll fight this son of a bitch. We were hoping to do it in court, but if you're going to make it impossible, then, damn you, we'll take you on your own terms."

Deloris Kirk came on the phone for a while, from the command post. She kept reminding her husband that they had discussed what to do in such a situation, but she seemed to have trouble holding his attention. Steeple got back on the line, and again he pleaded for Kirk to come out unarmed.

"Well, hey, Jan," Kirk said to Steeple. "If you're just trying to divert me, I'm going out and clean the bushes out."

"Art, you don't want to do anything silly," Steeple said.

By that time, Deloris Kirk was off the phone. From a snatch of conversation she had overheard on a police radio, she believed that the SWAT team was moving in. She insisted on talking to Chuck Fairbanks, the sheriff of Hall County, who was at an operational headquarters that the police had set up in a state road-repair depot in Cairo, and a phone connection was put through.

"Call all of those people away from my farmhouse," Mrs. Kirk said.

"We can't do that right now," the sheriff replied.

"Why not?"

"Because he threatened deputy sheriffs, that's why," Fairbanks said. "The judge issued a warrant for his arrest."

Sheriff Fairbanks and Mrs. Kirk seemed to be at a stand-off. Mrs. Kirk wouldn't respond to the sheriff's request that she telephone her husband and ask him to come out peacefully. The sheriff continued to say that he could not agree to allow her to go into the farmhouse. They were still talking when Art Kirk burst out of the back door of his house. He was wearing the green coveralls he normally wore around the farm. Strapped to his arms or jammed in his pockets, he had a gas mask and a hundred and sixty rounds of ammunition and a long-barreled .357 magnum pistol. He was wearing a motorcycle helmet. He was carrying an automatic rifle.

"The trooper who was stationed on the southeast perimeter of the house in a shelter belt area advises that he saw the subject come out of the east door, carrying what appeared to be an AR-15 or M-16 by the sight on its barrel," a report prepared by the county attorney a week later said. "This trooper yelled as loudly as he could in the direction of Kirk, 'Freeze — police.' He then saw a movement in his direction, saw muzzle flashes and heard automatic rifle fire. He returned the fire toward the muzzle flashes and lost sight of the subject." Another SWAT team member had also fired at the flashes. For some minutes, there was silence. Then the SWAT team asked some deputies to shine headlights on the area where the shots had come from. Arthur Kirk lay on the ground near a wire dog kennel, not far from his back door. He had been hit by two bullets. "The cause of death," an autopsy report said several weeks later, "is attributed to exsanguinating hemorrhage secondary to a gunshot wound of the anterior right shoulder and of the upper left thigh." In other words, Art Kirk had bled to death.

Arthur Kirk was born and raised where he died — on the two hundred and forty acres near Cairo that was his family's home place. His mother had been raised on the same farm. Her forebears were among the Germans who had arrived in the late nineteenth century in such numbers that they dominated Grand Island and the rich Platte Valley farmland nearby. Art Kirk's parents were not prosperous. In the years after the Second World War, they were still farming with mules. For a while, Art and his younger brother slept in a brooder house so that there would be enough room for their parents and sisters in the tiny two-room farmhouse. Eventually, the Kirks managed to build an adequate farmhouse, with indoor plumbing. Partly with the money the Kirk children made detasseling corn, a small tractor was bought to replace the mules. By that time, Art was old enough to help adapt the mule-drawn equipment to the tractor. He liked working with machinery. He liked working with farm animals. He was interested in trying various combinations of chemicals and fertilizers to increase crop yields. Art Kirk might have simply remained on the home place to farm except that he and his father did not see eye to eye when it came to farming. The elder Kirk was apparently not interested in trying his son's ideas on crop rotation or irrigation or equipment maintenance. In 1953, Art Kirk got a job with the gas company and moved in to Grand Island.

In a small farm-state city the size of Grand Island, a large part of the population consists of people who grew up on the farm and moved in to town — people whose connection to farming is made up of childhood memories reinforced every so often by a visit to the home place for a family meal or for a harvest that requires some extra hands. Art Kirk appeared to be one of those people. He and his wife, who had also grown up on a south-central Nebraska farm, began to raise a family in Grand Island. Kirk worked in the gas company's meter-repair shop for about ten years and then switched to the service truck, calling on people who needed a pilot light adjusted or a gas dryer repaired. Altogether, he worked for the gas company for nearly twenty years, but nobody who knew him had any doubt that he still had his heart set on being a farmer.

In 1971, Kirk persuaded Dan Stauffer, who sells farm real estate in Grand Island, to rent him a hundred and sixty acres of farmland that Stauffer owns on the road between Grand Island and Cairo. A common way to rent farmland is for the owner to take a share of the crops as rent, and Stauffer was impressed by what Kirk managed to produce. "He had the crudest damn equipment you ever saw in your life," Stauffer said later. "But the crops he raised were clean, and he had a good yield. He worked like mad all the time, and so did his wife." A few years later, Kirk began acquiring his father's farm on a land contract — an arrangement more or less like a home mortgage. When the elder Kirk died, in 1979, Art and Dee Kirk and their children moved from a house on Stauffer's land to

230 / AMERICAN STORIES

the Kirk home place. By then, Kirk was also renting twelve hundred acres from the federal government — land at the Cornhusker Army Ammunition Plant. A frugal, meticulous farmer with set ideas about how things had to be done, Kirk attacked farming mainly with a nearly limitless capacity for hard work. For relaxation, he hunted and fished. When he wasn't in the fields, he was likely to be in the woods with a shotgun, and neighbors thought of him as someone who didn't spend much time socializing. Aside from using guns for hunting, he collected guns — not an unusual pastime in rural Nebraska. He liked to own guns whose design he admired. He liked to reload his own shells. He liked to rebore guns. According to someone who shared his interest in firearms, Kirk's greatest joy in life was "to take a gun and get it perfectly sighted so that the variance was less than half an inch in a five-shot group at two hundred yards." As he settled down on his home place, where he had once plowed behind a mule, Art Kirk seemed to be fulfilling his dream, whatever the cost in toil. He was a farmer with a full operation — corn and soybeans and milo and some feeder cattle and hogs and horses — and he had nearly two thousand acres under cultivation.

Around that time, the notion that dreams had come true was common among American farmers. There had been a number of good crop years in a row. More important, farmland seemed destined to grow in value indefinitely. There was a lot of talk about how America would be feeding the world for the foreseeable future — talk meaning that farmers might be selling ever larger harvests at steadily increasing prices. The experts said that effective, ambitious farmers should expand, in order to spread the cost of expensive farm equipment and to acquire land before its price got even higher. The farmland of America was a finite commodity that could never be replaced, it was said, and you couldn't go wrong owning it. Credit was easy. Even if a loan on land did not, as bankers say, "pencil out" — that is, even if the interest on the purchase price and the other costs of production seemed to be greater than the price of the crops the land could be expected to produce — the bank often went along. The loan was secure, after all, because the farmer's holdings had become worth so much money.

Turning down the loan would just mean that the farmer would take his business to the bank down the street. The steady increase in land values, a Nebraska banker has said, "seemed to prove the pencil wrong." But the pencil was right all along.

Grain prices didn't go up, but interest rates did — so at one point farmers were paying interest as high as twenty-two percent on their loans. The value of farmland began to decline even faster than it had increased. In four years, the value of Nebraska farmland dropped by a third. Farmers who had been millionaires on paper a few years before began having trouble keeping up with their interest payments. As some farm-oriented banks got into financial difficulty, bank examiners started insisting that loans show some real prospect of being repaid by cash flow rather than simply secured by net worth. A lot of farmers — particularly farmers who had expanded their holdings during the boom — had to declare bankruptcy.

The experts said that some farmers — especially those sometimes called the Young Tigers, who bought up farmland almost as fast as the previous purchase could be appraised as collateral — had simply overextended themselves. The experts said that some farmers had been shown to be poor managers. That's not the way farmers saw it. Farmers, of course, are accustomed to being buffeted by elements beyond their control — the weather, for instance, or some flip-flop in world grain prices. This time, though, there was something particularly maddening about the combination of a boom — a boom celebrated by farm experts and bankers and government agricultural specialists as proof that expansion was the wave of the future — and a bust that cost some supposedly successful farmers the land that their more modest forebears had managed to hang on to for generations. This time, also, it was more intense. By some estimates, the farm foreclosures of the mid-eighties in the Midwest will be recorded as the greatest dislocation of Americans since the Depression. Some farmers blamed the bankers. In Minnesota, a farmer and his son shot and killed two bankers they had lured to their farm. Some farmers blamed the government or the grain embargo imposed in 1980, and organized tractor caravans to protest to the authorities. A lot of farmers

didn't know whom to blame. They carried around a bitter, unfo-
cused anger that sometimes erupted into blockades at farm sales or
shoving matches at courthouses. It became common for someone
serving papers on a farmer to do so with a weapon handy.

In the tumult — the foreclosures, the public meetings, the
demonstrations — Midwestern farmers have been exposed to the
message of some organizations that seem quite certain about
whom to blame for the plight of American agriculture, or for just
about any other problem in American society. The organization
that has received the most public attention is the Posse Comitatus,
a loosely knit crowd of prairie vigilantes who spend a lot of time
stockpiling food and undergoing paramilitary training for the day
when they will have to protect themselves against urban hordes
desperate for the food supply. According to Posse doctrine, the
Federal Reserve System and the income tax are both illegal, and
there is no legitimate law-enforcement authority beyond the sheriff and the local posse that may be formed among the citizenry,
with or without the sheriff's permission. Adherents sometimes
shoot at law-enforcement officials they don't consider legitimate;
the Posse owes part of its notoriety to an incident in February of
1983 in which one of its members, a North Dakota farmer named
Gordon Kahl, shot and killed two federal marshals who were trying to arrest him for a parole violation.

The other right-wing fringe organizations preaching to American farmers vary from the Posse Comitatus and from one another
in the details of precisely how the conspiracy works. Even people
who adhere to the same theories vary in the intensity of their
adherence — so some people may simply attack the Federal Reserve System as illegitimate, while others refuse to transact com-
merce except by silver or barter. Still, there is enough overlapping
in theory and in membership to form a loose body of fringe-right
beliefs. Lawyers are generally seen as the enemy, and court decisions are therefore dismissed as predictably unfair. There is a lot of
talk about the Constitution. There is a strong element of anti-
Semitism, some of it leaning on the information in hate tracts so old
that the place of business of some international Jewish bankers is

given as Berlin or Hamburg. There's a tendency to sympathize with the teachings of "identity churches" — churches teaching that Anglo-Saxons are the true descendants of Abraham and that Jews are the people of the Devil. There is often a belief that the loans that banks have made to farmers are illegal and can be dissolved by one sort or another of do-it-yourself legal action — do-it-yourself legal action being the only sort of legal action available to people who believe that lawyers are among the conspirators lined up against them. There is a strong belief that a farmer has the right to keep anybody, and particularly representatives of the government, off his land — by force, if necessary. Some of the no-trespassing signs distributed by the fringe right begin "LEGAL NOTICE — To Federal Officers of the IRS, HEW, HUD, Environmental Health and other *Unconstitutional* agencies; and to all local members of planning & zoning boards. NO TRESPASSING." That sort of warning is sometimes referred to among the fringe right as a "federal post."

Art Kirk was not one of those farmers who overextended themselves through land purchases. The only land he actually owned was the home place; he had inherited a one-third interest in it and was buying the rest gradually, with payments to his brother and a sister. Still, he borrowed a lot of money from the bank. There was once a time when farmers borrowed operating money in the spring and paid off the loan after the fall harvest, but that time is long gone. Farmers now tend to have what amount to semipermanent bank loans. A farmer borrows money for planting expenses in the spring. He borrows money for a combine and other equipment. He may come in throughout the year to sign small notes — four thousand dollars for a used pickup, say, or twenty-five hundred dollars for sharpening blades and "general farm expenses" — as if he had a sort of drawing account. When he sells his crops, which are normally part of the collateral for his loan, he brings in the money, it's applied to paying off the interest and reducing the principal, the loan is refinanced, and the process starts all over again. In the early eighties, Kirk's loans began to show what bankers call deterioration; he wasn't producing enough income to take care of all the interest, so each year his principal got larger and the interest on it even harder to pay off. By the spring of 1984, his debt at Norwest Bank of Grand Island was approaching three hundred thousand dollars.

How did Art Kirk get that far behind? There had been some bad crop years, of course. He was paying high interest on operating loans. Although Kirk was the sort of farmer who would haggle over the price of a spare part and adapt scrounged secondhand machinery to his needs, there are some who say that he never really mastered the business aspects of modern farming — that he was trying to make up with labor in the field what he lacked in finesse with the calculator. According to someone who knew him well, "He didn't understand bankers or lawyers. He thought they were all bad and greedy. He thought they were out to get his money. A farmer *needs* a banker. He *needs* a lawyer. He *needs* a good accountant." There are some who say that Kirk was distracted by family problems. The Kirks were having so much difficulty trying to control their teenage son that at one point Dee Kirk tried to persuade the Hall County Sheriff's Department to put the boy in jail. Some years before, one of Art Kirk's sisters had committed suicide by shooting herself in the head with a .357 magnum; in 1982, one of the Kirks' daughters — a married daughter who had been having emotional difficulties — came to her parents' home, picked up Art Kirk's .357 magnum, held it to her head, and killed herself.

As Kirk's loan deteriorated, so did his patience. "He became more and more bitter with the establishment," someone who saw him during that period has said. "I think he was beginning to realize that he was getting in deeper and deeper and there was no way to get out." Testifying in an investigation of Kirk's death, Richard Falldorf, who handled Kirk's loan at Norwest Bank, put it this way: "It was just difficult to get Art to answer rational-type questions with rational-type answers." In February of 1984, the lease came up on the twelve hundred acres of ordnance-plant land that Kirk had been farming — the federal government leases out the land for three or five years through sealed bids — and he had to decide whether to bid on a new lease. The bank would agree to back him only on a rental figure that penciled out. Kirk made the bid, but he didn't get the land, so he was faced with the task of making a dent in his enormous loan with the income on the home place and the hundred and sixty acres he was renting from Stauffer. Kirk had always been known as a man with a quick temper, and his temper had grown worse. It was said that he usually kept a gun in his coveralls, even while he was plowing. It was said that when some local kids got too close to his land one day he fired shots over their heads.

In May of 1984, Kirk drove in to Grand Island to attend a meeting of an organization called Nebraskans for Constitutional Government, which has been described by its Grand Island representative, a man named Robert Mettenbrink, Sr., as a group that meets to study the Constitution. At times, the lesson has been led by a speaker from the Posse Comitatus. That night in May, the visiting speaker was Rick Elliott, of Fort Lupton, Colorado, the founder of an organization called the National Agricultural Press Association, or NAPA. Although Elliott had talked from time to time about a plan for NAPA to provide farm reports, the only apparent connection NAPA had with the press was that anyone who joined got a NAPA press sticker for his pickup truck and that Elliott was putting out a newspaper called the *Primrose & Cattlemen's Gazette* — an odd and erratically published mélange of conventional ranch news ("HEREFORD BREED DEMONSTRATE STRENGTH AND QUALITY AT COLORADO STATE FAIR") and some of Elliott's other interests ("HOW THE JEWISH QUESTION TOUCHES THE FARM"). Elliott had been traveling around the Midwest — particularly southern Minnesota and Iowa — telling farmers that there was a legal and nonviolent way to solve their financial problems. He said that all loans made since 1974 were illegal under federal truth-in-lending legislation. He said that by joining NAPA and following its guidance farmers could, without hiring lawyers, file lawsuits that would result in their bank loans' being declared null and void. He said that NAPA could find low-interest loans for farmers. He said all this in vigorous, dramatic speeches that were laced with patriotic references and historical anecdotes and citations of federal codes. The Kirks joined NAPA, and when Robert Mettenbrink opened a Nebraska chapter in Grand Island, Deloris Kirk worked for a while in its office. According to Mrs. Kirk, her husband had returned home from that first meeting and said, "Mama, I'm sure at last we found the answer to our troubles."

That view would not have been shared by Norwest Bank. In June, the bank found out that Kirk had sold seventy thousand dollars' worth of stored corn and thirty thousand dollars' worth of cattle — property that, by the terms of his note, belonged partly to Norwest — but hadn't brought in the receipts. The bankers had a talk with Kirk, but he still didn't produce any money. What he did instead was to file a case in the federal district court in Lincoln asking that the Norwest loan be declared null and that the bank be ordered to pay him several million dollars in damages for a number of reasons, among them that the bank's conduct "has led to Plaintiff being accused of stealing his own property which Plaintiffs have proof of ownership by bills of sale and checks which is surely the most wanton form of conduct on the part of Defendants that would make a skunk belch from odor while leaving Plaintiff with horrendous damages." Kirk didn't use a lawyer; Robert Mettenbrink notarized the papers.

The chief judge of the federal district court in Nebraska, Warren K. Urbom, was not impressed by Kirk's legal reasoning. Except for one claim that didn't include enough information to permit a judgment, the case was dismissed without a hearing in October. Of the citations of law that Kirk had made, Judge Urbom wrote, "Many of these provisions have absolutely nothing to do with the facts alleged." In fact, the homemade cases inspired by NAPA had been dismissed wholesale by federal judges in the Midwest, and at least one judge had spoken of the possibility of assessing future plaintiffs court costs for taking up the court's time with frivolous litigation. "These cases display a disturbing pattern of identical styles, identical statutory and case-law citations, and even identical typographical errors," Judge Urbom had written in a decision in August of 1984. "Given the meritlessness of the claims, I have to suspect that these complaints are being filed for purposes other than good-faith assertion of legal claims. Whether the plaintiffs have the purpose of harassment or are deceived by some third party into believing there may be merit in their claims, I do not know." The Kirks had a newspaper clipping quoting Judge Urbom's August decision. They also had a smudged photocopy of a clipping from the *Rochester* (Minnesota) *Post-Bulletin* that went further than Judge Urbom had in criticizing what he referred to as the third party. "Rick Elliott, who is helping farmers prepare lawsuits against their lenders and says he can get low-interest loans for farmers, has a criminal record that stretches from 1949 to 1972," the *Post-Bulletin* reporter, Bruce Maxwell, wrote. Maxwell listed convictions for perjury and bad checks and selling stocks without a license. He also reported that the NAPA programs Elliott operated were being investigated by attorney-general offices in several states.

Once Judge Urbom had dismissed Kirk's suit, Norwest's lawyers entered a claim to the property that was security for Kirk's loan — his farm equipment and whatever crops had not been sold and the unaccounted-for hundred thousand dollars. Papers were drawn up notifying him of the date on which the state court would hear the bank's claim and ordering him not to dispose of any more secured property before that date. As was required by Nebraska law, Norwest turned the papers over to the civil section of the sheriff's office for service. The Norwest people also informed the Sheriff's Department that during their last conversation on Kirk's farm he had been wearing a .45. They may have mentioned that he was suspected of being a member of the Posse Comitatus. The Sheriff's Department, which had served papers on Art Kirk before, already knew him to be a man with a lot of guns and a quick temper. It was decided to send three deputies, and to send them armed.

When the events of that day are discussed in Grand Island, a lot of people are described as having done what they did because they couldn't be put in the position of doing otherwise. The bank, it is said, couldn't be put in the position of ignoring a debt of three hundred thousand dollars and a debtor who had sold a hundred thousand dollars' worth of secured assets. The bank had a responsibility to its depositors and to its investors. It was required to answer to bank examiners. The sheriff and the county attorney, it is said, couldn't be put in the position of permitting a citizen to avoid service of court papers by threatening deputies with a gun. Since the threatened deputy had responded by telling Kirk that he was under arrest, to which Kirk's response had reportedly been to mention the possibility of shooting the deputy's head off, it was decided that a warrant could be obtained charging Kirk with resisting arrest with a dangerous or deadly weapon. To judge from Art Kirk's conversation on the telephone that evening, he may have believed that he could not be put in the position of permitting armed deputies on land that had been federally posted. Once the warrant had been obtained, the county could not be put in the position of having its law-enforcement officials driven off the Kirk farm again — and that meant alerting the Troop C SWAT team.

"I am just afraid we're going to need some help, 'cause I'm afraid the guy's going to do some shooting," the chief deputy sheriff said that afternoon in a telephone call to the state police captain in charge of Troop C.

"Well, you understand if the SWAT team goes out there and there's any shots fired, they'll take him down — they won't worry about the consequences," the captain said.

"Well," the deputy sheriff said, "I don't know that the guy leaves us any choice, does he?"

In deciding to call in the SWAT team, Sheriff Fairbanks was, of course, conscious of the murders that had taken place when law-enforcement officials tried to arrest Gordon Kahl in North Dakota. A couple of months after the North Dakota shootings, Fairbanks had helped organize a Nebraska Sheriffs Association briefing in Grand Island on the Posse Comitatus and other fringe groups — a briefing at which the sheriffs were told that a number of Nebraska farmers and ranchers had been engaging in combat maneuvers.

Late in the afternoon, the SWAT team was officially called in.

Negotiators were named. An operational headquarters was set up in Cairo, and a command post was established at Troop C. Arrangements were made for an ambulance to be on hand in Cairo. "At approximately 8:00 pm, the command post was advised that the SWAT team was deployed in the vicinity of the Kirk farm," the county attorney, Stephen Von Riesen, said in his report. "The negotiators interviewed Mr. Titsworth, and it was agreed that he should be the first person to call the Kirk residence."

Among Nebraska farmers, one response to the news of Arthur Kirk's death was outrage. From some initial news reports that didn't go into what Kirk believed politically, or precisely why the SWAT team had surrounded his house, Art Kirk seemed to be a harassed farmer trying to defend his family's land against foreclosure — a tragic real-life version of the plucky farm folks that people like Jessica Lange and Sam Shepard and Sally Field had been playing in Hollywood movies. When Kirk, a man who hadn't done much socializing, was buried, several hundred people turned up for the funeral service. One local business took an advertisement in the *Independent* announcing that it would be closed for two hours so employees could attend "the funeral of Arthur Kirk, who was shot to death by State Police while trying to defend his family farm." Farmers held protest meetings. The headquarters of the Norwest Bank, in Minneapolis, sent a security team to the Grand Island branch. Kirk's pastor wanted to know why a churchman hadn't been called in. Kirk's wife wanted to know why she hadn't been allowed to go to her husband. A lot of people wanted to know why it was imperative for Arthur Kirk, a man who held no hostages and didn't seem to pose an immediate threat to the community, to be confronted with such force of arms. At least two state senators called for an inquiry into the circumstances of Kirk's death, and the governor eventually asked a retired district judge, Samuel Van Pelt, to conduct an investigation. The *Independent* got a lot of letters to the editor, most of them expressing sympathy with Art Kirk and condemnation of the law-enforcement authorities. "A large Chicago bank goes on the rocks," one letter began. "What happens? Several banks from around the world donate and the federal government comes with I forget how many billion dollars . . . A farmer goes broke, they can't get to him to sell him out, so they kill him."

The Hall County authorities and the state police defended themselves vigorously. They pointed out that a number of widely held assumptions about the incident were not true. The SWAT team was there to arrest Kirk on a felony charge, for instance, not to foreclose on his farm. The bank had made no claim to Kirk's land. The superintendent of the State Patrol said that SWAT teams were a device for controlling violence rather than raising the level of violence; the SWAT teams were organized in 1975, he said, and until Art Kirk started shooting his automatic rifle that night they had never been involved in an exchange of gunfire. The burden of the case made by the authorities was that Art Kirk had been a dangerous man, more like Gordon Kahl than like Sam Shepard. The morning after the *Independent* carried the story of Kirk's death, its lead headline was "LINK BETWEEN KIRK AND VIGILANTE GROUP PROBED." The State Patrol released transcripts of Kirk's telephone conversations on the night of the shooting — transcripts full of vituperation and threats and obscenity and bigotry. At a news conference, police displayed twenty-seven weapons that had been seized from Kirk's farmhouse after his death. Stephen Von Riesen, the county attorney, revealed that papers seized from the house at the same time included Posse Comitatus propaganda. They also included material from organizations like the Committee to Restore the Constitution and the National Commodity and Barter Association and the Anti-Lawyer Party and the Christian Nationalist Crusade, whose booklet "Jews and Their Lies," by Martin Luther, carried an epigraph of singular ecumenism: "Attention Reader: This book is not published for sectarian purposes. The publishers, as indicated above, are also publishing the edicts of more than 20 popes who dealt with the Jewish problem. Their edicts are as strong as anything contained in this work by Dr. Martin Luther."

Stephen Von Riesen maintained that those who wanted to assign blame for Art Kirk's death should have been looking not toward law-enforcement officials but toward the organizations that sell desperate farmers pipe dreams about how to escape their problems. "It's always easier to blame some amorphous conspiracy," Von Riesen said not long after Kirk's death. "Farmers have reached the point where the normal ways of handling problems aren't working. They're faced with losing their farms, and they're susceptible to radical, spurious approaches to the problem. Arthur Kirk was a victim of these groups that told him that there is a free lunch. There isn't any free lunch. If you borrow money, you have to pay it back."

Deloris Kirk continued to blame the police and to support NAPA. In fact, she seemed to draw closer and closer to the organization after her husband's death. Requests for interviews were referred to Robert Mettenbrink. When Mrs. Kirk held a press conference in Grand Island just after her husband's death, Mettenbrink introduced her, and Rick Elliott was also on hand. Mrs. Kirk was asked at the press conference how people could help, and she suggested that everybody read five works "that they're trying to destroy" — the United States Constitution, the Nebraska Constitution, the Bible, and two booklets associated with the fringe right. She appeared at NAPA rallies to say that her husband had been a happy man from the moment he heard Rick Elliott speak. It was a testimonial that lost some of its impact a few weeks after the shooting, when the *Independent* ran its first large story on Elliott's run-ins with the law. He had just been charged by the attorney general's office in Colorado with nineteen felony-theft counts having to do with NAPA and the *Primrose & Cattlemen's Gazette*.

When Deloris Kirk was asked at her press conference if she considered her husband a martyr, she said, "No, I think he was a victim." It was easy to see Art Kirk as a victim, although there was a lot of disagreement about whose victim he was. Some people agreed with Stephen Von Riesen that Kirk was the victim of those who led him to believe he could get his loan declared null with a do-it-yourself lawsuit and could keep the sheriff off his land with a legally worthless piece of paper. A lot of people saw Kirk as the victim of the pressures that farmers have had to face — a desperate man driven so far from rationality that he could believe that the Mossad, the Israeli intelligence agency, was pulling the strings in Hall County, Nebraska. Some people thought that there was plenty of blame to go around. The *Independent*'s editorial on the shooting said, "There are people who are profiting from the plight of farmers, some indirectly and even innocently because they are themselves deluded, and some more maliciously defrauding them," but it also said that the fact that Kirk owed the bank far more than he could ever hope to repay from the income on his land "says something to lenders and borrowers alike." Some Nebraskans who despised the message that groups like NAPA and the Posse Comitatus bring to farmers also thought that what Arthur Kirk chose to read in his own house was nobody's business and no justification for the state's show of force at the Kirk farmhouse that night.

In his report to the governor, Judge Van Pelt said that someone analyzing the circumstances of Arthur Kirk's death could identify several junctures at which a different decision might have avoided catastrophe. If the bank hadn't pressed its legal case or if the Sheriff's Department had sent out one unarmed deputy instead of three armed ones or if Deloris Kirk and some friends who went to counsel with Art Kirk after the incident with the deputies had stayed around or if Jan Steeple had gone to the Kirk farm to talk things over or if an arrest had been attempted while Kirk was cutting beans instead of while he was barricaded inside his house or if the SWAT team deployment had been delayed until Kirk had a chance to cool off, the Judge said, Art Kirk might have survived. Still, Van Pelt found that at each juncture the decision reached had been understandable, given the knowledge and resources available at the time. In other words, a lot of people had acted as they might have been expected to act, and at the end Art Kirk lay bleeding to death in his farmyard. It was not an analysis that offered much comfort to the Nebraska farmers who had been so upset by the shooting in the first place. A lot of them have a lot of Art Kirk's problems.

1985

COVERING
THE COPS

IN THE NEWSROOM of the *Miami Herald*, there is some disagreement about which of Edna Buchanan's first paragraphs
stands as the classic Edna lead. I line up with the fried-chicken faction. The fried-chicken story was about a rowdy ex-con named
Gary Robinson, who late one Sunday night lurched drunkenly into
a Church's outlet, shoved his way to the front of the line, and ordered a three-piece box of fried chicken. Persuaded to wait his
turn, he reached the counter again five or ten minutes later, only to
be told that Church's had run out of fried chicken. The young
woman at the counter suggested that he might like chicken nuggets
instead. Robinson responded to the suggestion by slugging her in
the head. That set off a chain of events that ended with Robinson's
being shot dead by a security guard. Edna Buchanan covered the
murder for the *Herald* — there are policemen in Miami who say
that it wouldn't be a murder without her — and her story began
with what the fried-chicken faction still regards as the classic Edna
lead: "Gary Robinson died hungry."

All connoisseurs would agree, I think, that the classic Edna lead
would have to include one staple of crime reporting — the simple,
matter-of-fact statement that registers with a jolt. The question is
where the jolt should be. There's a lot to be said for starting right
out with it. I'm rather partial to the Edna lead on a story last year
about a woman about to go on trial for a murder conspiracy: "Bad

244 / AMERICAN STORIES

things happen to the husbands of Widow Elkin." On the other hand, I can understand the preference that others have for the device of beginning a crime story with a more or less conventional sentence or two, then snapping the reader back in his chair with an abbreviated sentence that is used like a blunt instrument. One student of the form at the *Herald* refers to that device as the Miller Chop. The reference is to Gene Miller, now a *Herald* editor, who, in a remarkable reporting career that concentrated on the felonious, won the Pulitzer Prize twice for stories that resulted in the release of people in prison for murder. Miller likes short sentences in general — it is sometimes said at the *Herald* that he writes as if he were paid by the period — and he particularly likes to use a short sentence after a couple of rather long ones. Some years ago, Gene Miller and Edna Buchanan did a story together on the murder of a high-living Miami lawyer who was shot to death on a day he had planned to while away on the golf course of La Gorce Country Club, and the lead said, ". . . he had his golf clubs in the trunk of his Cadillac. Wednesday looked like an easy day. He figured he might pick up a game later with Eddie Arcaro, the jockey. He didn't."

These days, Miller sometimes edits the longer pieces that Edna Buchanan does for the *Herald,* and she often uses the Miller Chop — as in a piece about a lovers' spat: "The man she loved slapped her face. Furious, she says she told him never, ever to do that again. 'What are you going to do, kill me?' he asked, and handed her a gun. 'Here, kill me,' he challenged. She did."

Now that I think of it, that may be the classic Edna lead.

There is no dispute about the classic Edna telephone call to a homicide detective or a desk sergeant she knows: "Hi. This is Edna. What's going on over there?" There are those at the *Herald* who like to think that Edna Buchanan knows every policeman and policewoman in the area — even though Dade County has twenty-seven separate police forces, with a total strength of more than forty-five hundred officers. "I asked her if by any chance she happened to know this sergeant," a *Herald* reporter once told me. "And she looked at her watch and said, 'Yeah, but he got off his shift twenty minutes ago.' " She does not in fact know all the police officers in the area, but they know her. If the desk sergeant who picks up the phone is someone Edna has never heard of, she gives her full name and the name of her paper. But even if she said, "This is Edna," there aren't many cops who would say, "Edna who?" In Miami, a few figures are regularly discussed by first name among people they have never actually met. One of them is Fidel. Another is Edna.

It's an old-fashioned name. Whoever picks up the phone at homicide when Edna Buchanan calls probably doesn't know any Ednas he might confuse her with. Edna is, as it happens, a rather old-fashioned person. "She should have been working in the twenties or thirties," a detective who has known her for years told me. "She'd have been happy if she had a little press card in her hat." She sometimes says the same sort of thing about herself. She laments the replacement of typewriters at the *Herald* with word processors. She would like to think of her clips stored in a place called a morgue rather than a place called an editorial reference library. She's nostalgic about old-fashioned criminals. As a girl growing up around Paterson, New Jersey, she used to read the New York tabloids out loud to her grandmother — a Polish grandmother who didn't read English — and she still likes to roll out the names of the memorable felons in those stories: names like George Metesky, the Mad Bomber, and Willie Sutton, the man who robbed banks because that's where the money was. She even has a period look about her — something that recalls the period around 1961. She is a very thin woman in her forties who tends to dress in slacks and silk shirts and high heels. She wears her hair in a heavy blond shoulder-length fall. Her eyes are wide, and her brow is often furrowed in concern. She seems almost permanently anxious about one thing or another. Did she neglect to try the one final approach that would have persuaded the suspect's mother to open the door and have a chat? Will a stray cat that she spotted in the neighborhood meet an unpleasant end? Did she forget to put a quarter in the meter? Despite many years spent among people who often find themselves resorting to rough language — hookers, cocaine cowboys, policemen, newspaper reporters — her own conversation tends to sound like that of a rather demure secretary circa 1952. Her own cats — she has five of them — have names like Misty Blue Eyes and Baby Dear. When she is particularly impressed by a bit of news, she is likely to describe it as "real neat." When she discovers, say, a gruesome turn in a tale that might be pretty gruesome already, she may say, "That's interesting as heck!"

Among newspaper people, Edna's line of work is considered a bit old-fashioned. Daily police reporting — what is sometimes known in the trade as covering the cops — is still associated with that old-timer who had a desk in the station house and didn't have to be told by the sergeant in charge which part of the evening's activities to leave out of the story and thought of himself as more or less a member of the department. Covering the cops is often something a reporter does early in his career — an assignment that can provide him with enough war stories in six months to last him through years on the business page or the city desk. Even Gene Miller, a man with a fondness for illegalities of all kinds, turned rather quickly from covering the cops to doing longer pieces. The *Herald*, which regularly shows up on lists of the country's most distinguished dailies, does take a certain amount of pride in providing the sort of crime coverage that is not typical of newspapers on such lists, but it does not have the sort of single-minded interest in juicy felonies that characterized the New York tabloids Edna used to read to her grandmother. When Edna Buchanan began covering the cops for the *Herald*, in 1973, there hadn't been anyone assigned full time to the beat in several years.

In the years since, Edna has herself broken the routine now and then to do a long crime piece or a series. But she invariably returns to the daily beat. She still dresses every morning to the sound of a police scanner. Unless she already has a story to do, she still drops by the Miami Beach department and the Miami municipal department and the Metro-Dade department on the way to work. She still flips through the previous night's crime reports and the log. She still calls police officers and says, "Hi. This is Edna. What's going on over there?"

·　　·　　·

Like a lot of old-fashioned reporters, Edna Buchanan seems to operate on the assumption that there are always going to be any number of people who, for perverse and inexplicable reasons of their own, will try to impede her in gathering a story that is rightfully hers and delivering it to where God meant it to be — on the front page of the *Miami Herald*, and preferably the front page of the *Miami Herald* on a Sunday, when the circulation is at its highest. There are shy witnesses who insist that they don't want to get involved. There are lawyers who advise their clients to hang up if Edna Buchanan calls to ask whether they really did it. (It could be libelous for a newspaper to call someone a suspect, but the paper can get the same idea across by quoting his denial of guilt.) There are close-mouthed policemen. There are television reporters who require equipment that gets in the way and who ask the sort of question that makes Edna impatient. (In her view, television reporters on a murder story are concerned almost exclusively with whether they're going to be able to get a picture of the authorities removing the body from the premises, the only other question that truly engages them being whether they're going to get the picture in time for the six o'clock news.) There are editors who want to cut a story even though it was virtually ordained to run at least sixteen inches. There are editors — often the same editors — who will try to take an interesting detail out of the story simply because the detail happens to horrify or appall them. "One of them kept saying that people read this paper at *breakfast*," I was told by Edna, whose own idea of a successful lead is one that might cause a reader who is having breakfast with his wife to "spit out his coffee, clutch his chest, and say, 'My God, Martha! Did you read this!' " When Edna went to Fort Lauderdale one day to talk about police reporting with some of the young reporters in the *Herald*'s Broward County bureau, she said, "For sanity and survival, there are three cardinal rules in the newsroom: never trust an editor, never trust an editor, and never trust an editor."

Edna likes and admires a lot of policemen, but, listening to her talk about policemen, you can get the impression that they spend most of their energy trying to deny her access to information that she is meant to have. Police officers insist on roping off crime scenes. ("The police department has too much yellow rope — they want to rope off the world.") Entire departments switch over to computerized crime reports, which don't accommodate the sort of detailed narrative that Edna used to comb through in the old written reports. Investigators sometimes decline to talk about the case they're working on. (Edna distinguishes degrees of reticence among policemen with remarks like "He wasn't *quite* as paranoid as the other guy.") Once, the man who was then chief of the Metro-Dade department blocked off the homicide squad with a buzzer-controlled entrance whose function was so apparent that it was commonly referred to as "the Edna Buchanan door." Homicide investigators who arrive at a scene and spot Edna talking intently with someone assume that she has found an eyewitness, and they often snatch him away with cautioning words about the errors of talking to the press rather than to the legally constituted authorities. Edna discusses the prevalence of witnessnapping among police detectives in the tone of voice a member of the Citizens Commission on Crime might reserve for talking about an alarming increase in multiple murders.

Once the police arrive at a crime scene in force, Edna often finds it more effective to return to the *Herald* and work by telephone. The alternative could be simply standing behind the yellow rope — an activity she considers fit for television reporters. She may try calling the snatched witness. With a cross-indexed directory, she can phone neighbors who might have seen what happened and then ducked back into their own house for a bolstering drink. She will try to phone the victim's next of kin. "I thought you'd like to say something," she'll say to someone's bereaved wife or daughter. "People care what he was like." Most reporters would sooner cover thirty weeks of water-board hearings than call a murder victim's next of kin, but Edna tries to look on the positive side. "For some people, it's like a catharsis," she told me one day. "They want to talk about what kind of person their husband was, or their father. Also, it's probably the only time his name is going to be in the paper. It's their last shot. They want to give him a good sendoff."

There are people, of course, who are willing to forgo the sendoff just to be left alone. Some of them respond to Edna's call by shouting at her for having the gall to trouble them at such a time, and then slamming down the telephone. Edna has a standard procedure for dealing with that. She waits sixty seconds and then phones back. "This is Edna Buchanan at the *Miami Herald*," she says, using her full name and identification for civilians. "I think we were cut off." In sixty seconds, she figures, whoever answered the phone might reconsider. Someone else in the room might say, "You should have talked to that reporter." Someone else in the room might decide to spare the upset party the pain of answering the phone the next time it rings, and might be a person who is more willing to talk. Edna once called the home of a TV-repair-shop operator in his sixties who had been killed in a robbery attempt — a crime she had already managed to separate from the run-of-the-mill armed-robbery murder. ("On New Year's Eve Charles Curzio stayed later than planned at his small TV repair shop to make sure customers would have their sets in time to watch the King Orange Jamboree Parade," Edna's lead began. "His kindness cost his life.") One of Curzio's sons answered, and, upon learning who it was, angrily hung up. "Boy, did I hate dialing the second time," Edna told me. "But if I hadn't I might have lost them for good." This time, the phone was answered by another of Curzio's sons, and he was willing to talk. He had some eloquent things to say about his father and about capital punishment. ("My father got no trial, no stay of execution, no Supreme Court hearing, nothing. Just some maniac who smashed his brains in with a rifle butt.") If the second call hadn't been productive, Edna told me, she would have given up: "The third call would be harassment."

When Edna is looking for information, slamming down the phone must sometimes seem the only way of ending the conversation. She is not an easy person to say good-bye to. Once she begins asking questions, she may pause occasionally, as if the interrogation were finally over, but then, in the sort of silence that in conventional conversations is ended with someone's saying "Well, O.K." or "Well, thanks for your help," she asks another question. The questioning may not even concern a story she's working on. I was once present when Edna began chatting with a Metro-Dade homicide detective about an old murder case that he had never managed to solve — the apparently motiveless shooting of a restaurant proprietor and his wife, both along in years, as they were about to enter their house. Edna would ask a question and the detective would shake his head, explaining that he had checked out that angle without result. Then, after a pause long enough to make me think that they were about to go on to another case, she would ask another question. Could it have been a mistake in the address? Did homicide check out the people who lived in the equivalent house on the next block? Did the restaurant have any connection with the mob? How about an ex-employee? What about a bad son-in-law? Over the years, Edna has come across any number of bad sons-in-law.

Earlier in the day, I had heard her use the same tone to question a young policewoman who was watching over the front desk at Miami Beach headquarters. "What do you think the rest of Bo's secret is?" Edna said as she skimmed log notations about policemen being called to a loud party or to the scene of a robbery or to a vandalized garage. "Is Kimberly going to get an abortion?" At first, I thought the questions were about cases she was reminded of by the log reports. They turned out to be about "Days of Our Lives," a soap opera that both Edna and the policewoman are devoted to. Fifteen minutes later, long after I thought the subject had been dropped, Edna was saying, "So is this new character going to be a friend of Jennifer's — the one in the car wreck?"

Bob Swift, a *Herald* columnist who was once Edna's editor at a paper called the *Miami Beach Sun*, told me that he arrived at the *Sun*'s office one day fuming about the fact that somebody had stolen his garbage cans. "I was really mad," he said. "I was saying, 'Who would want to steal two garbage cans!' All of a sudden, I heard Edna say, in that breathless voice, 'Were they empty or full?' "

·   ·   ·

"Nobody loves a police reporter," Edna sometimes says in speeches. She has been vilified and shouted at and threatened. Perhaps because a female police reporter was something of a rarity when she began, some policemen took pleasure in showing her, say, the corpse of someone who had met a particularly nasty end. ("Sometimes they try to gross you out, but when you're really curious you don't get grossed out. I'm always saying, 'What's this? What's that?' ") When Edna was asked by David Finkel, who did a story about her for the *St. Petersburg Times*, why she endured the rigors of covering the cops, she replied, "It's better than working in a coat factory in Paterson, New Jersey." Working in the coat factory was one of several part-time jobs that she had as a schoolgirl to help her mother out. Aside from the pleasures Edna associates with reading crime stories to her Polish grandmother, she doesn't have many happy memories of Paterson. Her other grandmother — her mother's mother — was a member of the Daughters of the American Revolution; Edna still has the membership certificate to prove it. That grandmother, in the view of her DAR family, married beneath her — her husband was a Paterson schoolteacher — and her own daughter, Edna's mother, did even worse. She married a Polish factory worker who apparently had some local renown as a drinker and carouser, and he walked out when Edna was seven. As soon as Edna finished high school, an institution she loathed, she joined her mother in wiring switchboards at the Western Electric plant. Eventually, she transferred to an office job at Western Electric — still hardly the career path that normally leads to a reporting job on the *Miami Herald*.

The enormous change in Edna's life came partly because a clotheshorse friend who wanted to take a course in millinery design persuaded her to come along to evening classes at Montclair State Teachers College. Edna, who had been interested in writing as a child, decided to take a course in creative writing. She remembers the instructor as a thin, poetic-looking man who traveled to New Jersey every week from Greenwich Village. He may have had a limp — a war wound, perhaps. She is much clearer about what happened when he handed back the first short stories the students had written. First, he described one he had particularly liked, and it was Edna's — a sort of psychological thriller about a young woman who thought she was being followed. Edna can still recall what the teacher said about the story — about what a rare pleasure it was for a teacher to come across such writing, about how one section reminded him of early Tennessee Williams. It was the one radiant New Jersey moment. The teacher told her about writers she should read. He told her about paragraphing; the first story she turned in was "just one long paragraph." She decided that she could be a writer. Years later, a novelist who had been hanging around with Edna for a while to learn about crime reporting recognized the teacher from Edna's description and provided his telephone number. She phoned him to tell him how much his encouragement had meant to her. He was pleasant enough, Edna told me, but he didn't remember her or her short story.

Not long after the writing course, Edna and her mother decided to take their vacation in Miami Beach, and Edna says that as she walked off the plane she knew she was not going to spend the rest of her life in Paterson, New Jersey. "The instant I breathed the air, it was like coming home," she told me. "I loved it. I absolutely loved it. I had been wandering around in a daze up there, like a displaced person. I was always a misfit." Edna and her mother tried to get jobs at the Western Electric plant in South Florida; when they couldn't arrange that, they moved anyway. While taking a course in writing, Edna heard that the *Miami Beach Sun* was looking for reporters. The *Sun*, which is now defunct, was the sort of newspaper that hired people without any reporting experience and gave them a lot of it quickly. Edna wrote society news and local political stories and crime stories and celebrity interviews and movie reviews and, on occasion, the letters to the editor.

Edna Buchanan may be the best-known newspaper reporter in Miami, but sometimes she still sounds as if she can't quite believe that she doesn't work in a factory and doesn't live in Paterson, New Jersey. "I've lived here more than twenty years," she says, "and every day I see the palm trees and the water and the beach, and I'm thrilled with how beautiful it is. I'm really lucky, coming from a place like Paterson, New Jersey. I live on a waterway. I have a house. I almost feel, My God, it's like I'm an impostor!"

When Edna says such things, she sounds grateful — a state that an old newspaper hand would tell you is about as common among reporters as a prolonged, religiously inspired commitment to the temperance movement. Edna can even sound grateful for the opportunity to work the police beat, although in the next sentence she may be talking about how tired she is of hearing policemen gripe or how irritated she gets at editors who live to pulverize her copy. She seems completely lacking in the black humor or irony that reporters often use to cope with even a short hitch covering the cops. When she says something is interesting as heck, she means that it is interesting as heck.

Some years ago, she almost went over to the enemy. A Miami television station offered her a hundred and thirty-seven dollars more a week than she was making at the *Herald*, and she had just about decided to take it. She had some ideas about how crime could be covered on television in a way that did not lean so heavily on pictures of the body being removed from the premises. At the last moment, though, she decided not to accept the offer. One reason, she says, is that she faced the fact that crime could never be covered on local television with the details and the subtleties possible in a newspaper story. Also, she couldn't quite bring herself to leave the *Herald*. "If I had been eighteen, maybe I would have done it," she says. "But the *Herald* is the only security I ever had."

Even before the appearance of "Miami Vice," Miami was the setting of choice for tales of flashy violence. Any number of people, some of them current or former *Herald* reporters, have portrayed Miami crime in mystery novels or television shows or Hollywood movies. Some of the show-business types might have been attracted mainly by the palm trees and the beach and the exotica of the Latin drug industry: the opening shots of each "Miami Vice" episode are so glamorous that some local tourist-development people have been quoted in the *Herald* as saying that the overall impact of the series is positive. But the volume and the variety of real crime in Miami have in fact been of an order to make any police reporter feel the way a stockbroker might feel at a medical convention: opportunities abound. Like most police reporters, Edna specializes in murder, and, as she might express it in a Miller Chop at the end of the first paragraph, so does Miami.

When Edna began as a reporter, a murder in Miami was an occasion. A woman who worked with Edna at the *Miami Beach Sun* in the days when it was sometimes known as "Bob Swift and his all-girl newspaper" has recalled the stir in the *Sun* newsroom when a body washed up on the beach: "I had a camera, because my husband had given it to me for Christmas. The managing editor said, 'Go take a picture of the body.' I said, 'I'm not taking a picture of a washed-up body!' Then I heard a voice from the other end of the room saying, 'I'll do it, I'll do it.' It was Edna."

In the late seventies, Miami, like other American cities, had a steady increase in the sort of murders that occur when, say, an armed man panics while he is robbing a convenience store. It also had some political bombings and some shooting between outfits that were, depending on your point of view, either running drugs to raise money for fighting Fidel or using the fight against Fidel as a cover for running drugs. At the end of the decade, Dade County's murder rate took an astonishing upturn. Around that time, the Colombians who manufactured the drugs being distributed in Miami by Cubans decided to eliminate the middleman, and, given a peculiar viciousness in the way they customarily operated, that sometimes meant eliminating the middleman's wife and whoever else happened to be around. Within a couple of years after the Colombians began their campaign to reduce overhead, Miami was hit with the Mariel boat-lift refugees. In 1977, there were two hundred and eleven murders in Dade County. By 1981, the high point of Dade murder, there were six hundred and twenty-one. That meant, according to one homicide detective I spoke to, that Miami experienced the greatest increase in murders per capita that any city had ever recorded. It also meant that Miami had the highest murder rate in the country. It also meant that a police reporter could drive to work in the morning knowing that there would almost certainly be at least one murder to write about.

·   ·   ·

"A personal question," one of the Broward-bureau reporters said after Edna had finished her talk in Fort Lauderdale. "I hope not to embarrass you, but I've always heard a rumor that you carried a gun. Is that true?"

"I don't carry a gun," Edna said. "I own a gun or two." She keeps one in the house and one in the car — which seems only sensible, she told the reporters, for someone who lives alone and is often driving through unpleasant neighborhoods late at night. It also seems only sensible to spend some time on the shooting range, which she happens to enjoy. ("They let me shoot an Uzi the other day," she once told me. "It was interesting as heck.") A lot of what Edna says about her life seems only sensible, but a lot of it turns out to have something to do with violence or crime, the stuff of an Edna story. Talking about her paternal grandfather, she'll say that he was supposed to have killed or maimed someone in a barroom brawl and that his children were so frightened of his drunken rages that the first sign of an eruption would send some of them leaping out of second-floor windows to escape. As an example of her nearsightedness, she'll mention some revelations in Paterson that seemed to indicate that she had been followed for months by a notorious sex criminal without realizing it. When Edna talks about places where she has lived in Miami, she is likely to identify neighbors with observations like "He lived right across the street from this big dope dealer" or "He was indicted for Medicare fraud but he beat it."

Edna's first marriage, to someone she met while she was working at the *Miami Beach Sun,* could provide any number of classic Edna leads. James Buchanan had some dealings with the anti-Castro community and was close to Frank Sturgis, one of the Watergate burglars. Edna says that for some time she thought her husband was simply a reporter on the *Fort Lauderdale Sun-Sentinel* who seemed to be out of town more than absolutely necessary. The story she sometimes tells of how she discovered otherwise could be written with an Edna lead: "James Buchanan seemed to make a lot of unexplained trips. Yesterday, at the supermarket, his wife found out why. Mrs. Buchanan, accompanied by a bag boy who was carrying a large load of groceries, emerged from the supermarket and opened the trunk of her car. It was full of machine guns. 'Just put the groceries in the back seat,' she said."

Edna tried a cop the next time, but that didn't seem to have much effect on the duration or quality of the marriage. Her second husband, Emmett Miller, was on the Miami Beach force for years and was eventually appointed chief. By that time, though, he had another wife, his fifth — a wife who, it turned out, was part owner of what the *Herald* described as "an X-rated Biscayne Boulevard motel and a Beach restaurant alleged to be a center of illegal gambling." The appointment was approved by the Miami Beach City Commission anyway, although one commissioner, who stated that the police chief ought to be "above suspicion," did say, "I don't think we're putting our city in an enviable position when we overlook this."

Since the breakup of her marriage to Miller, Edna has almost never been seen at parties or *Herald* hangouts. "I love to be alone," she says. One of the people closest to her is still her mother, who lives not far from Edna and seems to produce ceramic animals even faster than she once turned out fully wired switchboards. Edna's house is a menagerie of ceramic animals. She also has ceramic planters and a ceramic umbrella holder and a ceramic lighthouse — not to speak of a watercolor and a sketch by Jack (Murph the Surf) Murphy, the Miami beachboy who in 1964 helped steal the Star of India sapphire and the deLong Star Ruby from the American Museum of Natural History — but ceramic animals are the predominant design element. She has penguins and turtles and horses and seagulls and flamingos and swans and fish and a rabbit and a pelican. She has a ceramic dog that is nearly life-size. She has cats in practically every conceivable pose — a cat with nursing kittens, a cat carrying a kitten in its mouth, a curled-up cat. Edna is fond of some of the ceramic animals, but the fact that her mother's productivity seems to be increasing rather than waning with the passing of the years has given her pause.

All of Edna's live animals are strays. Besides the cats, she has a dog whose best trick is to fall to the floor when Edna points an imaginary gun at him and says, "Bang! You're dead!" Some colleagues at the *Herald* think that a stray animal is about the only thing that can distract Edna from her coverage of the cops. It is assumed at the *Herald* that she takes Mondays and Tuesdays off because the weekend is traditionally a high-crime period. (Edna says that the beaches are less crowded during the week, and that working weekends gives her a better chance at the Sunday paper.) Around the *Herald* newsroom, Edna is known for being fiercely proprietary about stories she considers hers — any number of *Herald* reporters, running into her at the scene of some multiple murder or major disaster, have been greeted with an icy "What are *you* doing here?" — and so combative about her copy that a few of the less resilient editors have been reduced almost to the state in which they would fall to the floor if Edna pointed an imaginary gun at them and said, "Bang! You're dead!" Edna's colleagues tend to speak of her not as a pal but as a phenomenon. Their Edna stories are likely to concern her tenacity or her superstitions or the remarkable intensity she maintains after all these years of covering a beat that quickly strikes many reporters as unbearably horrifying or depressing. They often mention the astonishing contrast between her apparent imperviousness to the grisly sights on the police beat and her overwhelming concern for animals. While I was in Miami, two or three *Herald* reporters suggested that I look up some articles in which, as they remembered it, Edna hammered away so mercilessly at a retired French-Canadian priest who had put to death some stray cats that the poor man was run out of the country. When I later told one of the reporters that I had read the *Herald*'s coverage of the incident and that almost none of it had been done by Edna, he said, "I'm not surprised. Probably didn't trust herself. Too emotionally involved."

Policemen, Edna told the young reporters in Fort Lauderdale, have an instinctive mistrust of outsiders — "an 'us-and-them' attitude." Edna can never be certain which category she's in. Any police reporter these days is likely to have a less comfortable relationship with the police than the one enjoyed by the old-fashioned station-house reporter who could be counted on to be looking the other way if the suspect met with an accident while he was being taken into custody. Since Watergate, reporters all over the country have been under pressure to cast a more suspicious eye on any institution they cover. Partly because of the availability of staggering amounts of drug money, both the Miami and the Metro-Dade departments have had serious scandals in recent years, making them particularly sensitive to inspection by critical outsiders. The *Herald* has covered police misconduct prominently, and it has used Florida's public-records act aggressively in court to gain access to police documents — even documents involved in Internal Affairs investigations. A lot of policemen regard the *Herald* as their adversary and see Edna Buchanan as the embodiment of the *Herald*.

Edna says that she makes every effort to portray cops as human beings — writing about a police officer who has been charged with misconduct, she usually manages to find some past commendations to mention — but it has never occurred to anybody that she might look the other way. Edna broke the story of an attempted coverup involving a black insurance man named Arthur McDuffie, who died as a result of injuries suffered in an encounter with some Metro-Dade policemen — policemen whose acquittal on manslaughter charges some months later touched off three nights of rioting in Miami's black community. There are moments when Edna seems to be "us" and "them" at the same time. Keeping the picture and the press release sent when someone is named Officer of the Month may give Edna one extra positive sentence to write about a policeman the next time she mentions him; also, as it happens, it is difficult to come by a picture of a cop who gets in trouble, and over the years Edna has found that a cop who gets in trouble and a cop who was named Officer of the Month are often the same person.

"There's a love-hate relationship between the police and the press," Mike Gonzalez, one of Edna's best friends on the Miami municipal force, says. A case that Edna covers prominently is likely to get a lot of attention in the department, which means that someone whose name is attached to it might become a hero or might, as one detective I spoke to put it, "end up in the complaint room of the property bureau." Edna says that the way a reporter is received at police headquarters can depend on "what you wrote the day before — or their perception of what you wrote the day before."

Some police officers in Dade County won't talk to Edna Buchanan about the case they're working on. Some of those who do give her tips — not just on their own cases but on cases being handled by other people, or even other departments — won't admit it. (According to Dr. Joseph Davis, the medical examiner of Dade County, "Every police agency thinks she has a direct pipeline into someone else's agency.") Cops who become known as friends and sources of Edna's are likely to be accused by other cops of showboating or of trying to further their careers through the newspaper. When I mentioned Mike Gonzalez to a Metro-Dade lieutenant I was talking to in Miami, he said, "What Howard Cosell did for Cassius Clay, Edna Buchanan did for Mike Gonzalez."

Gonzalez is aware of such talk, and doesn't show much sign of caring about it. He thinks most policemen are nervous about the press because they aren't confident that they can reveal precisely what they find it useful to reveal and no more. Edna's admirers among police investigators — people like Gonzalez and Lloyd Hough, a Metro-Dade homicide detective — tend to admire her for her skill and independence as an investigator. "I'd take her any time as a partner," Hough told me. "Let's put it like this: if I had done something, I wouldn't want Edna investigating me. Internal Affairs I don't care about, but Edna . . ." They also admire her persistence, maddening as it may sometimes be. Hough nearly had her arrested once when she persisted in coming under the yellow rope into a crime scene. "She knows when she's pushed you to the limit, and she'll do that often," Hough told me. "And I say that with the greatest admiration."

A police detective and a police reporter may sound alike as they stand around talking about past cases — recalling the airline pilot who killed the other airline pilot over the stewardess, or exchanging anecdotes about the aggrieved bag boy who cleared a Publix supermarket in a hurry by holding a revolver to the head of the manager — but their interests in a murder case are not necessarily the same. If an armed robber kills a convenience-store clerk, the police are interested in catching him; Edna is interested in distinguishing what happened from other killings of other convenience-store clerks. To write about any murder, Edna is likely to need details that wouldn't help an investigator close the case. "I want to know what movie they saw before they got gunned down," she has said. "What were they wearing? What did they have in their pockets? What was cooking on the stove? What song was playing on the jukebox?" Mike Gonzalez just sighs when he talks about Edna's appetite for irrelevant detail. "It infuriates Mike," Edna says. "I always ask what the dog's name is, what the cat's name is." Edna told me that Gonzalez now advises rookie detectives that they might as well gather such details, because otherwise "you're just going to feel stupid when Edna asks you."

There are times when Edna finds herself longing for simpler times on the police beat. When she began, the murders she covered tended to be conventional love triangles or armed robberies. She was often dealing with "an up-front person who happened to have bludgeoned his wife to death." These days, the murders are likely to be Latin drug murders, and a lot fewer of them produce a suspect. Trying to gather information from Cubans and Central Americans, Edna has a problem that goes beyond the language barrier. "They have a Latin love of intrigue," she says. "I had a Cuban informant, and I found that he would sometimes lie to me just to make it more interesting." It is also true that even for a police reporter there can be too many murders. Edna says that she was "a little shell-shocked" four or five years ago, when Dade murders hit their peak. She found that she barely had time to make her rounds in a thorough way. "I used to like to stop at the jail," she has said. "I used to like to browse in the morgue. To make sure who's there."

Edna found that the sheer number of murders overwhelmed each individual murder as the big story. "Dade's murder rate hit new heights this week as a wave of unrelated violence left 14 peo-

ple dead and five critically hurt within five days," a story bylined
Edna Buchanan began in June of 1980. After a couple of paragraphs comparing the current murder figures with those of previous years, the story went on, "In the latest wave of violence, a
teenager's throat was cut and her body dumped in a canal. A
former airline stewardess was garroted and left with a pair of scis-
sors stuck between her shoulder blades. Four innocent bystanders
were shot in a barroom gun battle. An 80-year-old man surprised a
burglar who battered him fatally with a hammer. An angry young
woman who 'felt used' beat her date to death with the dumbbells
he used to keep fit. And an apparent robbery victim was shot dead
as he ran away from the robbers." The murder rate has leveled off
since 1981, but Edna still sometimes writes what amount to
murder-roundup stories. "I feel bad, and even a little guilty, that a
murder no longer gets a story, just a paragraph," she says. "It dehu-
manizes it." A paragraph in a roundup piece is not Edna's idea of a
sendoff.

On a day I was making the rounds with Edna, there was a police
report saying that two Marielitos had begun arguing on the street
and the argument had ended with one shooting the other dead.
That sounded like a paragraph at most. But Edna had a tip that the
victim and the killer had known each other in Cuba and the shooting was actually the settling of an old prison score. That sounded
to me more like a murder that stood out a bit from the crowd.
Edna thought so, too, but her enthusiasm was limited. "We've already had a couple of those," she told me. Edna has covered a few
thousand murders by now, and she's seen a couple of most things.
She has done stories about a man who was stabbed to death because he stepped on somebody's toes on his way to a seat in a
movie theater and about a two-year-old somebody tried to frame
for the murder of a playmate and about an eighty-nine-year-old
man who was arrested for beating his former wife to death and
about a little boy killed by a crocodile. She has done stories about a
woman who committed suicide because she couldn't get her leaky
roof fixed and about a newspaper deliveryman who committed
suicide because during a petroleum shortage he couldn't get

enough gasoline. She has done stories about a man who managed to commit suicide by stabbing himself in the heart *twice* and about a man who threw a severed head at a police officer twice. She has done a story about two brothers who killed a third brother because he interrupted a checkers game. ("I thought I had the best-raised children in the world," their mother said.) She has done a story about a father being killed at the surprise birthday party given for him by his thirty children. She has done a story about a man who died because fourteen of the eighty-two double-wrapped condom packages of cocaine he tried to carry into the country inside his stomach began to leak. ("His last meal was worth $30,000 and it killed him.") She has done any number of stories about bodies being discovered in the bay by beachcombers or fishermen or University of Miami scientists doing marine research. (" 'It's kind of a nuisance when you plan your day to do research on the reef,' fumed Professor Peter Glynn, of the university's Rosenstiel School of Marine and Atmospheric Science.") Talking to Edna one day about murder cases they had worked on, a Metro-Dade homicide detective said, "In Dade County, there are no surprises left."

Edna would agree that surprises are harder to find in Dade County these days. Still, she finds them. Flipping through page after page of routine police logs, talking to her sources on the telephone, chatting with a homicide detective, she'll come across, say, a shopping-mall murder that might have been done against the background of a new kind of high school gang, or a murderer who seemed to have been imprisoned with his victim for a time by a sophisticated burglar-gate system. Then, a look of concern still on her face, she'll say, "That's interesting as heck."

1986

ZEI-DA-MAN

OR JOHN ZEIDMAN, as he approached twenty, China
seemed to bring everything together. In the view of his parents, it was about time. Particularly for John's father, Philip Zeidman, the first eighteen years or so of John's life had not always
been easy going. For one thing, John went through school as what
his father considered "a notorious underachiever — practically to
the point of taking pride in it." Philip Zeidman, a successful Washington lawyer, could see that what appeared to be almost willful
academic sluggishness on John's part might have been "a reaction
to the Type A parent" — meaning himself — but that didn't seem
to make it significantly less exasperating. Philip Zeidman has been
an achiever since childhood. He was a chairman of committees as
an undergraduate at Yale in the middle fifties; he is a chairman of
bar committees now. At thirty, he was the general counsel of the
Small Business Administration. When he went into private practice, in 1968, after a stint as a special assistant to Vice President
Hubert Humphrey, he found himself with a franchisers' trade association as his first client — he had organized some hearings on the
nascent franchising industry while he was at the SBA — and his
practice expanded with the proliferation of outlets for slickly
packaged hamburgers and ice cream and doughnuts. Nobody ever
mistook him, though, for someone who simply happened to be in
the right place at the right time. He is a person of astonishing

energy — a lister of things to be done, a logger of air miles, an amasser of honors, a tender of contacts, an organizer of task forces. He is the sort of person who answers answers to thank-you notes. He often strikes those he meets as an unreconstructed example of what is sometimes referred to as "a high-powered Washington attorney." To some people, of course, that means an overbearing or self-important attorney. "But anybody could see through that in ten minutes with Phil," a relatively recent acquaintance who was surprised to find herself liking Zeidman said not long ago. Before ten minutes has elapsed, in fact, Zeidman is likely to have told a joke that makes it clear that he sees through it himself. He can say that when he began private practice he quickly became known as the attorney who knew more than anyone else in the country about franchise law, and then add that, considering the state of the industry at the time, that was a distinction reminiscent of what Bosley Crowther once wrote in a movie review about Laurence Harvey: the seventh-greatest living actor of Lithuanian extraction.

Nancy Zeidman, John's mother, would not have been mistaken for the Type A parent. She and Philip met just before college at a weekend of parties sponsored by an organization that existed to bring Southern Jewish teenagers together; Philip, who grew up in Birmingham, was, it almost goes without saying, the co-president of the organization that year. She grew up in Atlanta, and she has more of the softness of a Southern accent left in her speech than her husband does. She is also given more to reflection than to activism. Her professional life has been concerned more with how best to adjust to the things that happen than with how to make things happen. Since the late seventies, she has worked with the St. Francis Center, an organization devoted to counseling the terminally ill and their families.

Even for someone of Nancy Zeidman's calmness, John was sometimes a trial. He bore the double burden of being the only boy and the middle child — two and a half years younger than his sister Betsy, who was, in fact, an achiever, and six years older than Jennifer, who was adored by the entire family as the baby. "He was always fighting for attention," Nancy Zeidman has said of John as a child. "If he was in the room with you, there wasn't much room for you, and he always wanted to be in the room with you."

John was still fighting for attention when he entered high school at Sidwell Friends, which all the Zeidman children attended. He had grown into a husky, nice-looking boy — strong enough to choose shot-putting as his Sidwell sport. Clinton Wilkins, the principal of the upper school at Sidwell, thought of him as "a bull in a china shop." If he didn't like people, he told them so. In grade school, he had followed more or less the same policy toward classes: if he didn't like one, he might simply leave. In high school, he was more interested in arguing politics or just hanging around with his pals than in pursuing his studies. If Philip Zeidman had permitted himself any dreams about having his son follow in his footsteps at Yale — or, by that time, follow in his and Betsy's footsteps — they were dashed somewhere around second-year French.

It was possible to see John Zeidman as someone who had chosen not to be measured by his father's notions of success; that is not an unfamiliar type in highly regarded private schools in Washington. It was also possible to see him as a sort of unformed version of his father — an awkward and boisterous and strong-willed version, still without the volume control and the saving wit. "You *knew* he was there," Clint Wilkins has said. "He was indomitable. He had a great sense of curiosity. You could tell that these qualities could be harnessed someday, and there would be tact, restraint, graciousness." Everyone agreed that John had a great sense of curiosity, and there were friends of the family who regarded him as just a sweet, warm-hearted, particularly exuberant teenage boy. Still, when Philip Zeidman, an articulate man, tries to sum up what John was like as a teenager, he is likely to smile and say, "He could be a pain in the ass."

As John was finishing his senior year at Sidwell, in 1979, Philip Zeidman and another lawyer with some government connections were completing arrangements for a three-week tour of China, and John got to come along with his parents as his graduation present.

As far as Philip Zeidman could see, the trip was one more wasted opportunity for John, who seemed to spend most of his time tossing a Frisbee around. Mary Earls, another member of the party, remembers John as responding to sights that the guides seemed particularly proud of by saying in a stage whisper that the Taiwanese version was no doubt infinitely preferable. John was not due to begin college that fall; he had been accepted by Duke as what is called there a January freshman. His parents set a simple rule about where he could spend the fall semester: anywhere but home. They had decided that he needed what one of their friends referred to as a parentectomy.

John decided to spend the fall in Boston. He worked as an intern at the public television station, and he attended an early-morning English composition class at Boston University. He saw a lot of Mary Earls and her husband, Felton, a child psychiatrist then at Harvard. Along with Mary Earls, he took a Chinese cooking course, and that led to a job as a bus boy in the teacher's Chinese restaurant. He learned to be on his own, and he learned, in his mother's words, "that he wasn't such bad company after all." By all accounts, he grew up a lot. "He was driven by a need to have an identity — to be somebody, to be his own person," Felton Earls has said. "And what I saw happening in those months is that he was discovering himself." When John entered Duke, in January of 1980, he was greatly changed from the bull in the Sidwell china shop. He was still a bit bumptious. He was still talkative enough to be distinguished from the other people named John in the dormitory by the nickname Z the Mouth. But he had harnessed a lot of his energy. He did well in his studies. He was active in a movement concerned with the allocation of dormitory space on the campus. And he eventually had a strong focus: he had decided that he wanted to study in China.

John applied himself to the study of Chinese in a manner that would presumably have astonished the teachers at Sidwell Friends, who after any number of attempts to teach him French had informed Nancy Zeidman that he simply had no aptitude for languages. His parents were delighted by what had happened to John. Just having dinner with him in a Chinese restaurant, where he would take charge of orchestrating the meal in Chinese, was enough to make plain his pride at having found his own field and his own notions of achievement. Although he had taken only a year of Chinese, he applied for a University of Massachusetts program that offered a junior year at Peking Normal University. He was accepted — the acceptance contingent on his taking a language course in China during the summer. In June of 1981, just after the end of his sophomore year at Duke, John Zeidman headed for China.

He simply loved it. It was almost as if a situation had been designed to take advantage of the qualities that John had exhibited all his life. Where someone more likely to be inhibited by an imperfect accent might hesitate to strike up conversations with strangers, John barged right in. Where someone more conscientious about obeying rules and regulations might have believed everything he read about restrictions on what foreigners could do in China, John assumed he could do anything. Where someone who had grown up valuing coolness and restraint might have been shy about reaching out toward Chinese students, John organized barbecues. He found his way around Peking on a bicycle and on public transportation. ("The motto of the Peking bus system," he said on one of the tapes he sent home, "is 'There is no such thing as a full bus.' ") On a trip between his summer language classes and the beginning of the academic year at Peking Normal University, he insisted on traveling "hard class" by train, both to save money and to force himself to speak Chinese. ("For one who has never been lacking in his use of the English language, August 7, 1981, will go down in history. With one exception, I neither spoke nor heard an English word . . . The one exception was when the train loudspeaker played a Chinese singer singing 'Jingle Bells' in English.") He spent a lot of time with Chinese families and even reported that he had met a "very nice girl." ("Don't worry, Mother, she's not coming home. Her name is Duo Li. I have been helping her with her English and she has been helping me with my Chinese. She is less shy than most Chinese girls, which is great, since we can talk and she doesn't giggle all the time.") He made fun of reporters who wrote that it wasn't possible for foreigners in China to complete the simplest transaction ("I think it would be helpful if some of these reporters left their apartments occasionally") and didn't forget to make fun of himself for being so certain that they were wrong ("Tomorrow, I use my self-bought train ticket and go to Shanghai. That is, assuming I bought the right ticket").

The Shanghai trip was to visit Felton and Mary Earls, who had just arrived for a three-month stay. Mary Earls, a neurophysiologist, was a guest of the Chinese Academy of Sciences; her husband had a World Health Organization fellowship at a local hospital. As someone who had put in some travel time in hard class, John took great pride in leading the Earls family around through the back streets and cheap restaurants of Shanghai, at a pace that Felton Earls later estimated at a hundred and fifty miles an hour. Back in Peking to start the semester, John was enough of an old China hand to respond to the unappetizing food at the dining hall by searching the neighborhood until he found a dumpling-and-noodle joint named Forever Red, where two students with male-American-teenager appetites could stuff themselves for less than a dollar.

John's tapes home were filled with reports on his economics class and his trips around the city and even the latest Chinese jokes. "Everything is really going well," he began a tape on September 26, 1981 — his twentieth birthday. He thanked his sister Jennifer for a tape she had sent and for a tape of "M*A*S*H" that he knew was on the way. "That and a bowl of Raisin Bran and a glass of cold milk and going home for a weekend would do me just fine for my birthday," he said. "I'm not homesick yet, but it would be fun to be home for a few days." Rosh Hashanah fell three days after John's birthday that year. In Washington, Philip Zeidman was up early, trying to sneak in a couple of hours of work before services. When the telephone rang and he picked it up to hear the scratchy line that usually indicated China, he figured that it was John calling to wish the family Happy New Year or treating himself to a birthday chat. The call was from China, but the caller was the person in charge of the University of Massachusetts program there. She said that John was in the hospital. She said that he was critically ill.

• • •

"Dear Patrick," Anne Thurston wrote. "Something very sad is happening here now. One of the students with the University of Massachusetts program — a young man from Duke who spent the summer at the Nationalities Academy studying Chinese — has contracted encephalitis. His name is John Zeidman. I met him in August . . . a nice guy — friendly, outgoing, 20 years old." Anne Thurston, who was in Peking to do research for a study of victims of the Cultural Revolution, lived in the dormitory that housed the students in the UMass program. Her husband, Patrick Maddox, was in the United States — also a China scholar, Maddox is the associate director of the John King Fairbank Center for East Asian Research, at Harvard — and she wrote long, detailed letters to him regularly. In that first letter about John Zeidman's illness, she reported that John had been examined by some eminent American neurologists who, by chance, were in Peking on their way back from a conference in Japan, and that their prognosis, which she had heard secondhand, was not good: "The American doctors, as I understand it, are saying quite frankly that he will probably die."

The Zeidmans had spoken by phone from Washington with one of the American doctors. They had learned of the neurologists' presence in Peking from one of the first calls that Phil Zeidman made after he learned of John's illness — to a neurologist he knew at Johns Hopkins, in Baltimore. That was one of about a hundred long-distance calls the Zeidmans made in the next twenty-four hours. "We began to cast the net," Phil Zeidman says when he explains how he responded to that first call from China. Who knew about encephalitis? What could the State Department do? Who could be helpful if John had to be evacuated? Was there a drug somewhere? It was quickly decided that the Zeidmans would fly to Peking as soon as possible. Betsy, who was then working in New York, came home to be with Jennifer. Mary Earls, reached in Shanghai, agreed to make her way to Peking — no small undertaking without advance arrangements — and take charge until the Zeidmans could get there. When she arrived at the hospital — the Infectious Diseases Hospital No. 1 — she found that John was paralyzed and unable to talk but still semiconscious. She held his hand, and she talked to him. She thought he understood her. When she told him that his parents would soon be there, she thought tears came to his eyes. Not long after that, John slipped into a coma.

Among the doctors who saw John in the first couple of days, there was no serious disagreement about the diagnosis. He had a strain of viral encephalitis called Japanese B — a strain that is virtually unknown in the United States but is common in parts of Asia, particularly in rural areas during the summer. Japanese B is normally transmitted to human beings by mosquitoes that have bitten infected birds or swine. By the time John Zeidman went to China, a vaccine to prevent Japanese B was available in some countries — not including the United States — but no one had ever found a drug that was effective against it once it had been contracted. The treatment has consisted simply of trying to avoid complications like pneumonia and breathing difficulties — Mary Earls authorized a tracheostomy while Philip and Nancy Zeidman were still on their way from Washington — and hoping that the patient pulls out of his coma. Apparently, some patients do. As the students in the UMass program frantically searched for information about Japanese B, they heard any number of stories about amazing recoveries that left the patient none the worse for the experience. The tales of recoveries, though, were not based on the efficacy of any particular treatment. John was in a condition not responsive to the wonders of modern medicine, and he was in that condition because of a maddeningly trivial happening: he had been bitten by a mosquito.

As the Zeidmans flew over the Pacific, they had no way of knowing whether they would find John alive when they reached China. They were not even certain that he would be in China; there had been talk of evacuating him, perhaps to an American Air Force hospital in the Philippines. After the American neurologists had all examined John, in fact, they did advise Mary Earls to authorize an evacuation. For several hours, she resisted the advice. There was, after all, no treatment for Japanese B. She thought that the Americans, who had been in China only a couple of days, were reflecting the shock that "great Western high-tech slick academic neurologists" were likely to experience at their first exposure to the relatively primitive conditions of a Chinese hospital. In her work in Shanghai, she had been impressed by the "quiet competence" of the Chinese, and she was impressed by the attentiveness of the care that John was getting at the hospital. Finally, she relented, and an American military-hospital plane arrived from the Philippines. It returned without John. After an examination, the medical officer in charge had decided that John was too sick to move. And so it was that when Philip and Nancy Zeidman arrived, after a nineteen-hour trip from Washington, they found their son in a room at the Infectious Diseases Hospital No. 1, in a deep coma.

Although the Zeidmans took a room at the Peking Hotel, they basically moved into the hospital — into a sort of waiting room next to the room John was in. To Philip Zeidman, the Infectious Diseases Hospital No. 1 looked like "an abandoned training camp." It had unpainted cinder-block hallways. Whatever paint there was in the rooms seemed to be peeling. There was one telephone. There was no operating room. To someone whose visions of a hospital included spotless linens and disposable needles in sterile packages, the Infectious Diseases Hospital No. 1 was not noticeably clean. There was an inner courtyard — a drab, grassless inner courtyard, since the grass was pulled up in Peking some years ago as a means of insect and vermin control — and the wind brought a fine covering of dust into the rooms. It often seemed cold. John had bought a huge down Chinese Army coat, and Phil Zeidman usually had it on, even when he was in bed.

Still, the Zeidmans found themselves in agreement with Mary Earls that the Chinese were doing everything in their power for John, particularly when it came to nursing care. There were two or three nurses in John's room at all times. They cracked ice from a huge block in front of his bed and used it to keep his fever down. They squeezed the juice from watermelon — prized medicinally in China — and fed it to him through tubes. They washed him regularly. They turned him regularly to prevent infection and bedsores.

They made circles of gauze to place under his heels. They talked to him. In Chinese, his name came out as Zei-da-man. As Phil Zeidman tried to sleep next door, he heard the wind in the courtyard and the rumble of carts carrying oxygen tanks up and down the halls and, from John's room, the nurses' voices crooning "Zei-da-man, Zei-da-man."

The Zeidmans were usually not the only people sleeping in the waiting room. Some of the students in the UMass program had organized themselves into a sort of duty roster so that there would always be someone at the hospital to translate; often, a couple of them spent the night in sleeping bags on the floor. "Because they are also frightened, not only by the trauma but also by their first brush with the absolute, we have tried to console them as they tried to comfort us," Philip Zeidman wrote in a letter home a few days after he arrived in Peking. "We have urged the Chinese authorities to provide blood tests, inoculations, and the like, and we will not rest until that is done." As it turned out, some of the steps that the Chinese took to assuage the fears of the students — spraying the dormitory with an insecticide similar to DDT, for instance, and taking blood tests with needles of dubious cleanliness — frightened them all the more. Trying to comfort one another during the long hours in the waiting room, the Zeidmans and the UMass students came to feel something like a family. "We all get so down at the dorm not being able to help," one young woman in the program wrote to Betsy and Jennifer Zeidman, neither of whom she had met. "One day after arriving, I told your mother that I really needed a hug from her, and she gave so much love as I cried in her arms." The Zeidmans could console their own daughters, of course, only by shouts over the scratchy telephone wires or by telex or by mail. In his letters, Philip Zeidman told Betsy and Jennifer how much John had spoken of them to the other students. "They know more about you than you can imagine," he wrote. "They know of every letter and card you sent him. And they know — as you simply must know and believe and always remember — that he loved you, and he knew that you loved him. Whatever may be brought by the hours or days ahead, you must nurture that knowledge, and the memory of the good times we had as a family together. We pray to God that we shall again, as a total family."

Nancy Zeidman didn't think that would ever happen. By temperament and by experience, she was more inclined than her husband to become resigned to the almost certain consequences of the mosquito bite. Unlike her husband, she happened to come from a family that had acquired an awful familiarity with death at an early age. In her work, of course, she counseled people who were trying not to stave off the inevitable but to deal with it. Almost from the moment she arrived in Peking, she had accepted as a fact that her family was no longer a total family. "I took one look at him," she said later. "I had seen enough dying people, and what scared me more than anything after looking at his face was that he was going to survive with severe brain damage."

Phil Zeidman was far from resigned. "I have an activist nature, and I would simply focus on the question 'What can we do?' " he has said. "Get an airplane? Get a vaccine? Get a valve?" He continued to cast the net. The one telephone in the Infectious Diseases Hospital No. 1 became, de facto, his telephone. An American businesswoman who had an office in Peking lent him the use of her telex machine, and there was constant traffic between there and the Zeidman law office in Washington — detailed reports to provide American consultants with data on John's temperature and pulse rate and blood pressure. Phil Zeidman kept making notes on his yellow legal pad. Was there a better respirator somewhere? Was there an experimental drug somewhere? Was there a doctor somewhere? "Let me ask you whether, based upon what you have heard, if you could snap your fingers and every expert in the United States were sitting here by our sides, would it make any difference?" he asked one doctor by long-distance telephone, after giving a detailed report on what a team of Chinese doctors had told him. "Is there a person anywhere in the world that might make a difference in this situation?"

A day or so before that call, about a week after John became ill, Anne Thurston wrote that the Americans in the waiting room seemed more hopeful, buoyed by the fact that John had survived for a critical period, but "my Chinese friends seem to have switched from the optimists to the pessimists. Now, in contrast to the stories of miraculous recovery that I was hearing earlier, other people are telling me that ninety-nine per cent of Chinese who contract encephalitis die." Two days later, she reported a turn for the worse. After a crisis with John's breathing, the doctors concluded that there had been extensive brain damage. "I cannot imagine any other couple handling this with as much love and affection and strength as they are," she wrote. "After hearing the news today, they put their arms around each other and cried, and Mr. Zeidman said to his wife that John is fighting for his life and that because he is still fighting, they must continue to fight with him, that they must do it for him and that if he makes it, then they can think about recovery and what the brain damage will mean."

One of the Chinese doctors in charge of John's case also broke down that day. He told Philip Zeidman that he was treating John as if he were his own son, and then he began to cry. "He said that he, like the Zeidmans, has a son and two daughters, and that if his son were to die, he doesn't know what he would do," Anne Thurston wrote. "But one still senses certain cultural differences, that the Zeidmans would feel the same were it one of their daughters in that hospital room, too, that it makes a difference to the Chinese that John is an only son. The doctor said, though, that they are doing everything possible for John, that they have gathered together the best expertise in Peking, and that there is nothing more that can be done. He is right, I know."

The Zeidmans realized that everything possible was being done, and they certainly realized that there were cultural differences. At times they became irritated at the conditions in the hospital and frustrated by problems in communication. At one point they were infuriated by a long delay in the arrival of a surgeon. They were bitterly angry at the fact that nobody had ever mentioned the possibility of being inoculated against Japanese B viral encephalitis and at indications that the Chinese government had seriously underreported its occurrence. They knew of the extraordinary care being given by the nurses they could hear talking to their son. They knew there was no treatment that could actually cure Japanese B. Still, the net that Phil Zeidman was casting was being cast partly in the hope of catching an American doctor.

Among those in America seeking medical opinions based on the detailed telexes from Peking were Philip Zeidman's sister, Adele, and her husband, Daniel Silver, who is the rabbi of a temple in Cleveland. One of the doctors they consulted was David L. Jackson, who had been the director of the intensive-care unit at University Hospitals, which are affiliated with the Case Western Reserve School of Medicine. From the telexes, Jackson judged that there was a danger — among other dangers — of John's suffering oxygen toxicity from long-term use of a respirator that was not equipped with the sort of pressure valve that is now used routinely in American ICUs. Having once visited some hospitals in China, he was aware that the life-support equipment and techniques at the Infectious Diseases Hospital No. 1 were likely to reflect the fact that the Chinese medical system is not in a position to give priority to intensive care. Jackson was not only a former ICU director but a neurologist. He was also the director of the Center for the Critically Ill at University Hospitals, a multidisciplinary institute concerned with what happens during critical illnesses not simply to the patient but to his family and to those who are treating him. And, as it happens, he is the sort of activist who tends to respond to the situations he's presented with by asking the same question Philip Zeidman asks: "What can we do?" It didn't take him long to agree to go to China to see what he could do to help the Zeidmans.

Jackson arrived with the pressure valve in his pocket. He had made some elaborate plans for reassuring the Chinese doctors that he wasn't arriving "like the U.S. Cavalry" to take over, but they seemed relieved to have him assume management of John's case. In treating people who are so ill that there's a question about whether it makes sense to employ extraordinary life-support techniques, Dr. Jackson's policy has always been "Where there's a reasonable doubt, err on the side of support." In John's case, the doubt

276 / AMERICAN STORIES

was narrow, but Dr. Jackson was convinced that it existed. He believed, for instance, that John's paralysis made it difficult to be absolutely certain about what seemed to be a lack of significant reflexes. Settling in at the hospital, close enough to John's bed to hear the hum of the respirator, Jackson concentrated on life support. The day after he arrived, he found himself involved in what he considered a life-threatening emergency: John turned blue, and his pulse rate jumped to a hundred and eighty. Concluding that a lung had collapsed, Jackson inserted a needle into John's chest to draw out the air — and then waited for forty-five minutes while the Chinese acquired a chest tube from a neighboring hospital. In general, Dr. Jackson did not consider the lack of equipment at the hospital an insurmountable obstacle, but he was beginning to think that an attempt should be made to move John to a modern intensive-care unit. The decision was sealed when the hospital had a brief power failure. When the power came back on, David Jackson told the Zeidmans that he was in favor of an evacuation.

A lot of telexes went out. A lot of people in Washington, some of them senators, got phone calls. A number of American Defense Department and Chinese government procedures were compressed. The plan was to fly John to an American Air Force hospital in the Philippines on an Air Force plane whose equipment included what amounted to a traveling intensive-care unit, and then to take him in stages to the Johns Hopkins Hospital. On the day before the plane was to arrive — three weeks after John had fallen ill — Dr. Jackson presided over lengthy rehearsals for getting John and the equipment that had to accompany him from his bed to the door of the hospital. The stretcher-bearers were UMass students. One student, chosen because he was about the same size as John, went through the rehearsals lying motionless on the stretcher.

That day, the UMass students also attended a meeting at which the results of the blood tests were given: many members of the group had high antibody levels, it was announced, which meant they had been exposed to encephalitis and had fought it off. That was comforting news, although, Anne Thurston wrote to her husband, the meeting had brought home with a jolt what she had so often read about the Chinese not having the strong concept of the individual that exists in the West: they had not considered it necessary to say who had high antibody levels and who didn't. "Mrs. Zeidman came to the second part of the meeting today to say good-bye," her letter continued. "It was as moving an event as ever I have witnessed. She began by saying that . . . despite the grave risks, Dr. Jackson had decided that it is still more dangerous for John to stay here than to be moved. He must be placed in an intensive-care unit. She said that even so John's prospects are bleak. She said that . . . the help the students have given is beyond thanks, that it would have been impossible for them (the Zeidmans) without that help. She said that she and her husband will remember each and every one of those students for as long as they live, that whatever happens, their home will always be open to them at any time day or night, for any reason, that they can call collect at two in the morning, come to stay for a day or a week or six months, that they are a part of the family and will always be treated so. She explained how difficult these now some 18 days have been for her and her husband and how the students made it possible for them to continue. She asked for a moment of silence. And then she said goodbye to the students, one by one. Oh God, was it sad."

The evacuation team arrived in a swirl of American technology. The team included a neurologist, an anesthesiologist, a general surgeon, and an internist. There were two nurses and two corpsmen. There was a video-camera team. There were machines that clicked open and snapped into place. The evacuation team went into action with the precision of a drill team. The evacuation procedures, Anne Thurston wrote to her husband, were "really quite incredible, fostering a sort of twinge of nationalistic pride that is ordinarily quite foreign to me." The twinge of pride did not change her view of what the outcome of the evacuation was likely to be. "I can only believe now that John is being flown home to die," she wrote. "But that is really where, if he must, I would want him to die — not here in a dimly lit room in a strange hospital where communication, by virtue of both culture and language, seems so excruciatingly difficult. And somehow I feel that he left in a blaze of glory, with sirens screaming and flags unfurled, and paths being cleared to make his way rapid. And there is a sense that he left with the weight not just of his family and of his friends behind him but with the weight of his countrymen and country as well, that they helped those sirens scream and the banners unfurl. And that makes me proud."

There were those who saw the impressive procedures less as a medical evacuation than as a "burial ritual" — the result of Philip Zeidman and David Jackson, the two activists, asking the question "What can we do?" long after anything could be done for John Zeidman. Philip Zeidman and Dr. Jackson acknowledged that the possibility of a significant recovery was, as Dr. Jackson put it, "a long shot at best." But not trying, Jackson has said, would have left everyone with too many unanswered questions. It was not simply that Philip Zeidman had to satisfy himself that no avenue had gone unexplored, though. On one level, he believed he would succeed; all his life he had believed that "if you put enough resources behind something you can make it work." Once John was back in the United States, in fact, no avenue was left unexplored. No technique was left untried. No relevant specialist was left unconsulted. But all the sophisticated instruments available at Johns Hopkins could not repair the damage that had been done to John; they could only measure its depth. Eventually, the doctors all agreed that there was no reason to continue to extend John's life artificially with a respirator.

Nancy Zeidman had begun to resign herself to that possibility on that first night at the Infectious Diseases Hospital No. 1, but for days and days her husband couldn't bring himself to give the doctors his assent. "It was something I didn't come to terms with until much later, and after much greater agony," Philip Zeidman has said. "Because I was so sure that if you had enough determination, enough brains, enough money, enough friends, you could do anything. If you could *bring a boy out of China*, surely you could bring him back to life in America." William Wendt, an Episcopal clergyman who runs the St. Francis Center, spent a lot of time with Philip

Zeidman in those days. "He didn't try to persuade me of anything," Zeidman has said. "He shepherded me into becoming accepting — accepting of the fact that there are some things man cannot do."

Wendt encouraged Zeidman to write down his thoughts about John — in effect, to write a eulogy. He encouraged the interest that Zeidman had already expressed in projects that could be memorials to John — an effort to find out why vaccination against Japanese B encephalitis couldn't be made available to Americans going to China, for instance, and an effort to establish some sort of Chinese studies program in America. Finally, more than two months after John had been brought to the Johns Hopkins ICU, Philip Zeidman assented to having the respirator withdrawn.

The Zeidmans may have been prepared to face John's death, but they were not prepared for what happened: the ICU nurses staged what amounted to a rebellion. The nurses and one of the residents assigned to the ICU objected to having the respirator turned off. In part, their objection turned on some disagreement over the prognosis for John; the nurses had been encouraged by a slight EEG change that the doctors in charge believed was insignificant. Also, the plans for disconnecting the respirator — abruptly, at a prearranged time — struck the nurses as inappropriately well laid. Apparently, though, the main basis of the rebellion was that the nurses had grown attached to John Zeidman, the rare ICU patient they could identify with, and they couldn't bear to see him die. "Tell your nurses this isn't their child, it's mine," Nancy Zeidman told the doctor who was in charge of the ICU. "And if I can let go they can let go." For a while, it appeared that the Zeidmans might have to go to court. Then the doctor in charge of the ICU arrived at an understanding with the nurses, and the respirator was gradually withdrawn. On January 3, 1982, John Zeidman died.

Anne Thurston was still in Peking when she heard the news. "I feel as though I need time to mourn his death, to think about it," she wrote to her husband a few days later. "Because I learned something from that experience, about Mr. and Mrs. Zeidman and parents' love for a child, about the young students who pulled together so well to see him and his parents through, about Chinese conceptions of the individual and of death . . . In the end, knowing the extent of the brain damage he had suffered, I hope they all gave up the fight. Surely it is better that way. And a better battle has never been fought. It is seeming to me the longer I am here that the meaning of life is living up to its tragedies. John's death is tragedy writ large."

John Zeidman was buried on a bright, unusually mild January day. The Washington Hebrew Congregation was filled for the service. The eulogy that Philip Zeidman had written while John was in the Johns Hopkins intensive-care unit was read by John's uncle Rabbi Daniel Silver. It was a long eulogy; the last paragraph began, "If John were here now, he would be tugging not so gently at my coat-tails and whispering not so quietly, 'Enough, Dad, enough.'" It was filled with quotations — from the tapes John had made in China, from tributes others had written after he became ill, and even from a letter Philip Zeidman himself had written just after arriving in China. In that letter, he had tried to explain to family and friends that he and his wife were not resentful about John's having gone to China. "Perhaps we are as willing to accept what life has dealt John, and us, because these few hours have driven home to us what we grasped intellectually but did not fully appreciate emotionally until we arrived here: the importance of these few months in John's life," he had written. "The extraordinary nature of these months for John makes this tragedy especially poignant, of course. We have the sense that a flower has been uprooted at the very instant it was turning to the sun and opening its petals to bloom. But we are steadfastly determined to remember that John was doing exactly what he wanted to do, that they were the happiest days of his life. We want you all to remember that, as a shining candle in this awful darkness."

Just how much resentment Philip and Nancy Zeidman felt about their son's experience in China was bound to be of some interest to the Chinese government. In the era of Chinese-American cultural exchanges and economic cooperation that had begun in the early seventies, John Zeidman was the first American student to fall ill in China and die. By chance, his father was a man of remarkable energy and a lawyer with some influence in the capital of the United States; the Chinese could not be certain how those considerable resources were going to be used. In such a situation, after all, there were any number of understandable ways for parents to act. The parents of John Zeidman might have responded to his illness and death with pure anger — blaming China publicly for being less than candid about a serious health risk, lobbying against any program that put other Americans in such peril. They might have responded by bringing a lawsuit. The thought of legal action had crossed Philip Zeidman's mind, in fact, but he never seriously pursued it — partly because it just seemed inappropriate. ("John would have said, 'You can do it, but don't use my name.' ") The Zeidmans did have some bitter feelings toward China, but those were outweighed by the realization that John had loved it. In his eulogy to John, Philip Zeidman had announced his intention of working toward making the Japanese B vaccine available in the United States and of establishing as a memorial to John a program that would "encourage other enterprising young Americans to acquaint themselves with the Chinese language and culture, as John did; to take their own first steps in a great adventure, as John did; and perhaps in the process to find a part of themselves they did not know existed, as John did."

The bitter memories that remained part of the Zeidmans' impressions of China were just about blotted out by an episode that began a few weeks after John's funeral. Nancy Zeidman, while reading the *Outlook* section of the *Washington Post* one Sunday morning, came upon an article headlined "THE LESSONS OF AN AMERICAN'S DEATH." The death being discussed was John Zeidman's. The author — David Finkelstein, who had been a China specialist for the Ford Foundation — said that even though John Zeidman was a young man who had died "mourned only by his family and friends," his death "may have a deeper significance." According to Finkelstein, the circumstances of John's death demonstrated that China, however it had been romanticized in America, was still a rather primitive Third World country with a controlled press and filthy hospitals and a government so defensive about the society's inadequacies that it had tried to prevent the Zeidmans from providing John with American medical help.

The Zeidmans found out that they were not beyond rage. Discovering that someone they had never heard of had used the death of their son to bolster a political position on China infuriated them. The *Post* agreed to run a reply, and the following week a piece headlined "THE LESSON OF AN AMERICAN'S LIFE," by Philip Zeidman, appeared in the same space. It argued that Finkelstein had drawn a lesson that was "fundamentally at odds with the message of John Zeidman's death — and, more important, of his life." John had died not of inadequate care but of viral encephalitis, Philip Zeidman wrote, and specialists had confirmed that he would have died of it even if, by some miracle, he had been whisked immediately to Johns Hopkins. Zeidman said that the Chinese had, within the limits of their resources, treated his son with skill and dedication and love; the officials, far from being obdurate and defensive, had welcomed American doctors and cut red tape to make the medical evacuation possible. Quoting from John's letters ("I found a hotel that I could stay at for less than 50¢ a night. That's if I don't mind sharing the bed") and from a piece that Finkelstein had previously published in *The New Yorker*, a piece maintaining that China was a backward and essentially closed society, Zeidman said, "A closed society is likelier to open to some people than to others." Even Finkelstein's line about John's having been mourned only by his family and friends struck Phil Zeidman as a way of trivializing his son's death. John's funeral, he wrote, had been attended by eight hundred people.

As a dramatic reflection of a father's hurt and rage, Zeidman's *Post* article was an effective piece of writing. It was reprinted by a number of publications, including the *People's Daily* of Peking. The Chinese were obviously gratified by what John Zeidman's father had to say. They obviously had reason to draw their own lesson from John Zeidman's death. In retrospect, it seems that the publication of Philip Zeidman's article in the *Washington Post* marked the time when the Chinese began to recognize the potential of John Zeidman as a symbol of the friendship of Chinese and American people.

In arguing that Finkelstein had identified the wrong villains in the story of John's death, Philip Zeidman wrote, "He died because he had not been protected against the disease at the outset." By the time of the exchange in the *Post*, Zeidman was deeply involved in trying to make a vaccine available in the United States. He had written to people in the drug industry. He had written to congressmen he knew to have an interest in health legislation. He had made inquiries to other Western countries whose citizens regularly traveled to China. He had met with officials of the Department of Health and Human Services. A vaccine against Japanese B viral encephalitis, he found, fell into a category of pharmaceuticals similar to what have become known in recent years as "orphan drugs" — medicines that aren't used in sufficient quantities for drug companies to justify the cost of bringing them to the market. A vaccine was already being manufactured in Osaka, Japan — Zeidman, accompanied by a Japanese client who is also a close friend of the family, had gone there to check on it — and the best way of making it available in the United States appeared to be through a Centers for Disease Control program that would provide the vaccine within the context of studying its safety and efficacy. Qualifying for that program required documentation demonstrating, basically, that the vaccine had already been found safe and efficacious. Such documentation existed, but the Health and Human Services people seemed to have difficulty prying it out of the Japanese laboratory. When Phil Zeidman was told about the delay, he asked his Japanese client — whose company owns, among other things, several hundred Mister Donut shops in Japan — to talk to the head of the Osaka laboratory about expediting the flow of documents, and he almost immediately received a response from his client's translator that must be unique in the annals of pharmaceutical research: "Today, I visited him again with three boxes (30 d) of donuts and a

Mister Donut gift set (coffee and cups)." The documents were sent. In the summer of 1982, seven months after John Zeidman's death, the Vaccine Committee of the Public Health Service decided that, under a research status called Investigational New Drug, the vaccine from Osaka could be made available to Americans traveling to China.

In that period, Philip Zeidman's energies seemed focused on his son almost as intensely as they had been when John lay in the hospital. At times, Zeidman answered the most routine letters about John's death, often enclosing a copy of the eulogy in his reply. He worked furiously to establish a memorial program in Chinese studies. It had been decided that the program would be at Sidwell Friends — a Chinese history course, language courses that would be available to students from other Washington-area high schools, and an annual lecture by a prominent China scholar. A lot of questions got written down on Phil Zeidman's yellow legal pads. Who would know the best people to have on the advisory committee? Who would be the best person to deliver the inaugural lecture? Who knew him? Who could recommend a likely director? Who might be interested in contributing money? Zeidman cast his net toward his government contacts and his political contacts and his law-firm contacts and his franchise-industry contacts and his personal contacts. A lot of money — a good deal of it hamburger money and doughnut money and ice cream money — began to flow toward Sidwell Friends. Phil Zeidman wrote the contributors thank-you notes, and answered the answers. "Once I had decided that the Chinese Studies Program was the thing to do, it became possible to sublimate everything else to doing it," he said later. It was not simply that Zeidman was coping with his son's death through a flurry of activity. He remembers that in the days when John lay in a coma at Hopkins Bill Wendt had said something that was particularly helpful: "He doesn't have to be forgotten. You can continue his life in a meaningful way by doing something that would be meaningful."

The Sidwell administrators tried to understand what was fueling the pace that Zeidman had set for himself ("After all, this program is going to define his son for him"), but they didn't always find the pace easy to accommodate. In discussing the program, he sometimes took the role of a parent — a high-powered-Washington-attorney sort of parent — who was constantly impatient about his child's academic progress. Zeidman was impatient for the program to become bigger and better, and better known. The Sidwell people wanted it to grow organically, and they were concerned about the possibility that, in size and attention, it could get out of proportion to the school's other programs. "We spent an intense year with Phil in 1982–83," one of the Sidwell administrators later said. "Whatever we did, Phil thought it wasn't enough."

Zeidman found it even more difficult to engage his wife in the sort of aspirations he had for the Chinese Studies Program. Looking back on those days, he has said, "It was very difficult for me to understand at that time, as I now understand, that the fact that I was compelled and motivated and almost exhilarated — just as I was almost exhilarated in China at the triumph of getting a plane or a valve — didn't mean that these things exhilarated her." Nancy Zeidman figured that it would take all the energy she had to pull her family through, and that's what she intended to use it for. There was nothing about her grief that could be expressed on a yellow legal pad. Looking back on it now, Phil Zeidman regrets that he couldn't leave his wife to her private grief — "I didn't really understand at the time that people grieve at their own pace, in their own way," he says — but they both realize that his way of coping with John's death was bound to involve action. "In a way, it was very selfish," he says of his frenzied activity in those months after the funeral, when he was searching for means of making the vaccine available and getting the Chinese Studies Program established. "It made me think I was doing something constructive."

He was, of course, doing something constructive. By the time the first John Fisher Zeidman memorial lecture was given at Sidwell Friends, in the spring of 1983, the endowment for the program stood at more than a hundred and fifty thousand dollars. An advisory committee of impressive names was in place. A full-time director had been hired. The inaugural lecture was being delivered by John King Fairbank, the dean of American China scholars. The Chinese Studies Program pledged at John Zeidman's funeral had been established — a tribute to Philip Zeidman's persistence or to Chinese-American friendship, or maybe to the fact that John Zeidman turned out to have had an aptitude for languages after all.

In the view of the People's Republic of China, the Sidwell program was a tribute to Chinese-American friendship. The embassy in Washington had been helpful from the start — donating books, sending representatives to Sidwell events. At the end of 1983 — at the time Washington was preparing for an official visit by the Premier of China, Zhao Ziyang — the Chinese demonstrated their interest in a way that astonished everyone involved. The Premier's schedule in Washington, it was announced, would include, in addition to meetings at the White House and in Congress and at the National Council for United States–China Trade, a visit to the Chinese Studies Program at John Zeidman's school. There was intensive preparation at Sidwell Friends. An assembly was planned. A gift — a photograph of the Lincoln Memorial statue — was selected. Walk-throughs with the Secret Service were held. On the evening before the visit, snow began to fall, and Sidwell maintenance men worked through the night to keep the driveway clear. Early the next morning, it appeared that their efforts had been in vain: the State Department said the visit would have to be canceled, because the driving conditions had increased the time that had to be allowed to get the Premier's party to a meeting at the House of Representatives. That afternoon, the Chinese Embassy announced that the Premier insisted on visiting Sidwell and had canceled a formal farewell ceremony with Secretary of State George Shultz the following morning to make that possible. The next morning, he was there, in Chinese class, assuring the students that their accents were better than his and telling them that they should visit him in Peking. "We thought it was an 'If you're ever over there, look me up' sort of thing," Lucia Pierce, the director of the Chinese Studies Program, said later. "The next day, the embassy called and said, 'When do you want to come over and start planning your trip?' "

In the summer of 1984, twenty students from the Chinese Studies Program, accompanied by seven adults, went to the People's Republic of China as guests of the Premier of China. The Zeidman family had been invited, but Philip and Nancy Zeidman didn't think they could face going back to China so soon. The one member of the family who went was Jennifer Zeidman, then just completing her junior year at Sidwell. Jennifer's parents tried to prepare her for the sort of attention she was likely to get as the sister of Zei-da-man, but the attention, it turned out, was far more intense than they could have predicted. By then, the Chinese government had made John a full-blown hero of the new era in Chinese-American relations. The American government seemed to have gone along with the idea: a couple of months before the Sidwell party arrived, Ronald Reagan had ended a speech in the Great Hall of the People in Peking by telling the story of John Zeidman and the Sidwell program and the Premier's visit. The Sidwell tour was on the television news in China virtually every night. There were constant banquets and constant toasts. There were constant questions from reporters and television crews. There was a visit to John's old dormitory room, which had been made into what amounted to a small shrine.

Jennifer burst into tears when she was led into John's room, but the adults on the tour reported that in general she had managed remarkably well under the pressure of constant attention. In the essay required for one of her college applications, Jennifer wrote about the trip. She said that it seemed odd to have her big brother treated as a hero, because he hadn't actually done anything heroic, and even odder to be treated as a celebrity just because she was Zei-da-man's sister. She said that she understood the political motivation behind the trip but that she had been impressed by the genuine, warm hospitality. She said that, all in all, it was easy to be cynical but that she had decided not to be. The college application was to Duke, where she had first gone as a weekend visitor when her brother was a Duke sophomore, and where, largely through the initiative of a dean who had known John as an undergraduate, an annual John Zeidman Memorial Colloquium in Communications had been established. Her application was successful. Jennifer was also accepted at Yale, but Duke was where she decided to go.

Philip and Nancy Zeidman were proud of the way Jennifer handled the role thrust upon her in China. They had obviously been concerned about letting her make the trip. They had worried about the emotional pressure on her. Even though they knew that there was no rational reason to worry about her physical well-being, they had worried about her physical well-being. But she had very much wanted to go, and, Philip Zeidman said later, "we concluded that the only thing worse than her going was her not going." Before she left, she had a couple of shots — vaccine from a laboratory in Osaka — to inoculate her against the Japanese B strain of viral encephalitis.

1985

AFTERWORD

ALMOST ALL of the pieces in this book originally appeared in a series called "American Chronicles," which I began in *The New Yorker* in 1984. I had previously spent fifteen years traveling around the country for a series called "U.S. Journal" — a three-thousand-word piece every three weeks from somewhere in the United States. The idea behind "American Chronicles" was to concentrate on a longer version of one sort of "U.S. Journal" piece, the narrative. I wanted to tell the sort of stories you might tell in front of a fire, and those stories require some time to unfold.

The New Yorker happens to be a good place to tell a story. It's quiet. A lot of magazines, in trying to call attention to the piece ("Murder in Iowa Corn Country") or make it typographically appealing or help it along with a few pictures, become the equivalent of people who want to interrupt a story or get ahead of a story or blurt out the little bend in a story that the storyteller was planning to reveal in his own good time at what he figured was just the right place.

I sometimes described what I was looking for as a story that had a beginning and a middle and an end. After a while, I had cause to recall how often people who are about to tell a story in front of the fire say, "I don't know where to begin." Looking back through some of the stories I've told over the years, I notice that I have sometimes been so conscious of trying to puzzle out the beginning that I state explicitly where I think it is. A story I once wrote about a couple of teenage boys from South Texas who were found with half a million dollars of cash in the trunk of their car began, "It came to light because of a bad left turn." A story I once wrote about a Louisiana woman who jousted for years with a lawyer for the state bureau of records over the question of whether her parents should have been identified on her birth certificate as "colored" or "white" began, "Susie Guillory Phipps thinks this all started in 1977, when she wanted to apply for a passport. Jack Westholtz thinks it started long before that."

The end of a nonfiction story can be even harder to find than the beginning. Unlike a writer of fiction, a reporter does not have control over the characters; people are invariably uncooperative about arranging their lives to suit the rhythms and structure of the well-told tale. Also, any piece of nonfiction is shaped by when the reporter happens to show up — by when he freezes a story that may turn into some other story after he has left town. Because of that, the stories in this book have been left in their original context. Economic conditions are as they were; positions are held by people who may have since moved on or maybe even died. Some of what has happened since I left town is presented below. By now, of course, even that could have changed. Life goes on with or without a reporter present.

OUTDOOR LIFE

Louis Conner still lives in Sisters, although he has his own place now. He works as an apprentice plumber. The townspeople have been understanding from the start, and the flow of refugees from California and the Willamette Valley seems so steady that Louis can envision a time when the population consists mainly of people who have never heard of what happened between him and Ed Dyer. If it hadn't been for the civil case against the Forest Service, Susan Conner says, "we could have just gone on with our lives." Motions and depositions for that dragged on for several years. The Conners finally agreed to a settlement for an undisclosed sum rather than go through a trial.

TELLING A KENTUCKY STORY

Tom Chaney eventually left Horse Cave. He didn't feel completely comfortable there, he says, "more because of the bankruptcy than the marijuana." A friend happened to have a restoration project in Philadelphia that needed overseeing, and when that was over another friend had a souvenir shop in the restored Bourse Building that needed managing. In that shop, Tom has sold more miniature Liberty Bells than he would have thought existed ("Why the flatland tourists are swarming to buy those things"). Lately, he has been thinking of returning to one of his former professions, maybe newspapering.

THE LIFE AND TIMES OF JOE BOB BRIGGS, SO FAR

Sooner or later, John Bloom quit writing under his own name. For professional purposes he became Joe Bob Briggs. As Joe Bob, he has written newspaper columns and books, served as the host of the Movie Channel's "Joe Bob's Drive-in Theater," and operated a 900 number (1-900-JOEBOB). He sends a variety of messages — from a newsletter called "We Are the Weird" to Christmas greetings — to a list of people who may or may not know John Bloom. The first stanza of his 1987 Christmas message seemed particularly Joe Bobbian:

> I been thinking bout the baby Jesus
> And folks in China that got diseases
> And guys named Leon that smell like cheeses . . .
> Kinda makes you wonder, don't it?

RUMORS AROUND TOWN

The person brought to trial for shooting to death Martin Anderson was not a hit man but Thomas Bird himself. Lorna Anderson Eldridge, who was also charged in that killing, agreed to plead guilty to a reduced charge of second-degree murder and testify for the prosecution, but the judge gave her fifteen years to life anyway. Relying on a defense that was focused on attacking her credibility, Tom Bird was acquitted of murdering Martin Anderson. During his testimony he finally admitted that he and Lorna Anderson had been having an affair — but, he insisted, it had begun only after the death of his wife and her husband. Lorna testified that the affair had begun long before that, and that they had planned the murders together because divorce "wouldn't look right for the kind of ministry Tom wanted."

A COUPLE OF ECCENTRIC GUYS

Penn & Teller Get Killed was not a success with the critics or at the box office. In the fall of 1990, Penn and Teller hit the road again with a new show called "Penn & Teller: The Refrigerator Tour" (so named, Teller says, "because we open the show by dropping a refrigerator on our wretched selves"), and it opened on Broadway the next spring to enthusiastic reviews. Shortly before the beginning of the Refrigerator Tour, on an NBC special called "Don't Try This at Home," Penn ran over Teller with an eighteen-wheeler, right in front of Radio City Music Hall. Then he explained to the television audience how the trick was done.

COMPETITORS

Reuben Mattus retired from Häagen-Dazs in the summer of 1990, and began to think about the possibility of launching a new enterprise that would produce fat-free frozen desserts. Mattus still might not consider Ben Cohen and Jerry Greenfield "real ice cream people" — Cohen spends a lot of his time on a variety of good works, and Greenfield has never summoned up tremendous enthusiasm for being a business executive — but they both remain at Ben & Jerry's Homemade. Cohen concentrates on sales and marketing. (With distribution in forty-four states, Ben & Jerry's is now Häagen-Dazs's principal national competition in the field of super-premium ice cream.) Greenfield tends to the morale of the troops and to some special projects, the latest of which is a traveling vaudeville van to promote Ben & Jerry's. The acts offered by the van do not include the Dramatic Sledgehammer Smashing of a cinder block on the bare stomach of the noted Indian mystic Habeeni Ben Coheeni.

RIGHT-OF-WAY

Both Patricia Saltonstall and the Kidwells still live where they did when their argument began. They have never made peace, although their lawsuits have been dropped. Points of View farm continues to run a large ad in the *Rappahannock News* once a year recalling "our slain farm manager." Patricia Saltonstall continues to give an annual scholarship called the Rance Lee Spellman Memorial Award. Where the right-of-way meets 729, there is a sign for the Kidwells' and also a sign for Pat Saltonstall's two-house development farther back toward the mountain — Rancelee Vale.

GOLDBERG CAN GO HOME AGAIN

Larry (Fats) Goldberg says, "I've got a lot of deals cooking." So far, none has met his standards, although lately he has expressed enthusiasm for combining two of his earlier schemes in a place that would sell pizza-bagels ("It's a natural!") and has also spoken highly of the Kansas City eating tour ("This thing's big time!"). He did finish a new version of his diet book — the diet book about controlled cheating, not, alas, the one that requires eating the book. He is still thin. He is still a bachelor.

YOU DON'T ASK, YOU DON'T GET

In the spring of 1991, thirty-three years after Frankie Lymon's death, Emira Eagle Lymon's victory became official: she signed an agreement with the Morris Levy estate and BMI and Windswept Pacific. (Maxwell T. Cohen, Frankie Lymon's lawyer, had been dropped from the suit by the plaintiff along the way.) What one of the lawyers involved called "a fair chunk of the money" was put in escrow pending the outcome of the claim made by the surviving Teenagers to a share of the royalties.

I'VE GOT PROBLEMS

The financial pressure on the remaining farmers of the Great Plains has eased some, and so have the activities of groups like the Posse Comitatus. In May of 1986, Rick Elliott was convicted in Colorado on fourteen counts of theft and one of conspiracy, in connection with his operation of NAPA and the *Primrose & Cattlemen's Gazette*. He served about half of an eight-year sentence. According to the Center for Democratic Renewal, an agency that monitors hate groups, he was last heard of trying to organize NAPA chapters in Oregon and Idaho.

COVERING THE COPS

Edna Buchanan has been on leave of absence from the *Miami Herald*, writing books. She did a memoir of her crime reporting called *The Corpse Had a Familiar Face* and a mystery novel called *Nobody Lives Forever*. She is working on a sequel to *The Corpse Had a Familiar Face;* the title she has in mind is *Never Let Them See You Cry*. In 1986, the *Herald* submitted a selection of ten of Edna's crime pieces to the Pulitzer committee, and she was awarded the Pulitzer Prize for general reporting.

ZEI-DA-MAN

The Chinese Studies Program at Sidwell Friends was jolted by the events in Tiananmen Square. A student exchange that had become part of the program was suspended; a summer trip was canceled. After what Philip Zeidman calls a "careful and at times wrenching reassessment," the student exchange was reinstated, and he considers the program stronger than ever. It has by now received contributions of more than five hundred thousand dollars.